PENGUIN BOOKS

The Cut Out Girl

'An extraordinary story, harrowing, deeply affecting.
This fascinating story is guaranteed to haunt you' *People*

'With painstaking research and impeccable prose,
Van Es has crafted an awe-inspiring account of the
tragedies and triumphs within the world of the Holocaust's
"hide-away" children, and of the families who sheltered them'
Georgia Hunter, author of *We were the Lucky Ones*

'A deeply researched investigative book' *Jewish Chronicle*

ABOUT THE AUTHOR

Bart van Es was born in the Netherlands and is bilingual in English and Dutch. He now lives with his family in England. He is a Professor of English Literature at the University of Oxford and a Fellow of St Catherine's College.

The Cut Out Girl

A Story of War and Family, Lost and Found

BART VAN ES

PENGUIN BOOKS

PENGUIN BOOKS

UK | USA | Canada | Ireland | Australia
India | New Zealand | South Africa

Penguin Books is part of the Penguin Random House group of companies
whose addresses can be found at global.penguinrandomhouse.com.

First published by Fig Tree 2018
Published in Penguin Books 2019
001

Printed and bound in Great Britain by Clays Ltd, Elcograf S.p.A.

A CIP catalogue record for this book is available from the British Library

ISBN: 978-0-241-97872-6

www.greenpenguin.co.uk

MIX
Paper from
responsible sources
FSC® C018179

Penguin Random House is committed to a
sustainable future for our business, our readers
and our planet. This book is made from Forest
Stewardship Council® certified paper.

For
Charles de Jong and Catharine de Jong-Spiero
and
Henk van Es and Jannigje van Es-de Jong

Prologue: December 2014

'Without families you don't get stories.'

The woman who tells me this stands making coffee in her apartment in Amsterdam. Her name is Hesseline, Lien for short. She is over eighty and there is still a simple beauty about her: a clear complexion without noticeable make-up; a little silver watch but no other jewellery; and shiny, unpainted nails. She is brisk in manner but also somehow bohemian, dressed in a long, dark grey cardigan with a flowing claret paisley scarf. Before today I have no memory of ever having met her. All the same, I know that this woman grew up with my father, who was born in the Netherlands immediately after the war. She was once part of my family, but this is no longer the case. A letter was sent and a connection was broken. Even now, nearly thirty years later, it still hurts Lien to speak of these things.

From her white open-plan kitchen we move to the seating area, which is full of winter sunlight, filtered partly through stained-glass artworks that are fitted against the panes. There are books, museum catalogues and cultural supplements spread beneath a low glass coffee table. The furniture is modern, as are the pictures on the walls.

We speak in Dutch.

'You wrote in your email about being interested in the family history and about maybe writing a book,' she says. 'Well, the family thing doesn't really play for me. The van Esses were important in my life for a long time, but not now. So what kind of writing do you do?'

Her tone is friendly but also businesslike. I tell her a little about my work as a professor of English Literature at Oxford University – writing scholarly books and articles on Shakespeare and Renaissance poetry – but she knows most of this already from the Internet.

'So what is your motivation?' she asks.

My motivation? I'm not sure. I think hers could be a complex and interesting story. Recording these things is important, especially now, given the state of the world, with extremism again on the rise. There's an untold story here that I don't want to lose.

On this bright December morning we talk of world affairs, of Israel, of Dutch politics, and about the situation in Britain, where David Cameron's coalition government is nearing the end of its five-year term. We move quickly from subject to subject, almost as in an interview for a job.

After perhaps an hour she pushes away her empty cup and speaks definitively:

'Yes, I have faith in this. Shall we sit at the table? Do you have a notebook and pen?'

I had not wanted to arrive like a reporter, so I need to ask her for paper and something to write with, but we are soon seated at the dining table, which is made of pale laminate wood. I can ask anything I want about what she remembers: what people said and did; what she wore and what she ate; the houses she lived in; and what she dreamt.

We sit in the warm modernity of the apartment and our first meeting stretches on for hours. The documents – photographs, letters, various objects – appear only gradually as she thinks of them, but by mid-afternoon, with the light outside already fading, the table is covered in mementos. These include a children's novel with a bright yellow cover featuring a steamboat, and a ceramic tile with a cartoon on it of a drowning man. There is also a photo album of red imitation leather that has a well-worn spine. On the first page of the album there is a picture of a handsome couple with the words 'Mamma' and 'Pappa' written beneath in blue pen.

The woman on the left in the photograph is Lien's mother, whose name is Catharine de Jong-Spiero. She is perched on the edge of a rattan chair, the curved back of which envelops her. The sun is full in her face and she is smiling a little shyly. Her husband Charles, Lien's father, sits on the ground in front of her in his shirtsleeves, his large hands resting comfortably on his knees. He leans back against his wife, who has one of her hands on his shoulder, and he looks up with a confident,

ironical gaze. There is an air of nonchalance about him, laughing at the idea of a posed photograph in a way that his wife, with her fixed smile, finds harder to do.

The man's air of nonchalance is also there in a few more photographs pasted on the first page of the album. One shows him in the back of a motor car, surrounded by a group of dapper young men. In secret he holds his fingers, like bunny ears, behind the head of the friend who poses in front of him with a pair of gloves and a cane. In another he stands, hat in hand, in front of a large black doorway, his leg with its polished shoe thrust to the fore. There are about a dozen of these early pictures. The most crumpled of them – torn, folded and re-stuck with yellowing glue – is of a beach party of around twenty young men and women in bathing suits, smiling and embracing. A woman in white at the centre holds up what looks like a volleyball. 'Mamma, Pappa, Auntie Ro, Auntie Riek and Uncle Manie,' reads the handwritten text beneath.

Although I am unpractised at interviewing, a rhythm soon

develops to our conversation. I ask countless questions, probing away at some detail, scribbling down notes.

'What was the room like?'

'Where did the light come from?'

'What sounds could you hear?'

It is only when all the details of an episode are exhausted and she can tell me nothing further that we move on.

Darkness has fallen by the time that Lien mentions her poesie album: a kind of poetry scrapbook that nearly all girls in the Netherlands used to keep. At first she cannot find it, but then, after looking around in a side room, she suggests I stand on a chair and look on top of the bookshelf, where it lies wedged, kept safe from dust in a small transparent plastic bag. It is a grey cloth album of around eight by ten centimetres with a faded pattern of flowers on the cover. Inside, on the first of its facing pages, there is a set of rhymes that are signed 'your father' and dated 'The Hague, 15 September 1940'. They begin as follows:

This is a little book where friends can write
Who wish for you a future bright
To keep you safe throughout the years
With many smiles and never tears.

I stand for a moment reading the sloping hand. Opposite, on the left, there are three old-fashioned paper cut outs in pastel colours: at the top, a wicker basket of flowers; and below, two girls in straw hats. The one on the right smiles and looks happy, like Lien's mother in the photo, but the cut out girl on the left purses her lips as she clutches her posy. She glances sideways, as if unable to meet the viewer's eyes.

I

It is really Hitler who makes Lien Jewish. Her parents are members of a Jewish sports club (there is a team photo that shows her father dressed in thick socks and an open-necked shirt), but other than that, they are not observant. They eat matzah at Passover and, under family influence, got married at a synagogue. Lien, aged seven, however, thinks more about the Dutch equivalent of Father Christmas, St Nicholas, and still remembers her fury at being told that he does not really exist. She feels a trick has been played upon her by the adults and hides herself in rage and embarrassment in the cupboard beneath the stairs that lead to the apartment above.

That cupboard at number 31 Pletterijstraat, The Hague, is just across the hall from her bedroom, which faces you as you

come in through the front door. As you enter her room there is a line of four little windows right up against the ceiling, too high to look out of, that give a rather dim light. These windows connect to the back bedroom, where her parents sleep. The other bedroom, which looks out on to the road and connects to the kitchen, is sublet by Mrs Andriessen. She is elderly and rather a great lady, and, like everyone else, writes in Lien's poesie album. 'Dear little Lien, remain obedient and good, / and all shall love you, as they should,' she instructs the child. Lien pays more attention to the flower pictures that are stuck in by Mrs Andriessen than she does to this wise advice.

By 20 April 1941, when Mrs Andriessen writes her entry, it is not easy for Jews to be obedient in occupied Holland. Jews must carry identity papers stamped with a 'J'; they are banned from the Civil Service, from cinemas, cafés and universities; Jewish ownership of a radio is a criminal offence. But for Lien things are still just about normal. She goes to a mixed school, and the children's names written in her album with careful fountain pens are, for the most part, not Jewish:

'Let's remain friends for ever, dear Lientje, what do you think of that?' writes Ria.

'A sunny, happy life, may it remain yours for ever,' from 'your girlfriend, Mary van Stelsen.'

'Will you still remember me, even without this album page?' asks Harrie Klerks.

This last entry causes Lien some upset because, in spite of promising to work tidily, Harrie blots and spoils a page of the album so that it needs to be cut out with a paperknife. Still, Lien generously gives him a second try.

Lien's real worries, if she could formulate them, are not about the war but about her parents' marriage. When she was very young, just two and a half, she had to leave the flat above a shop that they then rented to go to live with Auntie Fie and

Uncle Jo and their two children in another part of town. Her parents got divorced. Mamma came to visit her, but she did not see Pappa for a very long time. After two years Mamma and Pappa got remarried and set up home in the Pletterijstraat, turning over a new leaf. Pappa has stopped travelling as much as he did when he worked as a salesman for Grandpa and he makes an effort to stay home at night, making children's puzzles out of wood at the table under the big light in the kitchen. For Lien he makes a little painting of Jan Klaassen and Katrijn, the Dutch Punch and Judy, which is her most treasured possession. Jan Klaassen and Katrijn are sitting in the sunshine on top of a grey cloud that is raining down beneath them, holding umbrellas in their hands as they smile. Perhaps Jan Klaassen and Katrijn are a bit like Mamma and Pappa, who are happy now that they are out of the rain?

Lien gets terrible stomach aches and does not like eating anything except desserts. She has medicines from the doctor and one time, when she got really thin, she had to go and stay for six weeks in an infirmary, where you have to drink a lot of milk and eat porridge. It would be horrible to go back there, so she tries to eat as much as she can of the farmer's kale and potato mash that Mamma makes her, but it always takes a very long time.

For his new job Pappa has a little factory like Grandpa's, which is really no more than a shed and can be reached through the yard at the back of the flat. He makes jams and pickles using vats of fruits and vegetables and various sizes of glass jar. Lien watches while Pappa works, but she is not allowed to help because this is a very clean job that children's fingers might spoil. Instead she is mainly to be found on the street, singing nursery rhymes and playing games like 'Where shall I lay my handkerchief?', with children huddled in a circle and one child going round and round until she finds someone to give the handkerchief to, who must then chase her to try to give it back. Lien loves this kind of playing; she is almost always outside when there is sunshine and will even put up with a bit of rain if there is fun to be had.

She also goes to ballet, which is very ladylike, and sometimes they have shows. In Mamma and Pappa's bedroom there is a picture of her in front of the stage scenery. It was taken after a performance: she is wearing her costume of black skirt and white blouse and she holds up a glove puppet on her right arm. The puppet is rather lumpy and bumpy and looks owlish, but it is supposed to be Mickey Mouse. Apart from the ballet costume she loves her two best dresses. One is blue-grey silk, which she bought with Mamma on a shopping trip to the Bonneterie, the enormous department store with glass doors and a high ceiling that swallowed them up when they stepped inside. Its floors are so shiny you can see your face in them, and when you look down from the inside balcony on to the entrance hall the people below you look like ants. The other favourite is a little bell-shaped dress (known as a clock

dress) of satin with petticoats underneath that her mother made by hand.

Lien's world is a world of school, street games, and of grannies and grandpas, aunts and uncles and cousins. There is family all around them: at the end of short walks from the Pletterijstraat or at the end of short rides on the tram. In the summer they take the tram to Scheveningen, where they play on the beach. Pretty, the family dog, loves it there – running as fast as she can on the wet sand, just touching the water, leaving a long line of four-toed impressions for the sea to wash away. When Lien throws a tennis ball for Pretty she gets it back, moments later, all soggy and sticky and covered in sand.

Her favourite cousins are Rini and Daafje. They are almost like a brother and sister because Lien stayed with them for such a long time when Mamma and Pappa could not be friends. On one of the many days they spend together, Rini writes a short moral verse in the poesie album about 'taking people as they come'. The poem is not particularly appropriate as Lien does very little judging of anything or anyone, but sometimes

it's easier just to write something standard, and that's fine if the handwriting and the stuck-in pictures are beautiful, so Lien writes something moral and improving in Rini's album as well.

And then there is Auntie Riek with cousin Bennie and the two little ones, Nico and baby Robbie, for whom Lien sometimes helps to care. There is a photo of Auntie Riek and Mamma squeezed on to a wooden chair, with Bennie (thumb in mouth) and Lien (with a white bow in her hair) perched precariously on their laps. Mamma sits on one arm of the seat, holding Lien with her left hand and Riek with her right. The chair looks terribly unsteady, the whole gang likely to topple over any minute, and though Mamma maintains her serious camera smile you can see that her sister-in-law is starting to laugh.

A favourite place is Uncle Manie's ironware shop nearer the centre of the city, filled to the ceiling with racks of screws,

door knockers, hammers and bicycle bells. One time Lien is given a beautiful pair of skates there, with white leather tops and long, sharp silvery blades. When it is winter Lien will be able to try them. She can already see herself gliding without effort past other children, racing ahead in the sunshine, turning a pirouette on the ice.

War in May 1940, when Holland is invaded, comes out of a blue sky in Lien's memory. Standing with her parents, she sees planes up above and they tell her, 'This is the war.' Apart from this, not much happens. There are German soldiers who sit at tables outside cafés and sometimes walk the streets. They are friendly. It is only slowly that things start to change.

From the autumn of 1941 onwards the names in Lien's poesie album become different. Or rather, they become more the same. Roosje Sanders, Judith Hirch, Ali Rosenthal, Jema Abrahams: those who write their names from September 41 to March '42 are all unmistakably Jewish, and this is because Lien now has to go to a Jewish school. The poems they write are still about friendship, angels and flowers, but the pastel cut outs of bouquets and girls in crinolines, which were stuck all over the early pages, are now rare. On 15 September 1941 new signs appear outside libraries, markets, parks, museums and swimming pools: 'Forbidden for Jews'.

2

It is January 2015. Having met with Lien for one day in December, I have come back to the Netherlands for a few weeks to continue our interviews. We have also decided that it would be good for me to visit the places where she lived. This is to spark her memory with photos and also to get a sense of the locations myself. So I am on my way to The Hague.

Historically speaking, The Hague was always considered a village and not a city. The quiz question 'What is the capital of the Netherlands?' is difficult to answer because the Dutch talk of a 'head city' rather than a 'capital', and the head city of the Netherlands is indisputably Amsterdam. The Hague is merely the seat of government. Though chosen as the meeting place of the States General of the new republic at the end of the sixteenth century, it was not granted the dignity of a university or even a town wall. The Protestant representatives of the seven provinces who broke away from the Spanish empire met there precisely because it was neutral and unthreatening. They held their meetings in a moated fortress, which today is still the home of the Dutch parliament. In The Hague there is no great port or tradition of trading but, all the same, its status as the birthplace of the Low Countries is apt. The city sits on sand dunes and the remains of a boggy shoreline that was first drained by subsistence farmers in the ninth century. Like so much of Holland it was raised by human labour from the North Sea.

Heading for The Hague, I drive along motorways that slice through the old sea floor, a monochrome carpet of identical squares. When compared to England, where I have lived since I was a teenager, the Dutch countryside feels seamlessly modern in its flat, perfectly organized uniformity. Every few minutes I pass a neat farmhouse of dark reddish-brown brick with a sharply pitched roof. In the yards of these farmhouses there are spotless tractors and feed silos and none of the agricultural lumber that is found on the other side of the North Sea. Even the livestock looks standardized: rectangular cows all stamped with variations of the same black and white. Straight, silvery ditches cut up the land into even portions that stretch into the morning mist.

As I reach the edge of the city, the farms are replaced by a succession of sleek steel and glass structures: car showrooms, distribution centres, noise barriers, and greenhouses inside which there is a controlled environment of carbon dioxide and light. These buildings, just as much as the farms, feel almost artificial. Holland, when seen through a car window, looks devoid of history of any kind.

Having turned off the motorway, I soon find myself in a district of tired red-brick terraced housing. I park on the Pletterijstraat, the street on which Lien used to live. At the start of the last century, when these houses were built, the city was booming. Posters with art nouveau illustrations promoted its virtues as a residential haven to farming folk from the overcrowded countryside and to immigrants from the colonies and the Near East. The Hague, suddenly, was not just a city but a city for the world. In 1900 it became the home of what would soon be called the Court of International Justice, housed in splendour at the newly constructed Peace Palace. As it had been at its origin, The Hague was, once again, a neutral meeting place for great powers. The Pletterijstraat, completed in 1912, held its place in this city of hope.

Today the street is still mainly residential, with a corner

shop and a couple of independent garages that sell second-hand cars. The ground-floor flat at number 31 is now a small therapeutic gymnasium with the logo 'Fysio Fitness' splashed in yellow on its frosted glass. I press the buzzer and wait until a tall young man in a tracksuit opens the door. He is one of the gym instructors. Behind him in the lobby are two older gentlemen in exercise clothing: bunched-up shorts, faded cotton jumpers, bright trainers, and socks that are a bit too long.

I am left on my own in the little entrance hall, with the class getting going in what used to be Mrs Andriessen's room. I can hear the exercise class in progress, with the instructor saying encouraging things.

To the right there is the cupboard where Lien hid when she discovered that St Nicholas was not real. In front of me is her old bedroom, now an office with healthcare qualifications pinned up on the walls. The windows let in some pale January light.

It does not take long to see the three-room apartment. Everything is decent, ordinary, and of a reasonable size. Behind the office is the bedroom of Lien's parents, which now contains a massage table and an anatomical skeleton wearing a red bobble hat. Connected to this is a galley kitchen with a kettle and some fitness leaflets on the worktop. The scrubby backyard has become a storage place for random objects: a metal bin, a snow scoop, a bicycle, some breeze blocks, a stack of plates and some broken chairs. Looking over the fence I try to work out where Charles de Jong's little factory would have stood.

Having been in the flat for less than ten minutes, I make my way out, waving politely to the gym instructor and the old men.

Back in the street and with nothing obvious to do next, I suddenly ask myself what I'm up to. Although I work as an academic, I am no expert on Dutch history or on Nazi persecution. Is visiting the addresses where Lien's story takes me really research? Slightly on edge, with that question hanging over me, I begin to walk down the street.

Towards the end of the interwar period this area was becoming increasingly Jewish. In 1920, when the houses were new, there were just seven Jewish families on the Pletterijstraat. By 1940 there were thirty-nine. Almost directly opposite Lien's house stood the Jewish orphanage, which moved into its specially commissioned premises in 1929 and soon afterwards began accepting German refugees. Thirty-five thousand moved to the Netherlands after the Nazis took power.

Those coming to these terraces in the 1920s and 1930s were not from the old Sephardic Jewish families, who had escaped to the Netherlands from Portugal in the late fifteenth century. The newer arrivals were German and Polish, but they too were following an established route. Since the eighteenth century many Eastern Ashkenazi Jews, whose first language was Yiddish rather than Hebrew, had migrated to Holland. The first German, or 'Hoogduitsch', synagogue was built in The Hague in the 1720s. Over the years, tens of thousands would make their journey across the continent. Here there were no pogroms, it was possible to join guilds, to become a freeman of the city, and even to pass the status of freeman down the family line. Although there were areas of the city that were more Jewish than others, there were no lines of division. From generation to generation, the immigrants took on the tastes and the habits of their compatriots and became straightforwardly Dutch. So when Napoleon took direct control of the Netherlands in 1811 and ordered the registration of surnames, many Jews took the opportunity to naturalize theirs. Joseph Izak, for example, as a long-standing citizen, opted for the plain, native-sounding 'Joseph de Jong'.

The Portuguese, as the first settlers, remained distinct from these newer, more working-class arrivals. They were a kind of aristocracy, closely integrated with political power and trade. These Sephardic Jews, who had emerged as moneylenders after 1179 when the Lateran Council forbade the charging of interest amongst Christians, had escaped southern persecution and prospered in the seventeenth century in the great ports of Europe's northern coast. Though less than 0.01 per cent of the population, Sephardic Dutch Jews owned a quarter of the sugar plantations in Surinam, and they were crucial to the financial structures of the new republic. It was the Portuguese-Jewish banker Isaac Lopez Suasso, for example, who advanced the necessary 2 million guilders, and arranged the hire of 6,000 Swedish mercenaries, when William III of Orange set out to claim the British Crown in 1688.

If anything, the Sephardic community in The Hague was even more accepted than that in Amsterdam. It was in The Hague, in 1677, that the sceptical Jewish philosopher Baruch Spinoza was buried in great splendour in the Protestant New Church. This was an astonishing gesture of acceptance, even if the church authorities broke up the grave soon after, for non-payment of fees.

Village status, combined with its function as a royal residence, made The Hague an easy place for special pleading. Thus when, in 1690, there was a little local difficulty over some passages in the Talmud, a solution was not hard to arrange. The problem involved the carrying of objects in public on the Sabbath, which was clearly forbidden. The question, though, was what counted as 'in public'? In Amsterdam it had been decided that the whole city, as a walled unit, could reasonably be defined as 'a home'. The Hague, unfortunately, did not have town walls. Learned rabbis had determined, however, that if the two stone bridges over its canals were to be replaced by drawbridges, then The Hague too would, logically, be a home.

In consequence a Jewish delegation approached the governing magistrate. Might the bridges be modified at their cost? Two years later, in the true spirit of political accommodation, they were demolished and replaced.

German and Polish immigrants living in the Pletterijstraat in the 1920s and 1930s were hardly in a position to incur such expenses, even supposing they had the commitment to that degree of ingenuity in interpreting God's laws. Yet, although not rich, the River District was perfectly pleasant. Then, as now, it was a place of diversity, where different races and religions lived neighbourly lives. There was, it is true, some resentment amongst non-Jews at the level of migration and, in response, the government had put a cap on numbers. Depending on what circle you moved in, Jews could be feared as socialists, as capitalists, as Zionists, as poor and low-skilled, or as rich and over-qualified, taking the best jobs. In the 1930s it could be hard for Jews to get a restaurant booking. Still, even in 1937 there was only a 4 per cent vote for the Dutch fascist party, the NSB.

Leaving the old orphanage behind me, I take a turn off the Pletterijstraat on to a side street, hoping to find a café. I pass a primary school with neat *Jugendstil* lettering over its doors announcing its year of completion: 1923. Since that time a mural has been added that shows a giraffe looking out of a painted window with a smiling girl seated on its back. At ground level there are other figures of children on the brickwork and a Perspex sign that tells me this is a Protestant Christian school. Further up the street I can see a kind of shopping precinct, so I head up in that direction in search of a coffee.

When I get there the precinct is something different from what I expected. It is as neat and tidy as it looked from a distance, with attractively lit shopfronts, but the rows of windows show only women in lingerie perched on bar stools with dark red, dimly lit cubicles to the rear. Some of the windows have closed curtains; others display messages such as 'sensual massage', 'two women', or 'kinky sex'. Across the street from me there is a steel outdoor urinal where two men are urinating while they survey the scene.

As I walk through, feeling intrusive, it is difficult not to make eye contact with the women. My gaze moves quickly from one window to another, and I am conscious of my presence as a time-waster as well as a representative of the general crowd of men. Behind the glass in the warm light and with their thick layers of make-up the women look almost ageless, like bored but desperate sales assistants hovering at the front of a shop. A blonde young woman looks across at me, smiling, and then, as I pass, goes back to checking her phone.

In three or four minutes I have passed through the precinct and am back on the main road that leads to the station. From here I can loop back to the Pletterijstraat and get to my car.

Once again I am struck by the strangeness of this familiar country, which I left as a three-year-old forty years ago, returning only for the holidays every summer. I am now probably more English than anything, which is why the neat precinct for prostitutes is so foreign to me. The Dutch are pragmatic about these matters: it is logical to have sex or drugs or euthanasia out in the open, honest and regulated, and if it ends up less than a hundred yards from a primary school that cannot be helped.

This last hour, I feel, has been an immersion into the Low Countries: perfect motorways, a Protestant primary school, a red-light district, and the former home of a Jewish family now converted into a physiotherapy gym. This is a country of tolerance: letting people get on with things, not minding others' business if it does not interfere with your own. This makes the Netherlands progressive. But might it also explain why the Germans were so often allowed to act as they did? The Netherlands of the 1930s was still what was called a society of 'pillars': separate strands, such as the Protestants, the Catholics and the Liberals, who brushed shoulders and exchanged polite greetings, but who rarely went further than that. One followed the law and kept things tidy. Everything else was another's business, no need to interfere.

Of the 18,000 Jews in The Hague in 1940, 2,000 survived. Of the 400 old Portuguese Jews, so deeply embedded in the fabric of the state and the city, just eight returned. The entire Jewish orphanage, which stands across the road from me, was liquidated without survivors on 13 March 1943.

3

'Jew'. In May 1942 Lien sees her mother at the dining table in the kitchen with a large sheet of yellow cloth. There is a pattern of stars upon it with black outlines, each with a word printed at its centre: 'Jew'. Around every star there is a thin dotted line to make it easier to cut out. They must now wear these stars on each item of outside clothing, so Mamma carefully stitches a star reading 'Jew' on to the silk of the Bonneterie dress.

The children on the street whom she knows are the same as ever, but those on the way to school are not so kind. Sometimes they throw stones. Then one day a group of children runs up and grabs her, pushing her into a side street, chanting, 'We have caught a Jew.' When she does not come home her father goes out to find her. The gang backs away when it sees him, but once he takes her hand a bold lad edges closer. 'Dirty Jew,' he mumbles, half embarrassed, poised and ready to run off. Pappa ignores him, but not with his normal calmness; there is a tremor to his fingers as he leads her away from the alley and back to the flat.

As they reach number 31 they see Mrs Andriessen standing in the stairwell of the apartment block, half out on the pavement, looking for them. There is a worried, searching expression on her face and then a tense half-smile of relief when she sees Lien. This feels odd because Mrs Andriessen is almost always to be found in her soap-scented room. The old lady turns and calls something into the open door of their flat, her cheeks shiny and red. She seems to be telling Mamma that everything is all right. Lien suddenly thinks that because Mrs Andriessen is allowed to stay with them at the Pletterijstraat she must also be Jewish, like they are, though she is not sure about that.

Aunt Ellie, on the other hand, is not Jewish, because she is not really an auntie, just a good friend of Mamma's who visits all the time even though she doesn't have to wear a star.

When the summer holidays come, Lien often stays in the yard or the kitchen or on the flight of steps at the front of the house. She gets to know Lilly, who lives at number 29 upstairs. Lilly draws four evenly spaced pencil lines into the album and copies a poem perfectly on to the middle of the page:

> *Roses big and roses small*
> *Soft as velvet on a wall*
> *But the softest petal part*
> *Is the rose of Lientje's heart.*

Lilly draws some extra lines diagonally in the left-hand corner of the page: 'I lay in bed and mucked about / so Mum got cross and started to shout.' Every time they read it aloud to themselves they start to giggle.

Then, one evening in early August, still in the holidays, Mamma comes into her bedroom, just as always, to tuck her in and kiss her goodnight. She sits down on the chair beside her, rests one hand on top of the covers and uses the other to stroke Lien's hair. 'I must tell you a secret,' she tells her. 'You are going to stay somewhere else for a while.'

There is a silence. Whatever comes after this becomes hazy, but this sentence, spoken in her mother's voice, stays fixed. Lien remembers that her mother was very lovely, and kind, and that she felt loved.

The excitement of the secret presses heavily the next morning when Lien sits at the top of the outside steps with Lilly and a few other children beside her, wanting very much to tell. It feels special to have a secret, but it is not fun to have to keep it for so long. When Mamma comes home Lien runs down the steps and catches up with her. 'Can't I tell?' she whispers. 'I think it's a really nice secret.' But Mamma won't let her; it is very important that nobody else knows.

That evening there is a gathering of aunts and uncles who squeeze themselves into the kitchen and then, as its gets ever fuller, find a place to look into it from the doorway of her parents' room. It is not a birthday party because there are no children (except for her and baby Robbie), but still Lien is the centre of attention: she has the gooey taste of chocolate in her mouth, which is almost unfamiliar, and is asked to sit on nearly everyone's lap. For some reason she decides to behave badly, laughing in the high-pitched squeal that Mamma doesn't like as she points to a spot on Aunt Ellie's nose, but, no matter how much she squeals and points at people, she is not told off. Her shrieks cut through the murmur of the other voices; the adults speak low to each other and have eyes only for Lien. Everything goes so quickly. There is no time for talking or even for thinking about the questions that emerge and then edge away, just out of sight, in her mind. It all feels rushed, but still the evening runs on for hours as a succession of hugs and whispers; she is only half-conscious of being carried slumbering to her bedroom in her father's arms.

In the morning, soon after she has had her bread and cheese, there is a lady at the door, even grander than Mrs Andriessen and not so old. She has a firm jolly manner just like the nurse at the doctor's surgery, saying nice things about her, and asking questions about her schoolwork and about what books she enjoys. Lien is embarrassed that she does not do much reading, though she remembers to say that she likes Jan Klaassen and Katrijn. The lady is quite young but not at all like a mother. It is a real adventure to be going with her, the kind of adventure that gives you a little feeling of sickness in your mouth. On the outside she is excited but on the inside she feels calm. They are unstitching the stars from her dresses – the two women's fingers moving very fast.

Lien can keep her own name and her surname, de Jong, but she must not say anything about Mamma or Pappa or family. She is not to be Jewish now, just a normal girl from Rotterdam whose parents have been killed in the bombing. If anyone asks, she must say that the lady is Mrs Heroma and that she is taking her to her aunt who lives in Dordrecht, which is a different town. It is important to stay very close to the lady, hugged tight into her body so that nobody who knows her can see that Lien is not wearing her star. Mamma says exactly the same things as the lady and gets her to repeat them, even though Lien feels she knows them already. Then, a kiss with a hug that hurts a little and she is outside in the Pletterijstraat, walking fast in step with the lady, trying hard to keep herself pressed into her coat. The bag of her things, including her poesie album and Pappa's puzzle, is over Mrs Heroma's shoulder and bangs its edge against her with every stride.

It is not far from Lien's house to the station, so their walk through the streets and then through the park (where Jews are forbidden) to the Hollands Spoor railway is over almost as soon as it starts. The station front looks like a palace, but there is no time to look at it because their train is about to depart. Lien thinks for a moment about her bedroom, close enough for her to run back.

Mrs Heroma talks to her about funny place names. There are lots in Holland, she says. For example, the Double Sausage

Street in Amsterdam, The Moustache in Groningen, or Duck-sick Road in Zeeland. There is also a road called Behind the Wild Pig. Lien thinks these names are funny. She likes Mrs Heroma and giggles as they watch the houses of The Hague pass faster and faster through the window of the train compartment, the *kchunk, kchunk* of the wheels on the railway growing louder and closer together. The smoke from the locomotive is dirty but it smells clean. 'Does Lien know any funny place names?' After a lot of thinking, she remembers Cow Thief Street, which Mrs Heroma had not known about. 'Cow Thief Street, that's a good one!' Mrs Heroma says.

Lien is about to say, 'It's not far from our house,' when she stops herself just in time.

Unlike The Hague, Dordrecht has only one railway station. It is also like a palace, only a bit smaller, without the princess towers of the station they left behind. They walk through another park – bigger than theirs at home, and sleepy in the afternoon sunlight – then through streets with little houses, nothing at all like the three-storey apartment blocks of The Hague. Her legs are tired now and it takes a bit longer each time to get to a new corner, but at each one Mrs Heroma tells her the street name and then a funny one from somewhere else in Holland, so Lien presses on. They reach the Mauritsweg (at which Mrs Heroma says 'Trousers Street'), then the Krispijnseweg ('Buttermountain Street') and finally the Bilderdijkstraat ('Rabbitpipe Street'), and they have arrived. All the houses that Lien has passed seemed little compared to the ones in The Hague, but these ones in the Bilderdijkstraat are the littlest of all. In fact the street doesn't really look like it has houses; it just has two long, low red-brick walls with doors and windows set in it, stretching as far as Lien can see.

In the road a group of boys is running and shouting. Mrs

Heroma, ignoring the commotion, walks straight to the door of number 10 and knocks hard on the little round window-pane. In her coat pocket, unbeknownst to Lien, there is a letter. It is written in the same steady hand that her mother used on the second page of the little girl's album. The letter, which still survives in Lien's apartment in Amsterdam, is dated August 1942. It reads as follows:

Most Honoured Sir and Madam,

Although you are unknown to me, I imagine you for myself as a man and a woman who will, as a father and mother, care for my only child. She has been taken from me by circumstance. May you, with the best will and wisdom, look after her.

Imagine for yourself the parting between us. When shall we ever see her again? On 7 September she will be nine. I hope it will be a joyful day for her.

I want to say to you that it is my wish that she will think only of you as her mother and father and that, in the moments of sadness that will come to her, you will comfort her as such.

If God wills it, we will all, after the war, shake one another by the hand in joyous reunion. Directed to you as the father and mother of:

Lientje

4

I am on a train approaching Dordrecht (colloquially known as Dordt), the city to which Lien was brought in the late summer of 1942. Seen from the railway bridge before we pull into the station, its Great Church rises up between pretty gabled houses, beyond which lie harbours and a heavy-industrial zone. Though small by today's standards, with a population of around 120,000, this city was once the biggest in Holland. Built on an island that was created by a confluence of rivers, its heyday lies back in the fifteenth century, when it became a natural centre for the handling of agricultural goods. For a while it was a merchant city. The silt-filled rivers, however, proved unsuitable for the larger ships that soon became necessary for ocean trading, which meant that, over time, Dordt was overtaken by its larger westerly neighbour, Rotterdam.

It was here, rather than in The Hague, that Dutch independence really started. In 1572 the city hosted the First Assembly of the Free States, at which William of Nassau, Prince of Orange, announced his open rebellion against the Spanish king. It was also here, at the Synod of Dordt, that the new republic, having proved victorious, decided on its state religion. From 1618 to 1619 the Protestant churches of Europe gathered to debate the great theological questions. On one side stood the followers of Jacobus Arminius, who felt that some kind of accommodation with Catholicism might be possible: perhaps 'grace' (that great act of divine forgiveness for man's innate sinfulness) could indeed be fostered by human action, such as penitence or good deeds? Opposing them were the Calvinists, who insisted on what they termed the 'total depravity' of human beings. According to Calvin, only a small band of individuals, already chosen by God before the beginning of time, would be saved from damnation, no matter how fervently the others might try to join that 'elect'. The Synod ended in a Calvinist triumph, and only four days after its conclusion the main protector of the Arminians, Johan van Oldenbarnevelt, was led to execution on the block. 'Total depravity' was thus confirmed.

After leaving the functional interior of the station, I look back over my shoulder at its classical façade and then head down the main street into town. My plan is to begin by visiting the small war museum. It is only a short walk, first through an area of modern office blocks and then through a set of pretty medieval streets that are full of cyclists and shoppers. At this hour of the morning these are mostly retired couples wearing practical clothing such as jogging bottoms and zip-up water-proofs in vivid colours like purple, lime green and pink.

The museum, which is located in a town house across from the old harbour, is like hundreds of others: a little faded and cramped, with over-bright lighting so that nothing looks real. In the entrance hall, pride of place is given to an army Jeep that stands in the middle of the foyer on a dais of artificial grass. Stiff mannequins sit inside it. Their clean helmets have tightly fitting chinstraps and they smile, eyes forward, like Lego men. Behind, there are maps showing the German landings and then the Allied liberation. Bold arrows show troop movements accompanied by numbers and dates. Elsewhere there are photographs and display cases full of weapons, documents and medals.

Dordrecht was one of the towns that saw real fighting when the Germans invaded. Paratroopers were dropped at first light on 10 May 1940 to seize the bridges. The city had a garrison of 1,500 soldiers, but the Dutch army, which had not fought a real war for more than two centuries, was spectacularly ill prepared. Few of the men had received full combat training and much of their ammunition was locked in a central depot for safekeeping, so they had only a minimal supply of rounds. In the early hours many of the defenders simply looked up to the sky in awe of the Junkers bombers. Others wasted their supply of bullets trying to shoot them down.

All the same, once the shock of the landing abated, there were pitched battles. On day one, dozens of German assault troops were killed or wounded and around eighty were taken prisoner, shipped to England just in time. Then on 13 May around twenty Panzers rolled into the city, of which fifteen were disabled at the cost of twenty-four Dutch lives. After just four days of fighting, however, Dordt, like the rest of the Netherlands, surrendered and the troops spent the last of their energy destroying their own equipment to prevent it from falling into enemy hands.

As the sole visitor to the museum, I feel a little intrusive. Around me the men who work here (I should imagine on a voluntary basis) are checking stocklists, cleaning objects from the display cases and reorganizing the small library of books about the war. As I stand scanning the battered spines, I turn to a man in a blue shirt with white hair who is sorting piles of volumes at a desk. He looks up, pleased at my interest in history and still more so when I tell him about Lien and her journey here from The Hague. At the mention of Mrs Heroma, who brought Lien to Dordrecht, a look of recognition crosses his face. He asks what information I have.

On my laptop, which I take from my suitcase, there is a photograph of a document: a yellow sheet of lined A4 paper covered in jottings, some crossed out. It is headed 'What should play a role in the construction of a new law?' The document is in the hand of Mrs Heroma, and I took the photo of it in Amsterdam. It came to Lien after Mrs Heroma's death. By the time that these jottings were made, long after the war, Dieuke Heroma-Meilink (known as 'Took' to her friends) was a Labour politician, first in Parliament and then at the UN. The annotations on the paper are practical, with Lien cited briefly as a case of an only child who had to join a larger family. A detail makes the situation human: as Lien's mother pulled the front door shut at the Pletterijstraat, Mrs Heroma heard her beginning to sob.

The man calls others towards him, and soon a small group is looking over my shoulder at the document on the screen. As I scroll through the images on my computer – the poesie album, the letters and the photographs – a strong feeling of shared interest fills the room. The one who really knows about this, I am told, is Gert van Engelen, a local journalist who also works for the museum. Emails are sent and messages are left on answerphones and meanwhile the group checks indexes and databases, giving suggestions as to where I might go to find out more. They feel almost like friends. By mid-afternoon I have a list of websites and publications and am watching a video recorded by the United States Holocaust Memorial Museum twenty-five years ago in which Mrs Heroma, somewhat reluctantly, reveals the things that she and her husband did during the war.

In the 1930s the Heromas lived in Amsterdam, where Jan Heroma, having first completed a degree in psychology, was studying at medical school. The two of them were politically progressive, deciding to live together rather than get married, sharing a flat with the future socialist Health Minister Irene

Vorrink (who was to become famous for decriminalizing recreational drugs in 1976). Having trained as a social worker, Took was employed by a trade union to provide political education for working-class women. At night in the flat, at a small desk with a typewriter, she translated German academic literature written by Jews into Dutch. This was necessary because, without these translations, German Jewish academics, persecuted at home by the Nazis, would find it difficult to find jobs in the Netherlands. To the Heromas, liberal, politically neutral Holland seemed a natural place of refuge.

By the time of the invasion, Jan Heroma had his own medical practice in Dordrecht, an elegant white terraced house at number 14 Dubbeldamseweg. An extra door had been fitted to allow patients direct access to the waiting room at ground level, and from there they could cross straight to the doctor's study. The couple themselves lived in an apartment upstairs.

At first, the German invaders did little to disturb ordinary

life in the Netherlands. They took over the reins of power (appointing Arthur Seyss-Inquart as Reichskommissar in charge of the civil administration), but the structure of government and the operation of services such as the police, the school system, shops, churches and businesses remained more or less the same. Anti-Jewish measures ramped up over time almost imperceptibly: exclusion from air-raid shelters; an 'Aryan Declaration' for members of the Civil Service; a requirement for the registration of all Jews. Then, from February 1941, mass arrests began, slowly at first. Those whom the Heromas had brought to apparent safety in their own country were now under threat, and the translations and new posts in the universities they had once provided were no longer of use.

From November 1941 onwards, regular ads were placed in the bottom left-hand corner of the classifieds page of the local paper. Next to announcements from the dentist, the fashion boutique and the concert hall, there were notices such as this:

J. F. HEROMA
PHYSICIAN
CHANGE OF
CONSULTATION HOURS
On Krispijn at 11 am
daily, apart from Saturdays;
PRIVATE CONSULTATION
daily from 1.30 to 2 pm

Where it mattered, people knew what these messages meant.

Across Holland, as the occupation gained in intensity, networks were being constructed to resist the Nazis: delicate lines of trust that connected couples like the Heromas in Dordrecht to distant others whom they had never met. These webs often clung to the holdfasts of pre-war society, such as medical associations, student fraternities, churches and political groups. Jan Heroma was a doctor and a member of the Social Democratic Workers' Party and also the friend of many Jews in the academic world. This made the house at number 14 Dubbeldamseweg a point of intersection. The little car that the Heromas owned made them unusually mobile, so that journeys between the houses of patients, sometimes far out into the countryside, traced fragile, invisible strands.

As Jan Heroma and his wife ferried people across the country and kept them hidden in their basement, others too were beginning to take action as part of networks in different towns. Jooske de Neve, for example, part of a resistance group called The Unnamed Entity, sat on trains from Amsterdam accompanying groups of Jewish children, herself shaking with a feverish headache of fear. Speaking long afterwards, she recalled that she could always detect the moment at which other passengers recognized the quiet cluster of boys and girls as Jewish. She just had to hope that they would not tell. Once, a set of train guards began moving through the carriage, checking IDs and tickets. A wave of panic overcame her, and she ran to the toilet and flushed a pack of false identity cards (which she was ferrying in addition to the children) on to the tracks below. It haunted her conscience for ever afterwards that these false papers were found.

In Utrecht, Hetty Voûte, a biology student, joined a group that called itself The Children's Committee. Searching for addresses to hide young boys and girls now separated from their parents, she cycled around the countryside, calling at random on farmers for help.

As she stood at the gate of one farmhouse, the owner told her, 'If it is God's wish that those children are taken, then that is God's wish.'

Hetty looked straight at him. 'And if your farm burns down tonight, then that is also God's wish,' she replied.

Back home in her room, in her bookcase she had a leather-bound volume with the title *The Assembled Tales of John Galsworthy* stamped on the spine. Within, there lay hidden a system of index cards that recorded the names and addresses of the 171 Jewish children she had saved.

Around the same time, in Limburg, at the southern tip of the country, another farmer was being presented with children to shelter, starting with a three-year-old girl who was left at his door. Looking back, one can see that it was hard for this man, Harmen Bockma, to keep his head above water. He already had a milk round early each morning and worked shifts at the local mine to make ends meet. To hide children he would need special spaces in his farmhouse, which would take money as well as time. And so, in order to get the paid leave from the mine that would be necessary for the work to be completed, Harmen Bockma cut off part of a finger from his own hand.

More stories such as these are to be found in the museum and in the Dordrecht municipal library. In a high-ceilinged café I talk with Gert van Engelen as he writes down email addresses and phone numbers in my notebook and suggests places of wartime significance that I might visit beyond and within the town.

Two final stories stick with me. One is the case of Ger Kempe, a student doing the rounds in search of funding for a resistance group hiding children, in late 1942. Having knocked at an unknown door, he was tentatively invited in by the old lady who answered it. Perched on a sofa in her sitting room, the young man delivered a speech that was met with awkward silence. The woman waited for a long time, giving no response, and then eventually told him to come back in a few days' time.

When he did so, expecting little or nothing, the old lady gave him 1,600 guilders: a fortune that saved many lives.

The second story concerns a number of female students. By late 1942 the situation for the remaining Jews in the Netherlands had become utterly desperate, so much so that mothers were now leaving babies and young children on doorsteps in the hope that they would be taken in. The German authorities, aware of this trend, put out an official notice: from now on, all foundlings would be assumed to be Jewish and even those who had earlier been accepted and adopted by Aryan families were to be hunted down by the police. The group of young students could see only one solution. They would register Jewish babies as their own children, fathered by German soldiers. This would bring the certainty of safety, but also, of course, tremendous shame to the women themselves. Years afterwards, An de Waard retold the story of her experience at the register office, where she was made to wait on public view for a very long time. Eventually, under the clerk's contemptuous gaze, she was able to register the child as 'William', a royal name, which for her was a little gesture of resistance. Like the five other babies saved in this manner, William survived the war.

Meanwhile, in Dordrecht, the Heromas continued to ferry, to care for and to hide Jews of all ages, although they were increasingly fearful that their activities were being tracked. Once, Jan Heroma headed out to look after a sick Jewish woman in hiding who, in spite of his best efforts, died of natural causes after several hours. As there was no way to remove her body without its being noticed, he dug a secret grave for her in the back garden under cover of night. In another case, he and Took rushed out to a house that had been hit by Allied bombing, aware that a Jewish couple were hiding inside. They guided the couple back to the Dubbeldamseweg, and hid them in the cellar. After this, Jan went out in his little car to fetch the bombed-out couple's daughter, who had been taken to a farmhouse far away. At first the girl, long separated, did not recognize her mother. Then, when she suddenly did, her delighted screams of recognition brought the terror of discovery to the house.

For months all went well, but then one night there was a knock at the door and policemen were waiting outside. In the dead of night, with Jews still hidden in the cellar, Jan Heroma was led away to prison and an uncertain fate.

During my time in Dordrecht I visit many places, but it is only towards dusk on the final day, just before taking the train back to The Hague, that I head to the Bilderdijkstraat to see the address where Lien first arrived in the town. It is a ten-minute walk from the station, so I go there trundling my suitcase, first through the park in the weakening sunshine and then along the broad pavements of a suburban trunk road that is beginning to fill with commuter traffic.

The Bilderdijkstraat itself is narrow and rather gloomy. For the first fifty yards both sides of the street have high grey panel fencing that is faded and marked by graffiti tags. After this, on the left, it opens out on to an urban playground filled with the smooth-edged concrete of bicycle and skateboard ramps. I come to a halt and look at the empty swings and slides, which are of a high-quality polished metal that makes them look like abstract works of art. A few trees grow on little islands of grey soil surrounded by asphalt, but there is no grass. About half a dozen teenage boys of North African appearance sit chatting, perched on the saddles of their bikes. Across the way, a corner shop advertises cheap international dialling and halal meats.

Since the 1970s the Netherlands has become a country of immigration. One fifth of the population were either born outside its borders or are the children of those who were. Integration, especially amongst the 2 million that are of non-Western origin, has, on the whole, been only moderately successful, and that feeling of isolation is evident on this street.

Looking for number 10, I begin scanning the doorways, my suitcase clunking on the pavement slabs. Towards the end of the road there is a block of new terraced housing, different from the low-rise brick tenements that surround it. Some of this is occupied, but other parts have steel grilles over the windows that seem to have been there for a good while. The new build has confused the number system, so I end up walking along the same stretch of pavement again and again. While the boys on bicycles are in no way threatening, they regard me with increasing interest as an oddity, as well they might.

By the time I decide that number 10 stood on what is now the playground, the sun is casting long shadows across the street. I reach for my phone and take a few pictures, first of the concrete skateboard ramp with the spindly trees around it and then of the row of houses that stands opposite. The entire terrace is a single flat-roofed unit. It is as if its long front wall was rolled in some factory and then had windows and doors punched out of it by an enormous machine.

As I return the phone to my pocket a door opens and a middle-aged man in a kameez comes towards me, asking suspiciously, with a heavy accent, what I am doing. Meanwhile, the boys on bicycles begin to hover around. Faced with their questions, I am suddenly evasive, explaining in a vague manner that I am conducting research about the Second World War.

Why is it that I do not tell this man about Lien, as I did at the Pletterijstraat? I have done so at addresses across Dordrecht, where I have sat happily chatting in people's front rooms over the last few days. Why do I feel guilty here?

It is because I sense a distance between us. It is because I assume that Jewish history will not be welcome in this place.

'You ought not to be spying on people,' the man tells me, and as he says this I suddenly see myself from the outside, with my wheeled suitcase and my phone camera and my scuffed, expensive, brown leather shoes. Perhaps if I had told the full story this might have forged a connection. Instead, we retreat away from each other, equally nervous, and I head out again towards the commuter traffic on the main road where the cars have now switched on their lights.

Walking back towards the station, I am reminded of the obvious fact that the Muslim community, in terms of the hatred directed towards them, is probably closer to the Jews of the previous century than any other. There are no easy parallels but, all the same, the language of Geert Wilders (whose Party for Freedom has hit 15 per cent in national elections) has an air of the 1930s to it. According to Wilders there should be a ban on the Koran and on the building of mosques. He has called the Prophet Muhammad a 'paedophile' and he calls Islam 'evil'. He has spoken of the threat of an 'Islamic invasion' and wants no more Muslims to enter the country at all. He has even demanded the abolition of Article 1 of the Dutch constitution, which outlaws discrimination on the grounds of religion. It is hardly surprising, given this background, that the inhabitants of the Bilderdijkstraat should feel suspicious. All the worse, then, that I came here trundling a suitcase, pointing a camera, only to look and not to tell.

5

Everything is different. The family in the Bilderdijkstraat in Dordrecht have a *mooie kamer*, a room at the front of the house that is kept for special occasions and for the rest of the time stays unused, cool and dark. After a few months of staying there, Lien gets very ill with suspected tuberculosis and she lies there on the sofa for days on end, watching the light of the day brighten and fade through the curtains, waves of cold and heat shaking her frame. 'Auntie', as she is told to call the mother of the new household, brings clear soup in a teacup with a piece of toast that cuts when it touches her throat. Auntie washes Lien's face with a damp towel and helps her to sit up. The room, like the rest of the tiny single-storey apartment, is sparsely furnished, with just two chairs facing the sofa on which she lies. Beside the unlit coal burner there is one precious object: a cabinet of dark polished wood with a china teapot and matching cups set out on top. The cups, which are never used, are pure white inside and they gleam even when the curtains are closed. If she picks one up and holds it to her eye, ever so gently, she can see her reflection in it. The curved sides of the cup bend the walls of the room so that they surround her like a burrow.

When you are ill the whole world exists at a distance. She senses movement outside on the street through the curtains and the front windows: men calling in the Dordt accent, so different from her own. At the end of nearly every sentence they say 'hey'. As the children arrive from school there is noise from the adjoining kitchen: voices, a chair scraping, a tap running. 'Be quiet – Lien is asleep next door, hey!' The kitchen is where the house comes to life. Mothers and children enter without knocking from the back of the house, bringing friends and news. Auntie's voice is the loudest:

'Do you know what they are charging for mince at the butcher's?'

'Nell is getting her meat straight from the farm, Kokkie told me, hey?'

Movement here is rougher than it was in Lien's old house. There is banging of pots and cutlery, and if Kees, who is nine, behaves badly his father will give him a whack on the arm. But everyone is welcome, the neighbours are friends, and there are always new voices at the dinner table. The men talk of workers' rights and of the bosses at the factory with a sense of confidence and strength. A strong smell of cigarettes pushes its way into the silence of the front room.

Even though it happened a few months after she first arrived, Lien's strongest memory of the house in the Bilderdijkstraat is that of being hot and feverish in the *mooie kamer*. When Mrs Heroma brought her, she also went in there, sitting on the sofa, looking across at Auntie, a big woman with a rosy-cheeked face, who told Lien about her new cousins. Besides Lien and Kees, there are two other children in the household: Ali, who is eleven; and little Marianne, who is nearly two. Ali and Kees first had a different mother, but she died.

After their talk in the front room, Mrs Heroma says good-bye, leaving Lien behind with Auntie, who takes her through into the back of the house. In the kitchen Lien is absorbed into the hubbub. Because there are so many people coming and going it is impossible to feel like a guest for long. As she enters, little Marianne totters on uncertain legs in the corner, half supervised by Ali, and then slumps into a heap. Lien feels grown up as she crouches to comfort her, and she and Ali soon have the girl in fits of laughter. When Lien does a ballet dance Marianne sits rapt with attention, looking up with adoring eyes. At bedtime, from Auntie's arms, Marianne gives Lien several wet kisses, leaving a little trail of cold baby spit on her cheek.

The first dinner is not so easy. She is given a deep plate with a mountain of potatoes, sprouts and a meatball, all covered in gravy. Everyone is already eating; the talk continues uninterrupted except for the regular scrape of spoons. Lien toys with a potato. The digestive medicine, which Mamma normally gives her with a glass of water before a meal, is in her bag. She raises her hand to ask if she can go and get it. It takes a long time for her to be noticed, but eventually Auntie calls out in her loud voice to ask what she wants. 'Medicine?' Auntie loudly repeats the word as if it is something in a foreign language. Lien slips away to fetch the brown bottle and holds it out, label first, so as to explain. Auntie's rosy face is all scrunched up with suspicion as she examines this object that Lien has brought into her house. Then she delivers her verdict. 'You don't need this, you can just eat your dinner with everyone else, hey,' Auntie tells her, and pours the thick white liquid into the sink. Returning to the stove, Auntie continues to take part in the conversation, turning only briefly to instruct Kees not to bolt his food.

Around her, the plates are already emptying. The moment one is finished, Auntie reaches over the seated person, picks up the plate, brings it to the sink for a vigorous wash, and then returns it steaming with fragrant tapioca. Gradually the kitchen fills with the smell of the hot pudding. Lien would like to leave her sprouts and potatoes and move on to her sweet, which was often what happened at home. The boy Kees, nearly finished, has stopped eating; he looks over at her with a conspiratorial, comradely air. Auntie, though, gives short shrift to the rebellion. The last of the tapioca is scraped from the pan and divided amongst the existing pudding eaters, who barely notice the ladle as it reaches down over their heads. Plates are cleared and not a word is spoken about the uneaten sprouts and potatoes. Lien is dumbfounded and feels a hollowness inside her – it is all so different – but she joins Kees and Ali to head outside.

After dinner they are allowed to play for another hour. Kees takes Lien with him and introduces her to his playmates. He seems proud of her. He is certainly proud of his ability to walk on the crumbling brick wall in the wasteland beyond the houses and scoffs when she notices afterwards that he has cut his knee. Lien merges easily with the huddle of children who stand watching Kees as he jumps from one brick stack to another. Although they notice her accent and listen vaguely to her story, she is soon part of the group.

As the late summer evening darkens a new consciousness settles over the children, who move almost in union like a flock of birds. They melt into the little terraced houses, exchanging brief words about tomorrow's plans. At number 10 the bustle is over. Auntie has finished cleaning the kitchen and is now knitting; Uncle sits reading, his face stern with concentration beneath the room's only light. Kees, Ali and Lien wash themselves at the sink and visit the loo. *"Trusten,'* says Auntie, which is short for *welterusten*, meaning 'goodnight'.

The children share one bedroom, with the adults and baby Marianne in the other. Within minutes, Kees and Ali are sleeping. Lien lies listening to their regular breaths. As far as she can remember she has never slept in a room with other people. For a moment she thinks of her bedroom in the Pletterijstraat. At home Mamma always comes to sit by her in the evening, stroking her hair before she kisses her goodnight.

*

Kees shakes her awake in the morning. It is still holiday time and today he is going to catch tadpoles. He knows a place where you can find them even in August, and Lien can come. They wolf down their bread and cheese at the kitchen table while Auntie watches and then scramble out the door. Outside the sun is shining, so she barely notices the chill as she runs, following Kees through the empty lanes.

After ten minutes they are already in an area of farmland and industrial depots, which is where the secret supply of tadpoles is to be found. The blocked-up ditch that is their home has a slippery slope of grass and brambles, and Kees edges down carefully, ploughing the soil with a stick in his right hand to keep himself steady, holding a jar in his left. He looks over his shoulder at Lien above him, then turns to paw at the water. Lien is not sure what he is trying to do, but after a few sweeps Kees seems satisfied. He holds his eye to the glass and then picks his way back up to her, the jar now filled with milky green liquid that sloshes over his hand.

Lien hardly dares touch the wet container, and it takes her a while to spot the strange tailed and legged creature swimming inside. She has never seen anything like it, though she has been told in school about tadpoles. It looks like a frog gone wrong. After a bit she is goaded into trying to catch one, and finds herself sliding a little on her way down the slope. Reaching into the brown-green water, she has the horrible sensation that there is something trying to climb its way into her shoe. Kees is confident about everything and calls down encouragingly, adding instructions to improve her technique, and soon there is a fellowship between them, which makes Lien more certain about what she is doing, and the air is filled with mutual cries of admiration as they work. At the end of the morning they have a whole set of the little monsters decanted into a single jar. After scrutinizing their catch through the glass, giving them names and characters, they pour the tadpoles back into the murk.

With this adventure behind them, Lien and Kees become firm friends. On other days there are different excursions. Kees teaches her to ring doorbells at people's houses and then scamper away to hide and look. They also climb the great bridge over the canal and peer down on the barges, which Kees tries to hit with little stones. He is very good at throwing and sometimes they hear the satisfying tinkle of glass. The town of Dordt, and the countryside around it, is their playground and they can disappear into it for a whole, unimaginably long, day at a time. The two of them follow rules that they themselves decide on, glorying in their liberty as only children can. When they return in the evening to the Bilderdijkstraat they feel like conquering heroes, worthy of the banquet of potatoes, sprouts and meatballs that awaits.

For the first time in her life Lien is free of her tummy aches. She eats happily in the small kitchen, she loves the talk and the bustle, she loves the freedom of running wild. At home she looks after little Marianne, telling her stories as she feeds her, one extra bit of story with each bite. Everyone follows the rules of the household – bedtimes, mealtimes, keeping your things tidy – but really she has to do almost nothing. Auntie cooks, washes and cleans, seemingly without having to think about it, and for dinner everyone is always welcome to bring friends. If Uncle is studying in the evening they have to be quiet. She is a bit afraid of him, but she also admires him terribly. Men and women listen when he talks to them, and they always do what he says.

After a month, she is back at school and it is her ninth birthday: 7 September 1942. She gets to choose her own dinner and she chooses sprouts. After breakfast, Auntie brings her some letters and packages from home. When Lien arrived in early August there were three dates ahead of her: her birthday (which was the most important); her mother's (a long way ahead, on 28 October, when she would surely be home); and then far away in the distance there was Pappa's, in December, further off even than St Nicholas. Now the first of these dates is upon her. Before anything else, she opens the packages: two big bags of sweets, including one of liquorice, of which she takes one piece and then two. There is also a knitted thing and a book that she puts to one side.

Four letters. It is strange to sit here in silence looking at them in the *mooie kamer*, where she has hardly been since she arrived. The first she reads is Pappa's, which has '7 SEPTEMBER' written in capitals in the top right-hand corner to make sure it is read on the proper day. She recognizes Pappa's faultlessly joined sloping writing, which is also there on the first page of her poesie album. The letter is four sides long:

Dear Lientje

I am writing this letter on the occasion of your birthday. I congratulate you on your ninth birthday and hope that you will have many happy returns in future years to remember this day. Then, of course, we will be together again and will celebrate this one an extra time. As Mamma is sending you a present (I don't know what it will be?) I will do the same and so enclose one guilder, with which you can buy something that you like, or you can use it to give others a treat if you have a ration card for sweets.

I have heard you are having a nice time there and that you are learning to swim. Can you swim well already?

We are always happy to hear news from you and if you ever have not so much to do, write to us with some news. It doesn't have to be a long letter and it will help you to practise your handwriting. You are probably back in school now? That must be nice, because then you won't be behind the others when you come back.

Hey, Lien, I saw the menu for your birthday meal; it looks delicious. I think we will eat exactly the same things on the day itself, because it is kind of also a celebration for us (is 'celebration' with an 'e' or an 'a'?).

If you sit there with the six of you I would really like to see your pudding. Draw it for me if you like, because that must be a big pudding. I don't know who had the last bite of it, but I think it was you. We will have to remember because when you come back we will start from where you left off.

Are you always the first or the last to be dressed in the morning? And with food? You can win that race, I think. You will have to write to me about all this and about how you celebrated your birthday.

Don't forget Mamma's birthday!! [Pappa squeezes in a tiny '28 October' here, deciding afterwards that she might have forgotten the date.] *Lientje, I hope that you have a very, very, very, very happy time of it and we here will have a nice glass of lemonade and let's hope that we will soon be together, the three of us, maybe even before Mamma's birthday. That would be the best present. Hey, Lien, the paper is nearly full and I had wanted to write so much more.*

Thank your foster-parents on our behalf, also for their kind letter to us, and look after yourself, then the time will go quickly, till we collect each other from the train.

I also have to pass on the congratulations of the family. Both grannies and grandpas, Auntie Fie, Uncle Jo, Rini, Daaf, Auntie Bep, Uncle Mannie, Auntie Riek with the three children, Uncle Bram and Auntie Ro. Have I forgotten anybody? Because they have all told me that I must congratulate you on their behalf. I had nearly forgotten to send a greeting from Pretty.

Lien, many more years after this one. Hip, hip, hip HOORAY.

from Pappa

The second letter is a short one from Mrs Andriessen:

Dear Lientje

Many congratulations on your birthday. I hope that you are healthy and are having a nice time. Also, best wishes to your housemates. You should have a pleasant day and let us hope that everything will be normal again soon, like it was. I am well. You'll see a small present for you. Now, Lientje, take my warm greeting, in thought.

Many kisses
from Mrs R. A.

The next letter is from Aunt Ellie, who had written a poem in Lien's album, decorated with a beautiful fan. She leaves a lot of space at the top of her big sheet of lined paper, below the place and date, 'The Hague, 2 September '42':

Dear Lientje

Many congratulations on your birthday and I hope that you will become a big girl to make Mamma and Pappa even prouder of you than they are now!

Aunt Ellie had wanted very much to come and see you, but it is better not to. Your present – you knew what it was anyway – you will get from somebody else now. Babs has knitted it beautifully, hasn't she?

I have heard that you are having a nice time and that everything will be fun.

If you want to see Aunt Ellie very much, just for a moment, you should ask your aunt and uncle if they can think of a way to do it.

But over there you have lots of new aunties and uncles and playmates, so perhaps you have forgotten us already long ago!

Dear little thing, I'm stopping with this. A nice happy day, I
hope that you can have one, and enjoy your lovely birthday meal.

Very many kisses from
Aunt Ellie

E. Monkernuis, Kanaalbrugweg 87, The Hague
The liquorice is from Granny and Auntie Bep!

Finally there is Mamma's letter, the one she wanted to save till last. Diagonally at the top is written 'Meant for 7 September':

Dear Lieneke

Heartfelt congratulations on your ninth birthday. Although I
cannot congratulate you myself now, because of this I still think of
you the whole day and I hope that you will have just as much fun
as you would with us at home. I will send you a book and some
nice things to eat and you will have to make do with that this year.
I have not been able to buy a watch for you. I hope that Aunt Ellie
will come to you herself – that would be very nice for you and for
me. If she doesn't go then the package will go in the post and you
will still get everything. I hope that you are now going to school and
that you will be happy and that you will appreciate what Auntie
and Uncle are doing for you, because that is a lot. I don't know if
Pappa can write to you, because he is out of town. But please believe
that he will also think of you the whole day and that he thinks it is
a shame that we cannot be together. But maybe everything will
come good again. Think of that, love. Write Mamma a little letter
back, but don't put it in the mail, because we don't live at the
Pletterijstraat any more. So just give the little letter to Auntie and
Uncle – they will make sure I get it. Or you can give it to Aunt Ellie,
if she comes.

Goodbye, angel, a really lovely day for the rest and thousands of kisses from your loving

Mammie

The book that Mamma sends her is called *About a Happy Holiday*. Its cover shows three children, drawn in pastel colours, who are standing on a quayside with a lady in a green hat looking protectively on. Behind them is an enormous ocean liner, at which the children are waving excitedly as it comes in to dock. The whole thing is cheerful colours: the bow of the ship is a solid triangle rising above the quay, and above this there is a long white line marked with regular black circles that are portholes. Right at the top, above the waving figure of what must be the captain, an orange funnel puts a little puff of

smoke into a bright yellow block of sky. In a picture like this, going away seems like a simple and beautiful thing.

Lien takes the book and places it high on a shelf in the *mooie kamer*, where it remains untouched.

There is an alien grown-up sadness in these letters, like the sadness she felt when Mamma and Pappa quarrelled and she had to go away to stay with Daafje and Rini. Suddenly Lien wants more than anything in the world to be home. Real home, in her own bedroom in the Pletterijstraat. But now she thinks that maybe her bedroom has a different girl living in it, just when she wants so much to be lying in her little bed with Mamma stroking her hair.

Lien feels a tightness in every part of her and sees that she is weeping, and once she knows it she cannot stop. The tears just keep coming. Her breathing gets all muddled and she begins to sob in hard, sharp bursts. Then grief overwhelms her like sickness, rolling over her as a great, dark wave.

Now she finds herself crying constantly, for days, for hours on end. There is no comfort possible; she just wants Mamma and Pappa with an all-consuming hollowness. Desperate, not knowing what to do with her, Auntie takes Lien for a walk in the park, where she just carries on crying, so unhappy that it hurts like a raw wound. Then both of them are weeping, hand in hand with the grey autumn sky above them, the leaves still dark green and brown on the trees. They just walk round and round the same paths, seeing the same faces, not speaking at all. As they cry together, Lien holds herself close to this warm, strong woman, and the feeling of loss is joined by a new feeling, of love.

6

The ceiling of The Hague's Central Station is like an Escher print of squares within squares. I stand looking up at it for a moment and then resume scanning the crowd. I am here to carry out research at the National Archives, just across from this building. There are papers there on the police service that was active in Dordrecht in the war years, hunting out hidden Jews. Steven, the cousin with whom I will stay, is due to meet me and after ten minutes I spot him. His lean frame and handsome cheekbones stand out; he is tall, even by Dutch standards. He is wearing a sort of baseball jacket with black jeans, black skateboarding trainers and a peaked cap. A little medal with faded ribbons sits askew on his chest. I feel the medal as he bends down to give me a hug.

We have not seen each other for at least a year, but when I emailed he was quick to answer that it was no problem for me to stay at his place, which is close to the station. I should arrive, he suggested, fairly late in the evening. He would pick me up, take me on a tour of his workplace, and then we could head home in the early hours. Steven has a mix of professions: a visual artist, festival MC and local politician, he also manages an arts centre cum nightclub that he set up himself, which is where we are heading now.

I hear the club before I see it. A dull regular thud. After a twenty-minute walk, we have reached a light-industrial zone, with warehouses and 1930s office blocks looming up in the darkness behind high steel gates. This is an area of deprivation, and the building in which the club is located is part of a project to try to revive it, attracting small businesses, but there is still a lot of empty space. The huge block stands out against the night sky in outline and makes me think of an oil tanker, weighed down, engines running, trying to get up to speed.

Once we are inside, the club, though half empty, envelops us. At the entrance, Steven trades air punches with a muscled bouncer and bear-hugs the girl at the desk. Beyond this there is dry ice and music, a series of large rooms with young men standing at turntables, each lit in different pulsing colours. The style of the place has an edge of irony to it. Room one is themed as a 1970s beach club, with a retro glitter ball and pinkish slides of a desert island projected on to the walls. Most punters at this time of night, I am told, will be tuned in via Internet radio, checking Facebook and Instagram, deciding whether to come.

By 2 a.m. the news is positive: the club is filling up. Parties of friends make their way past the bouncer and on to the dance floor, checking for familiar faces, ordering drinks. They compliment each other on their clothing and check their phones. Soon there is live Japanese painting in time to the music, and I watch as a great bird emerges from spots of colour on a white wall. The steel tanks on the ceiling, Steven proudly tells me, contain 2,000 litres of beer, which is piped to the bars. There are people now of all races, mainly young, who move with an aura of pleasure, raising their hands. A man who might be in his sixties – with a shaved head and grey stubble, dressed completely in black – stands beside me on the sidelines as he nods his head rhythmically to the sound. Later, in a courtyard, surrounded by smokers, we hold a brief conversation. He is a patents lawyer and travels Europe catching events such as this whenever he can. Berlin, he tells me, is especially great.

Berlin. That word's meaning has changed so completely. Today it means a weekend break or a conference. And Tokyo, from where the young men at the turntables come, is now a riot of neon advertising, Hello Kitty kitsch and minimalist design. The old Axis capitals have been conquered for the rainbow flag of youthful globalization, which is all around me in the club. This is the other side of the immigration that I saw in Dordrecht this morning: instead of marginalized and tribal, the young here are united by music and a set of witty, ironic Internet memes. But then this was there too, in another form, in the 1930s. Those pictures of Lien's father (first with the dapper young men in the motor car and then posing with his fedora hat and polished shoes) make me think that he would have fitted quite easily into this happy cosmopolitan crowd. And yet all that unity, at least in Berlin, was wiped away by the Great Depression, a catastrophe not entirely different from the crisis that laid waste to the industrial estates that lie all around us in darkness, locked up behind gates.

It is nearly morning when we get to Steven's apartment, which, like the club, is in a derelict building. Although marked for demolition, it can be used in the interim on a short-term lease. The huge rooms, more than twenty metres long, have high ceilings and rows of uncurtained windows that look out on to a skyline of silent lit-up roads. This was originally the testing laboratory of the Dutch trading standards agency, and the glass doors still bear their original labels. They read 'Destruction Experiments', 'Radiology' and 'Endurance Repetitions'. It feels like a film set, especially because Steven and his flatmates have placed various art objects on the floor in pools of light. There is a full-sized plywood paper sailboat that greets you on first entry, and opposite, at the far end of the room, a smashed chandelier that sits on top of a plinth. In the midst of all this is a kitchen island with a glass-fronted fridge and a stove.

Steven heads straight for the stove, puts the kettle on, and begins chopping a piece of ginger to make tea.

'No light in the toilet – you have to use your phone,' he warns me after I ask the way.

And soon we are talking with the city spread out below us. I hear about Steven's various projects: local Hague politics, an art residency in Japan, the club, and his girlfriend's work for an urban redevelopment corporation in Amsterdam. He asks me about my family: my wife's new job at the hospital, and especially about my eldest daughter, Josie, with whom he has a special bond. He sits roughly between her and me in age. She has had some tough years lately, but her life has turned a corner and he listens with enthusiasm about her move to London, where she now works. In all the flood of information my search into Lien's life barely gets a mention, which is partly because I am sheepish about it, wrapping it up in my description with various other bits of university work. The fact is that Lien's story is not a comfortable one for the van Esses: asking questions about it threatens the reopening of old wounds.

Half an hour later I am drifting towards sleep on a mattress in the music room, surrounded by piles of records, a keyboard and a drum kit, with the night sky already turning grey.

The next morning I sit at a large table in the modern, brightly lit reading room of the National Archives. In front of me there are three plain cardboard boxes. Others are reserved and waiting behind the desk. Beyond the glass doors at the back of the librarians' office you can see the archivists shifting material on trolleys that look as though they belong in a mortuary. With uniformed officers moving about in search of hidden cameras, warning readers not to lean over their papers, the place feels military and clinical at the same time.

Between 1945 and 1950 the Dutch authorities investigated around 230 police officers for their role in the Holocaust, a process that produced a vast amount of documentation, which now sits on shelves that stretch for over two and a half miles. Most of the prosecutions relate to Amsterdam. But Dordrecht, whose 300 Jews were almost all murdered, has a fair section of shelving reserved for itself.

The Jewish wartime death rate in the Netherlands, at 80 per cent, was more than double that of any other Western country, far higher than that in France, Belgium, Italy or even Germany and Austria themselves. For me, vaguely brought up on a myth of Dutch resistance, this comes as a shock.

There are various factors that help to explain the exceptionally low chance of survival. The population was urban, persecution began early, escape across the borders was almost impossible, and the registration process (which was aided by a blindly cooperative Jewish Council) was efficient. But the active participation of Dutch citizens – who did the work of informing on neighbours, arrest, imprisonment and transportation – also played a significant part. Unlike Belgium, where the SS were the Jew-hunters, or France, with its complicated mix of Vichy and direct military occupation, in Holland it was the native administration that brought death to the Jews.

Here, unlike anywhere else, a scheme of financial bounty was established. A price of seven guilders and fifty cents was placed on the head of every Jew. This was money that policemen, informers or civilian operators would receive personally, in cash. On top of this, the authorities established a system of competition, with two independent agencies being given the power of arrest. One of these was the ordinary police force, which set up various specialist units with names such as the 'Central Control', the 'Bureau for Jewish Affairs', or the 'Political Police'. The other was a semi-commercial company, the *Hausraterfassung*, a Dutch-staffed body whose technical job was the seizure of Jewish property, but which expanded its business to seize people as well. In spite of having just fifty agents, the *Hausraterfassung* tracked down around 9,000 Jews. Through such measures, the Dutch authorities quickly exceeded the targets that were set by their German masters and, in the end, delivered 107,000 'full Jews' to the death camps in the east.

In Dordrecht it was three men on the regular police force – Arie den Breejen, Theo Lukassen and Harry Evers – who did most of the work. From the moment Lien arrived in the city in August 1942, these individuals would have been trying to track her down.

I hesitate for a moment, sitting in front of my laptop, and then open the first box.

When I do so, it seems at first as though I have entered the world of Willem Frederik Hermans's classic post-war Dutch novel *The Darkroom of Damocles*. The last part of this book is set after the liberation, with investigators attempting to work out who was good and who was bad in the Netherlands during the war. The main protagonist, Henri Osewoudt, awaits their verdict, but, as years pass, the evidence (made up of stacks of incomprehensible photographs and contradictory witness statements) simply gathers on desks. As he describes this situation, Hermans plays a literary game with the symbolic objects of the photo negative and the mirror, so that, by the end of the book, the reader can no longer tell who is the hero and who is the villain.

The first box of Harry Evers's files gives the same impression. There are mysterious photos, several of which show the interior of a cupboard with hidden electrical circuitry. Others show sections of microfilm with lines of code. Mixed in with these, apparently at random, are handwritten letters, typed-up witness statements, and official forms. Some describe Evers's violence: the kicking in of doors and the vicious interrogations that he carried out as he searched for illegal items such as radios and guns. But then, like Osewoudt in Hermans's novel, Evers himself writes in outrage. He was, he claims, in reality a resistance fighter who only joined the Political Police after instructions from above. Members of the resistance write in to support this story. There were, they report, frequent tip-offs from Evers about raids that were coming; he helped with the repair of weapons; and he assisted in the shooting of a collaborator in the final stages of the war. Then, towards the bottom of the box, comes a report from the investigatory committee, dated 10 August 1945, which declares Evers innocent, a war hero even. Press cuttings follow, which tell the adventures of Evers the undercover man.

Mixed in with these, though, are letters of protest. Some in the resistance say that the verdict is a gross distortion. There are even copies of flyers describing Evers as a traitor. These flyers have been posted around the town.

The truth of the matter seems hard to work out.

Over the days in the archives, however, I open more boxes. A few survivors return to Dordrecht from Auschwitz, a few others emerge from hiding, and, as the witness statements mount up, first in the tens and then in the hundreds, doubt disappears.

One of the first to speak is Isidor van Huiden, a Jewish man who had lived just a few doors down from the Heromas on the Dubbeldamseweg. He tells the committee that, in the late afternoon of 9 November 1942, Evers and Lukassen, backed up by four policemen from Rotterdam, burst into his home, screaming and swearing, and began a search. After just ten minutes the family (who had crept into a hiding place) had all been discovered and were lined up under guard. Then, while the officers rifled through their papers and other belongings, the van Huidens heard piano music from the adjoining room. It was Evers playing show tunes after concluding the job.

The van Huidens were transported to the holding pen of the Hollandsche Schouwburg in Amsterdam, where they saw many of their Dordrecht neighbours, who told of violent interrogations in which Evers played a leading role.

They would not see those neighbours again.

Isidor himself was lucky because, as a member of the Jewish Council, he still had certain rights. He talked himself and his family out of the Hollandsche Schouwburg with the promise that he would move to the capital and remain at a registered address. The moment they were at liberty, they found a new and better place to hide.

Similar stories come out over the ensuing months of the investigation, and, as I work my way through the boxes, the full arc of Harry Evers's life comes into view.

He stares out vividly from various descriptions. A strong, thickset, blond man, a little puffy about the face. In age and social background he is typical of the Jew-hunters: unremarkable, modestly educated, fond of a drink. Born out of wedlock to a Catholic mother, Evers was brought up by his grandparents in Tilburg and then drifted through various occupations, including shipbuilding and car maintenance, before joining the Dutch army in the run-up to the war. His physical power and ability to inspire obedience got him promotion to sergeant, but he was denied elevation to the officer class.

Although for a time a member of a nationalist party, Evers was not especially political. His main interests were popular music, pornography and chasing girls. He conducted himself well during the German invasion and, after defeat in May 1940, he and some other ex-military men did talk big about forming some kind of resistance. Nothing, though, came of this half-baked plan.

In August 1940 Evers joined the police force. The army, clearly, was no longer an option. Some Dutch men did sign up to the SS or the Wehrmacht, but he was not really pro-German, even if, like most, he now accepted the new state of affairs. Instead, he got a specialist job in the price control unit, which monitored the black market. It soon became clear that he had a talent for tracking things down.

What was it that motivated Evers to transfer to the Political Police nearly two years later, in July 1942? He claimed afterwards that he did this on the instruction of a friend in the military resistance, but this is implausible. There was barely such a thing as military resistance in Dordrecht at this point and certainly not the fabled 'Section K' of which he would boast at his trial. True, Evers kept in contact with one of his old buddies who would eventually become a resistance man. He was always good at keeping his ear to the ground. But things were going well for the Germans. Resistance was absurd. He had just got married and he needed to move out of his boarding house. Proper Jew-hunting was about to begin, which meant that there was easy money to be gained from the Political Police. A man with experience of the underworld and the black market was just what was needed. So Evers signed up as a member of the Fascist Union, always knowing that he had credit as a Dutch nationalist to fall back on if things turned bad.

And, once he was in, it was heaven, better than he could have imagined. He knew people who knew things and he had a natural imposing presence, so it was easy to get to the truth. There were all-night sessions, handfuls of jewels and bank-notes that he could simply take. He developed little tics that gave him character, like toying with his handgun as he spoke, or playing piano at the end of a raid. He even obtained a piano of his own from the former house of a Jew.

It took talent to do things properly. Evers would check concrete floors for cracks that suggested hidden passages and would measure the distance between the height of a ceiling and the floor above. Power over women was a particular pleasure. There was a room next to his office that he used for the rape of the Jewish girls who happened to take his fancy. He liked to refer to his wife as his 'cauliflower' and to these women as his 'sprouts'.

As I read these things, I think of Lien in hiding.

Evers also caught children. One time he saw a little girl on a bicycle and noted to den Breejen that she looked 'like a Jewess', so they followed her home and found papers alight in the stove that proved he was right.

It is the case of Miepie Viskooper, a girl from Amsterdam aged seven, that is the closest to Lien's. She is the subject of witness statements 146 to 148.

Witness 146 is Johanna Wigman, a barmaid in her mid twenties who had taken the little girl into her care. On the night of 15 November 1943, Miepie was sleeping beside Johanna on a mattress. Then, at half past eleven, Johanna heard a break-in downstairs. She just had time to hide the child under the blankets before Evers and den Breejen burst in. The policemen demanded to know if her name was Johanna Wigman and then began their search. All too quickly Miepie was discovered. Den Breejen is recorded in the statement as saying, 'Here we have the Yid!' But then, as the men continued in search of other evidence, the little girl ran out.

Evers and den Breejen were furious and, for her act of protection, Johanna Wigman was sent to the concentration camp at Vught.

Witness 147 is the owner of the adjoining café, Cornelis van Tooren. He himself had a daughter, called Jannetje, of Miepie's age. Evers and den Breejen, he reports, had spent time searching the café before moving on to the neighbouring flat. After they left, he kept watch, and then, at around midnight,

Miepie ran into the bar. Evers came in right behind her, pointing his revolver, shouting 'It's the choke hole for you' at the little girl.

'I've only come to say goodbye to Jannetje,' she replied.

The worst is witness 148. This is Miepie's father, a small-scale confectionery manufacturer in the big city, the same as Lien's. Like Lien, Miepie was an only daughter, and again, just like Lien's parents, the Viskoopers thought their child would be safe if she hid with non-Jews, so they sent her away. They themselves also went into hiding, but they were caught. At the awful moment of their arrest there was at least the feeling that, for their daughter, theirs had been the right choice.

But then, as the couple were held at Westerbork, the Dutch transit camp for Auschwitz, Miepie was brought to her mother, under guard.

As I read this, I think of my own wife and children and imagine that unwanted reunion. I can see the smile of recognition on the face of the child.

The Viskoopers travelled together to Poland. Then, on arrival, Michel Viskooper watched as his wife and daughter were taken from him and driven away on a truck.

Michel, Miepie's father, was one of just 5,200 Dutch Jews who survived the death camps, but he returned to Holland alone.

I sit motionless in the reading room for a few minutes. After this I copy Miepie's case verbatim on to my laptop, typing as quickly as I can.

The wartime career of Harry Evers matches those of many collaborators recorded in the archives. Once the balance of power altered, they began to think about changing sides. In the summer of 1943, just as the transport of Dutch Jews was nearing completion, the Wehrmacht's advance into Russia was stopped. Already in the spring, former Dutch servicemen in non-essential professions had received a summons to forced labour camps in Germany, and by July a quarter of a million workers had been sent. First thousands and then hundreds of thousands went into hiding to avoid this fate. And as the authorities began to search for the missing men, the mood of the population turned far more strongly against the occupiers. Armed resistance, virtually nil at the start of the year, grew rapidly in the last two months of 1943. Meanwhile, the skies darkened with Allied bombers, and Evers, like others, started to worry about what he had done.

So, from the new year onwards, he began actively to help the resistance and took every opportunity to tell them about his bravery as a double agent working for the Germans under instruction from his own side. As time went on, he became ever more helpful. Finally, as Canadian tanks rumbled through the polders, he visited his old friends in their houses and in cafés and made them swear to be true to him at the point of a knife. Once the war was over, he even took the piano he had stolen and returned it, badly damaged, to the house of the Jew.

For nearly a year he remained at liberty, but then, on 13 February 1946, in the tax office near his childhood home in Tilburg, Evers was placed under arrest. He was carrying a loaded pistol and had kept a supply of grenades. Still, he went quietly enough.

In the end, he received an eight-year sentence, reduced to three years and six months on appeal. This was not out of proportion. After all, Albert Gemmeker, the famous 'laughing commandant' of Westerbork, who held a great party to celebrate the transport of the 40,000th victim to Auschwitz, served no more than six years. And afterwards Evers returned to society, enjoying a second marriage, although this one too ended quickly in divorce. When he died, aged seventy-three, in the early 1990s, there were still those in Dordrecht who hailed him as a hero and as the victim of an unfair campaign.

Eventually I retie the final bundle of papers. The next morning, Steven gets up early to see me off on the train. It is only as we are walking to the station, the same one used by Lien when she travelled to Dordrecht, that he points to the little medal with ribbons that sits askew on his chest. This, he tells me, was awarded to his paternal grandfather for heroism in the resistance. After he died, nobody else was going to wear it, so Steven wears it now.

The train doors hiss shut and the carriage starts moving. Steven remains on the platform, giving me a smile and a wave. As I move to the upper deck in search of a seat, I begin to question myself about the work I am doing. Lien asked me about my motivation. There are so many stories like hers and, besides, the bare facts have already been recorded for the Shoah Foundation archive, which was set up by Steven Spielberg soon after he completed his film *Schindler's List* back in 1994. Is there anything that I could add to that?

Around me, morning commuters are tapping on their laptops while the suburbs of The Hague rush ever more quickly by. On flawless tracks, the heavy carriage runs almost without a sound. Just as happened earlier when I was driving into The Hague on those flat and straight motorways, the smooth, unbending movement of the train makes me feel distant from the world outside the window. Rail travel in the Netherlands feels different from that in most other countries because almost nothing of the pre-war infrastructure remains. This makes the past less tangible than it is in England, where everything rattles and looks old. Yet this is the same journey that Lien made when she left her parents just over seventy years ago: it runs on the same ground. Switching my gaze from the view through the window to the modern interior of the carriage, I ask myself if it might be possible to write something that traces this invisible link between Holland's past and its present. I also wonder about my family and their relationship with Lien.

7

The second page of the red photo album on Lien's table in
Amsterdam is devoted to the early 1940s. 'Dordrecht' is written as a heading and underlined. There are nine photographs
in all. Across the top are two of the same pair of children, a girl
and a boy standing together but hardly touching: Ali and Kees.
The version on the left, which looks wintry, is the earliest. It is
probably from the time when their mother was still living; Ali,
the elder, is no more than three. She holds a doll with one
hand and with the other she steadies her brother, who is con-
centrating to stay on his feet. In the version on the right, taken
a few years later, Kees has already thrust himself forward,
smiling a little cheekily at the camera, cocking his head.

The photographer stands above the pair so that they look upwards, expectant, framed by too much space. Ali stands behind Kees now, in his shadow – figuratively as well as literally, one suspects.

Like most of the pictures on the page they are quite ordinary and rather inexpertly taken; expressions are hard to read. In the middle there are some passport snaps without names written beneath them: these are Lien's 'Auntie' and 'Uncle'. Uncle is the father of Ali, Kees and Marianne. Auntie is Marianne's mother and now also the stepmother of Ali and Kees. She is a little chubby and plain-looking; it is easy to imagine her as a farm labourer's daughter and then, from the age of fourteen, as a maid living in service, which is what she was until her late twenties when she and her husband met. As a child she was called 'fat Jans' by her family, although one could hardly get very fat on the bread and potatoes that were the staple diet of her early years. Uncle is more intense and wiry, but beyond this the photo gives little away. It makes me think of the neutral expressions on the identity cards that he smuggles for the resistance – one of the many secret activities he is involved in, which he will almost never talk about, even later in life. For his day job he is an engine fitter for the Electrical Motors Factory in Dordrecht, an expert at aligning machines so that they work in the best possible way. This means that he travels throughout the country, to mines and to printing presses for example, adjusting and maintaining the engines that were built in Dordt. Such work is excellent cover for a resistance man.

The conventional, restrained appearance of the couple actually says a lot about them. They are not given to emotional outbursts and they dislike pretension. They will do a great deal for you, but expressions of thanks will be dismissed with an awkward, slightly painful shrug. Their passions are lived out in the Social Democratic Workers' Party, the forerunner of the Dutch Labour Party: not revolutionary but communal, with a belief in institutions, in public provision, in the betterment of humanity by giving equal chances to all. The two of

them met at the evening classes that are provided by this organization – he already a young widower with two children, she an idealistic, warm-hearted girl of twenty-eight. There is nothing very romantic about them. Auntie likes mainly to talk about housekeeping, children and politics. She is practically minded and thinks little of the delicacies of appearance. 'Thin women are for looking at and fat women are for marrying,' her husband once told her, and she repeats this with satisfaction to her friends. He is rather stern and expects obedience, and if on a rare occasion she exceeds the boundaries that he sets for the household he will order her out of the room. This is not the behaviour of a model husband. There is an edge to him, but there is also an air of authority; he is unfailingly honest, he has principles and he gets things done. Thus, although she is a little fearful and would rather do without his masculine passions, Jans is proud of her husband and of the family she is bringing up.

On the left of the page from the album there is a snap of little Marianne, smiling proudly, balanced on a white wooden bench. The picture is taken outside Mrs de Bruyne's house, which stands directly across from number 10 on the other side of the street. Mrs de Bruyne herself is sitting beside the

toddler, looking on. In the album she is labelled 'Fau Buyne' because that is how the one-year-old pronounces 'Vrouw Bruyne' and the name has caught on. Fau Buyne, a widow, is a close friend of the family, and often looks after Marianne if Auntie needs to go out. She looks young but she already has a grown-up daughter who lives around the corner. Fau Buyne is part of the great network of friends and neighbours that reaches along and beyond the Bilderdijkstraat, people with the same sorts of jobs and the same small incomes, getting by as best they can.

There are two photographs on the page that do not feature family members. One, labelled 'Annie Mookhoek', is similar in style to the others and shows a slim, pretty girl in a checked dress wearing thick socks and dark shoes. Again, the photographer has placed her, full length, at the centre of the picture, where she stands, posing self-consciously, with her arms at her sides. There is a tangle of green scrubland around her, which

has the odd effect of making her float free of the background, almost as if she were rising upwards into the sky. The bright sunshine makes the checked pattern of her dress blend with the patchwork of light and shadow. She seems to smile down from a great height. This smiling girl lives a few doors away, and if Lien is not with Kees she is bound to be with Annie, playing street games, going off to the swimming pool or exploring the countryside.

The final picture on this page is very different from the others. It is large and yellowed with rounded corners and features a dark-haired, sad-faced boy of perhaps nine years old. It has been folded in half and has a chunk torn away from it at the bottom, its edges creased and eaten into like a parchment that is centuries old. The pose is that of a formal portrait from the nineteenth century, with the boy's head and shoulders carefully framed – the opposite of the clumsy snaps that make up the rest of the page. 'Hansje' is written beneath in blue ballpoint pen. The torn chunk leaves a hole where the

boy's heart is, at exactly the point where a Jewish star would be fixed.

The people pictured on this page of the album are Lien's everyday companions as the months pass in Dordrecht. Her crying, which started so suddenly, eases off over the weeks as she settles more and more into the routine of life in the Bilderdijkstraat. Nothing is said about such things in the family. In fact nobody ever talks about feelings or mothers and fathers; Auntie and Uncle are just steady, dependable and fair. If you fall over and scrape your knee, then Auntie will dab it with iodine, give you a kiss and usher you back outside.

There is always fun to be had with Kees or Annie or with the other children on the street. The games they play are a little bit different from the ones she is used to, but once you know the rules about how many steps to take, or how long you have to cover your eyes before you start running, or how many marbles you can hold at one time, then they are really just the same.

One afternoon in September when they are both in the kitchen, Lien asks Kees to write in her poesie album. At first she is afraid that maybe he will think it is all silly girls' stuff, but he takes the book from her hands without saying anything and sits down at the table, for a long time just chewing the top of his pen. When eventually he starts writing, his tongue sticks out a little from the corner of his mouth. She is only allowed to look when he has completely finished, and when she does so she finds both pages are filled with Kees's best handwriting, which has little curls at the ends of the letters and sticks perfectly to the lightly drawn pencil lines. He has spaced his words out so that sometimes you need to read from top to bottom and sometimes from corner to corner:

For – get
me – not

Stay – safe and sound
till you – weigh
500 pounds.

Good morning Monday.
How is Tuesday?
And say to Wednesday
That next Thursday
I'll take the Friday train
For a Saturday and Sunday stay

Dog, cat, rat
Lientje is a
Treasure

To remind you
of
your
cousin
Kees

Almost all the letters are formed perfectly. It is only at the end of the word 'Lientje' at the top of the page that the ink blots and thickens a little where Kees first wrote 'Lien' and then added the *tje* on to the end of it – *tje* meaning 'little one', used for something or someone you hold dear.

Lien sees much less of Ali, who is too old now to play on the street and spends her time instead with her girlfriends, talking about clothes and hair and boys and other things that do not interest Lien at all. When Ali writes in the poesie album, she gives Lien a future that is very different from her childish games:

Dear Lientje

I wish you:
A handsome young man of your own,
A stunning and beautiful home,
A mountain of money,
Each morning all sunny,
With cows in the field and a horse in the stable,
A pig in the salt and a ham on the table,
All this and no fears,
For one hundred years.

To remind you of your cousin, Ali

Ali's handwriting, like everything else about her, is neat, regular and grown up.

It is odd to have Ali writing about this world of cows, horses and stables, which is not at all like the world of terraced houses and factory workers in which they live. Lien does see a lot of farms, though, outside Dordrecht, on expeditions looking for wildlife with Kees or on trips to see their granny and grandpa in Strijen, twenty minutes on the bus from where they live. Granny and Grandpa Strien (which is what everyone calls Strijen) have a three-room rented cottage in a village where there is no electricity, so at night you use an oil lamp, although mostly you have to go to bed as soon as it gets dark.

Lien often visits Strien with Kees and Ali at weekends. Riding together on the bus that bumps along the ridge of the dyke, they feel like royalty, looking out at the huge flatness of fields on all sides. At Granny and Grandpa's you get to sleep high up on a platform under the sloping roof, after climbing a ladder. From there you can peek down over the ledge at the room below you, but, almost at once, the kerosene lamp is turned off – the flame dying with a soft *pop* – and it is impossible to see anything at all. Lien has never known such darkness or such silence. When she stares into it, shapes float in front of her and there is a ringing sound in her ears.

In the morning she helps to feed the pig (who will soon be 'in salt' in the larder), the rabbits and the chickens. These all live in pens on the little strip of land that surrounds the cottage, where your shoes sink deep into the cold clay. The mouths of the rabbits are like the clay in their chilly softness as they snuffle the clumps of grass from Lien's palm. Built right against the dyke, which rears up like a mountain behind it, the cottage looks out over the dark water of a canal and beyond this on to a sea of fields, stretching until they vanish in the morning mist.

At breakfast Lien is squeezed between Kees and Ali. Granny – who speaks a countryside Dutch that Lien finds hard to follow – holds a loaf tight against her aproned stomach and butters the end. 'Who would like a stick?' she asks. Kees is quickest to raise his hand, so Granny cuts swiftly towards herself into the loaf and uses the knife to flick a chunk of bread in his direction, making it land right in front of him on the scrubbed wooden table, buttered side up. 'Who would like a stick?' Granny repeats.

In Strien the children roam free around the cottages, the edges of the fields, and on top of the dykes that look out across the river. There are aunts and uncles in the other cottages that are pressed in between the dyke and fields, and sometimes they eat there. The aunts are kindly and do not mind if you join them. Just like at Granny and Grandpa's there are long prayers before mealtimes, but with other children around you must not close your eyes too long during the praying because someone will take the nice bits of food from your plate. The farm workers just accept Lien as part of the crowd of children. If anyone asks, she is 'one of Pot's', because Grandpa's nickname is 'Pot'.

Strijen is mud country, perfectly flat. The Netherlands is really a vast estuary formed from Alpine rock that has been ground down over millions of years and carried here by the Rhine. As the land flattens, the great river loses power and in the east it drops smooth, rounded pieces of gravel. When it slows still further at the country's centre it deposits sand. Finally, the river becomes tidal and even slower, leaving the silt that forms the clays of the south-west. It is this river-land that has been turned into polders, with the Rhine (now split into separate broad channels that have their own names as rivers) kept back behind dykes and flowing high above the land.

Auntie is a child of this perfectly level mud country with its unbounded skies spread far below river and sea. Her father and her brothers are itinerant farm workers, earning just enough by moving from farm to farm as unskilled labour: sowing, weeding, harvesting, hauling the potatoes and sugar beet on to horse-drawn wagons so they can be carried to town. When there is no farm work to be had, the men leave home to labour on the barges out on the mudflats, where they gather reeds for roofing and the manufacture of baskets. These polder labourers, with hands like cracked leather, are the lowest order of Dutch society; they own almost nothing, as if ground down like the rock from the Alps, from boulders, to gravel, to sand, to mud.

Auntie has left this clay country and come to the city, first as a maid in service and now as the wife of an engine fitter, with his two children to care for, and Lien, as well as a child of her own. She has turned against the religion of her parents – their prayers and their Bible reading, their belief that thunder is the anger of God – and replaced it with a faith in socialism: the faith that men and women can be made better through collective effort; that a new world can be built through education, healthcare and public building, things held in common by all. The German invasion is a setback, but she and her husband are prepared for a fight.

*

Lien is now part of the rhythm of her new family. She does not think about the war or politics, except in the vaguest sense as something that governs the movements of an impossibly distant adult world. She does, of course, miss Mamma and Pappa. The intense hurt of those weeks following her birthday has abated, but there is still that deep sense of longing, the wish that seizes her when she least expects it, just wanting Mamma to be there. As the days darken, Lien begins to think of the second of the dates that were in her mind when she arrived in Dordrecht: Mamma's birthday, on 28 October. She has money to spend on a present and a letter to write. Because they cannot use the public postal service, Lien has to start in good time, so Auntie tells her to sit down at the kitchen table one rainy Thursday afternoon after school. It is funny to write as if a date that is still nearly a month in the future is already there:

1 October '42

Darling Mammie

Hooray, the happy day we've been looking forward to has finally arrived.

I am going to school now. In September I started going to school. I am sending you a little present. Next year a bigger present. And now we must do some singing, till your throat is sore.

Lien writes out all the words of the Dutch birthday song, so that her letter already gets to two thirds of the way down the first side of the big sheet of lined paper: 'Long may she live, long may she live, long may she live in gloooory. In gloooory . . .' There is now more song on the page than there is news. Finally, the song runs out. 'So,' writes Lien, as if she is herself breathless from the singing, 'now you must have a sore throat?' Writing to Mamma is not nearly as nice as it would be to go and see her; it is difficult to know what to say. A good part of the letter is now completed, but there is still a side and a quarter of empty lined paper to be filled with some kind of news.

> At first it was a bit strange and new at school. I had to get used to it. After a bit it got better. Luckily I am not behind with my studies. We are already doing fractions. I am not very good at them, but it is still going quite well. There is a boy here who is also not a Jew any more. And you are not a Jew any more. And it is nearly a quarter of an hour's walk to school. I have a master now, not a lady teacher. He is called Mr Heimenberg and he is a great joker. First he coloured a girl's cheeks red with red chalk from the blackboard . . .

And you are not a Jew any more. And it is nearly a quarter of an hour's walk to school. How did she go from one to the other? Lien does not think about it; her pen just keeps moving along the paper as she thinks half about Mamma and half about whether it will soon be dry enough for playing outside. She also starts thinking about Mr Heimenberg, the teacher. Caught up in the excitement, she gets confused and starts repeating her words:

> And then he also chalks her nose red. And then also a girl or a boy in Maths has to point out something and then he turns like this with the stick and they cannot get it. Finally he gives it to them and someone or other has to point it out.

Quite what this story is about remains unclear, no matter how many times you read it, but Lien's writing continues unperturbed:

81

For the rest, the children at school and on the street are quite kind. And the little girl, Mariannetje, nearly two years old, she is a mischievous darling. First she had to go on the potty. She calls it her 'po'. So I went to get the potty. Then Auntie said, 'So Marian-netje, come over here and then you can go on your potty.' But then she said, 'No, no popo – fibbering.' What she meant was that she didn't need the potty, she had told a fib.

Now Lien is nearly at the bottom of the sheet of paper, so that the last bit of her final sentence has to be squeezed on to unlined space:

I hope you have a lovely day, and we here will also celebrate a little bit. I will buy flowers and some nice food. I hope that next year we will be together again. Many kisses from Lientje, who misses you very much.

Will she really buy flowers and nice food for her mother's birthday? It feels like the correct and grown-up thing to say, just like the present she is sending feels correct and grown up: a little tile that has a cartoon on it, drawn in what looks like felt pen. It shows a man who is supposed to be drowning, although, to be honest, his chest is very dry-looking in its smart jacket, and his body sticks out high above the waterline. The shore is right beside him, frustratingly out of reach, but luckily a lifebuoy is flying through the sky on its way towards him. 'When danger is at its height, rescue is close at hand' is written beneath. Standing in the shop with Auntie it felt like a fitting present, and also it is not possible to send things that are bulky when using the secret post. Auntie praises Lien for fin-ishing her letter and packs it and the tile into an envelope, adding a little note of her own:

Is de nood het hoogst is, is de hulp het meest nabÿ ÷

Dear Lien's mother,

*I want just to add a few words to Lientje's letter. It did take her a
bit of effort to get it full this time, but she succeeded in the end!*

*She is still doing very well – she goes to school and I get very
good reports on how she is doing. She is well behaved and quick on
the uptake. She is always cheerful, but now and then she does miss
you and her father very badly.*

*Lientje chose the present herself. She would have preferred the
motto 'He who laughs last, laughs best', but they didn't have that
one in the shop.*

*As far as clothes are concerned, I am organizing things as seems
best to me. Everything that gets too small for our Ali fits her
perfectly. She has clothes enough, but there are a few things she has
grown out of. But anyway, it is all working fine.*

I often say to her that she is a half boy and then she replies, 'That's what Mother always said.'

I hope that your day is not too sad, if that is possible, and that next year we can congratulate you in person, together with your husband and your child.

We shall make it a bit festive here and Lien will certainly think of you the whole day.

If it is possible, do send us a letter and write to say if there is anything special you would like us to do for Lien.

All best wishes, also from Lientje's uncle Henk.

Her auntie, Jans

It is not easy to write this message or to get the girl to write to her far-off mother, and it is harder still when the envelope comes back unopened and has to be hidden from Lien's sight.

Meanwhile, Auntie continues with the washing, the cleaning, the cooking and the bringing up of children, trying as best she can. Lien's dresses (the Bonneterie blue-grey silk and the clock dress of satin made by her mother) need to be passed down the line to other children, they cannot be kept as mementos, even if they feel to Lien at that instant like treasures lost.

When Lien wants to write to her father for his birthday on 10 December, Auntie has to tell her that there is no address to write to, that their papers have been misplaced. That afternoon it is quiet in the kitchen, and Lien sits herself down in a corner. On her finger she has two little rings that were a gift from her parents, one silver and one gold. She takes them off and starts to roll them up and down along the floorboards, from one hand to the other and back. First one and then the second slips down through a gap by the wall into the darkness.

Lien does not remember thinking at all about her parents for a very long time after that.

The winter days are darker and colder and Lien spends more time at home, playing with Marianne in the kitchen or chatting with a friend in the adjoining room. Auntie does not often give kisses or cuddles, or speak of love, but she does give a sense of assurance, and that, more than anything, allows Lien to be a child. There is a clean, dry heat from the stove, and there is always a comfortable smell of washing or ironing or cooking in the air. When Lien comes home from school there is warm milk and a thick slice of bread with apple syrup on it. There are questions about how her day went, and there is news about what little Marianne has done today together with Auntie.

Over time more and more names of friends appear in Lien's poesie album. One contribution, from her classmate Nelly Baks, is a special favourite because of its flowing calligraphy and its strange rapturous language, an old style of Dutch that has fallen out of use:

Lieneke

Say, what stand'st thou there amongst the flowers,
Sweet tender plants and sprightly herbs?
'Twixt clod and stone whence come thy powers?
Oh, thou, who so mine heart disturbs!

This poem is from a book that is kept in a glass cabinet in the front room of Nelly's house. When no one is home Nelly sometimes creeps in there to look at it, and, even though she does not understand all the words, she has learnt it by heart.

Annie Mookhoek, Lien's closest friend, is also an admirer of the poem and she wishes that hers, which is the first in the Dordt section of the album (dated 1 September), had been as romantic as Nelly's. Now that it is winter, Annie Mookhoek is often to be found in the kitchen in the Bilderdijkstraat, also drinking warm milk and eating bread with apple syrup. This wild-eyed girl with flowing hair loves nothing better than princesses and stories of knights and castles from the olden days. As she and Lien sit in the children's bedroom next to the kitchen, the two of them talk of romantic adventures, of outlaws living a life on the run under an evil king, their girlish faces lit up with the excitement of it all. Then, taken up by the moment, Lien whispers to Annie that she has a real secret, one that nobody is allowed to know. Annie offers her ear for her to whisper. 'I am really a Jewess in hiding,' Lien breathes. 'Jewess': the word is intoxicating.

Annie turns, her eyes wide in amazement, looking anew at her friend. 'Is that really true?' she asks.

A few days later, Lien comes home to find Auntie strangely shivery, waiting for her in the kitchen, without either warm milk or bread with syrup. Lien feels a tight painful grip on her arm and is led to the *mooie kamer*. Auntie shuts the door and then turns to put both her hands on Lien's shoulders, pinching them with the same hard grip. She bends forward so close that the little girl sees the thin spiderweb of red lines on her cheeks. Annie has told her mother, who has passed this on.

'You must never, ever, tell that to anyone,' Auntie says slowly, stopping after each word.

Lien is sent to bed without any dinner, something that has never happened before. She lies there, staring upwards at the ceiling with dry eyes, hearing the scraping of chairs, the clink of cutlery on plates and the hubbub of voices through the thin door. Beyond these sounds, nothing at all enters her consciousness at this moment – neither fear, nor regret, nor any memory of home. Outside a dark entity presses upon her: some vast, hovering, invisible creature, perceptible only through the beating force of its wings.

There is one other person to whom Lien has confided her secret, but Hansje – the sad-faced boy from the photo album – has not told anyone else. More often now the two of them spend time together, outside even in the January chill. They play a game called animal graveyard in a spot by the half-built wall in the scrublands, where they will take a dead mouse, a frozen bird, or a softly iridescent butterfly with wings that crumble to the touch. Hansje and Lien dig the cold hard earth with a broken slate and build coffins and headstones, cutting the dates of burial into a piece of brick with a nail. Sometimes they cannot find any creatures that need burial, so they find live ones instead and help them on their way. They will crack the shell of a beetle or crush the pink ribbed tube of a worm found hidden under a rock. The ceremonies are just the same for the 'helped' as they are for the already dead: soft words mumbled as the body is lowered into the grave. Lien and Hansje, who is also 'not a Jew any more', have something in common, although they never even whisper what it is.

The winter of 1942–3 is much milder than the one that preceded it, but there is still frost, icy rain and the occasional flurry of snow. Lien suffers from what are called 'winter feet': reddish-blue blisters and an itchy tingle around the toes. The cure for this is rather medieval: having to sit, each morning, with your feet in a bowl of your first urine, warm but rapidly cooling as the minutes pass. Apart from this – while Polish Jews fight in the Warsaw Uprising against the final liquidation of the ghetto, and while the German army faces defeat at Stalingrad – all is fairly quiet in Dordrecht. There is enough to eat, even if choice is more limited, and Lien has no thoughts at all about the progress of the war.

For her, life continues as normal. In fact, it becomes more normal over time. She is simply one of the family. As the thin ice cracks on ponds and ditches, she goes out to look for frog-spawn with Kees and fills great jars full of the jelly with its little black spots. They go more often to Strien and watch the ploughing and the sowing. The routine of life in the Bilder-dijkstraat is uninterrupted: friends still come to dinner; the games out on the street continue; and Auntie oversees every-thing with her warm, self-confident care. Lien and Kees are like sister and brother: during the holidays they spend their days together, up to no good. It is easy, learning things at school and being friends with other children and, as the days grow longer, Lien spends more and more of her time playing out in the sun.

One afternoon in the spring of 1943 she is out in the backyard with Mariannetje, who is now quite steady on her feet. They are playing a chasing game, with Lien as the chaser. The closer she gets to the escaping Marianne, the more frantic the little girl's steps become, until finally they are almost paralysed with delicious, giggling fear. Lien carries her with wobbly steps to the captive place, lets her run, and then catches her again. Auntie is working in the kitchen with the door open, chopping onions that then sizzle at the bottom of the big pan. The doorbell rings, which is unusual, and because Auntie is in the middle of something Lien is sent from the yard, through the kitchen and along the corridor to the front of the house to see who it is. Behind her, the kitchen is all scent, noise and light.

She sees a figure through the little glass window and pulls the front door towards her. There on the doorstep stand two men in police uniform – big and full of power – and before she can even look up to see their faces they charge past her into the house. Although she does not know it, these are Harry Evers and Arie den Breejen. Their heavy steps thump down the corridor and then Lien hears the smash of the kitchen door.

She stands confused momentarily.

The next instant, Auntie is there beside her, down at her level.

On the floor, below the pegs for the coats, there is an old pair of boots, probably Uncle's. Auntie pushes them towards her.

'Put these on, go to Mrs de Bruyne's, don't come back.'

And all at once she is out on the street, her feet so loose in the boots that she almost trips. The Bilderdijkstraat feels like a different place now, or, rather, it is the same but with time slowed down. The walk across the road to Mrs de Bruyne's, just a few steps away, feels like a journey even though Lien is moving as quickly as she can. She rings the bell and stands there, only looking forward at the door handle, not turning her head. If she had the watch that Mamma had hoped to give her, its hands would be standing still.

After what seems like an age, Mrs de Bruyne opens the door. One glance and just the first word of an unplanned sentence is enough for Lien to be pulled inwards and for the door to slam shut. They stand for a moment in silence. There are some stairs at the end of the corridor, and Mrs de Bruyne is staring towards them, transfixed. Lien can tell that 'Fau Buyne', who is so familiar, does not know what to do, even though she is an adult and ought to be in charge. Fau Buyne looks suddenly old. But then she shakes herself from her shoulders, takes Lien by the hand, very gently, and leads her into the front room, the *mooie kamer*.

'Stay in here, love.' She has a shake in her voice, like an old lady would have.

The door clicks shut and there is rapid movement behind it: steps that quickly fade. Lien stands on her own in the centre of the room, which is cool and dark, the white curtains almost entirely closed. This side of the street is in shadow, but across the road number 10 is still bathed in sunlight – it is just visible through the window – and Lien stands there in the shade, looking at the house she has just left. One of the uniformed men steps out of the front door and puts his hand over his eyes to shield them from the sun, briefly scanning the street. Lien does not move and, oddly, feels no fear. For a long time she just stands there, watching the men enter and exit, but in the end Lien sits down on the sofa, from where she studies the photographs on the wall that loom in the near-darkness, and listens to the ticking of the clock.

A *mooie kamer* is a place of transition: Lien sat in a place like this half a year ago when she first came to Dordrecht with Mrs Heroma. And eventually it is again Mrs Heroma who will come to collect her and bring her to a different house. After that, Lien will go onwards to new addresses and new people. But the house that she will always look back on as a refuge is number 10 Bilderdijkstraat, the home of Jans and Henk van Es.

8

I had always known that my grandparents sheltered Jewish children during the German occupation of the Netherlands. For many years I had meant to look into this, but, all the same, until December 2014 I knew almost no details about what actually happened at that time. There were no family stories about it. For me there was just the faint mental image of pale faces looking up from beneath the floorboards, too cartoonish to feel real.

My grandfather died when I was seven, and although my grandmother, Jans, was a significant figure for me until she died when I was in my early twenties, I had barely talked with her about the war. When I asked her about it she would say, 'We were not brave, but you had no choice if somebody turned up at your door.' With that the conversation ended and so the past receded into the background, seemingly dead because there was no talk to keep it alive.

Then, in November 2014, my uncle Kees passed away. He was the senior figure in the family, my father's loved and admired big brother. My most recent contact with him had been through his grandson, so Kees already felt to me in some ways like a figure from a bygone age. His death sparked something inside me. A generation and its stories were fading. If I was to do something before these people and their memories disappeared for ever, it had to be now.

There was no clear moment of decision, but still, while doing the washing-up one Sunday evening, I asked a question that would end up changing my life. My mother had come round for dinner, as she often does on a Sunday when Dad is away. I was pushing food from the plates into the recycling caddy, and drinking my tea, when I asked about Lien.

Lien. I remembered the name from my childhood: a Jewish girl who had stayed with my grandparents during the war. And after the war she had continued to live with them. But I had no memory of having met her, just a vague sense of an argument in the distant past and of a letter sent by my grandmother many years ago, which had severed contact for good. She was now never mentioned by the family, but, as far as I knew, she was still living and (in spite of my grandmother's wishes) my mother had kept in touch.

'Yes, Lien is over eighty now and she lives in Amsterdam, but I don't think she'll want to see you. It is not a happy story and it is best left alone. Anyway, the historical details have already been recorded. They were put on that Steven Spielberg archive years ago.'

But I was insistent and my mother enquired and, after a bit, I got an email address. On 7 December 2014 I sent the following email in Dutch:

Dear Lien

I am the son of Henk and Dieuwke van Es and I have for many years wanted to make contact. I just received your email address from Dieuwke and was very happy to hear that you would be willing to meet me. As it happens I will be in the Netherlands from 19 to 22 December. If it worked out for you I would very much like to come and see you on one of those days. Maybe for lunch, or to go and eat out somewhere, or coffee? I would like to get to know a family member. On top of this I would very much like to know about your experiences during the war and also after that with the van Es family. As part of my job I write academic books and I would like to write something about your story (I understand of course that the story is not some straightforward fairy tale). Maybe we could explore that idea? If that did turn into something I could also come to the Netherlands on future occasions as well.

At the very least I hope to speak to you at some point soon. My apologies for my poor Dutch (I do speak it pretty well).

Many thanks and I hope to see you soon,

Bart van Es

Two hours later I received a reply.

At 11 a.m. on Sunday 21 December I parked my car outside Lien's apartment in Amsterdam, walked to the entrance and pressed the buzzer reading 'de Jong', which I recognized as my grandmother's maiden name. By this stage I had looked Lien up on the Shoah Foundation website, but as this only featured a still image of her taken in the 1990s, plus a few basic facts, I still knew almost nothing about the sort of person I would find. The intercom buzzed and I was invited to climb to the second floor, where she stood waiting on the landing, surrounded by potted plants and posters of modern art.

'Let me look at you,' she said, standing back.

I was led, with mock formality, along an open walkway with a view of a planted courtyard.

'You look more like your mother,' Lien told me. I was struck by the thought that, when she last set eyes on him, my dad would have been close to the age I am now.

Our meeting that day ran on until long after darkness fell. At the end, it felt strange to break up our togetherness. In an odd way I felt older than her, given we'd spoken almost entirely about her life as a child. We see people at least as much by the stories they tell as by their outward appearance, and I had got to know Lien through the little and the big events in her life before she was nine. Part of her still felt vulnerable and inexperienced. I promised to return early in the new year.

As I travelled back, Holland's motorways looked more modern than ever: the car showrooms lit up like spaceships floating in the blackness, Audis and BMWs stacked one above the other on great shelves behind glass, their headlights blazing, powered by hidden electric cables, to show their hi-tech designs. As I drove on a road that was as straight as a beam of light, the black and white pictures of Lien's early life returned to me, such as the photo taken in 1938 that shows two girls sitting at an old school bench and, standing behind them, two boys wearing ties and short trousers. Lien wore a bow in her hair, as did her friend.

Even more than by the pictures, I was haunted by the mental image of Lien's mother planning to tell her daughter about the 'secret'. There was such self-possession in her parents' conduct, thinking through how best to help Lien onward with the minimum of fuss, to save her even if they could not save themselves. I could see before me that last, composed family meeting, with the aunts and uncles holding their niece for what would prove the final time. And last of all I was struck by her mother's letter to my grandparents: its measured sacrifice in giving up not simply her daughter but, still more precious, all claim on her daughter's love.

Later, having picked up my three children and with my eldest daughter, Josie, sitting beside me, I started to tell her about Lien's story, but found my voice breaking and had to stop.

Lien's mother had written to my grandparents to say that she hoped the eight-year-old girl would 'think only of you as her mother and father and that, in the moments of sadness that will come to her, you will comfort her as such'. After the war, my father grew up with her as a sister. Why, then, at my grandmother's funeral, was Lien unmentioned and unseen? How could such a connection break? How could my grandmother have sent her that letter, breaking off contact, signed coldly 'Mrs v Es'?

Two weeks later I was back with Lien in her apartment and talking now of the time after the raid on my grandparents' house in the Bilderdijkstraat. She was moved quickly between households, staying in one place for no more than a few days. 'The crying became less, each time, in exact proportion to the moves I had made,' she said.

9

A succession of rooms, visited only briefly, sometimes for a night, sometimes for a week. They blur into one another, present only in fleeting memories, such as that of an afternoon spent staring upwards at the sunshine framing the edges of a blackout blind. Lien makes no decisions, loses self-awareness for hours, but she is not afraid. Everywhere there are new routines to follow: where to wash, when and what to eat, how to eat, where to sleep. On the first night away from the van Es family she stays with Mrs de Bruyne's daughter, just a few streets away from the Bilderdijkstraat. When she gets to the camp bed in the upstairs bedroom there is a bag containing her clothes and a few belongings, but no word of what has happened or what is planned. Lien asks no questions. She eats when she is supposed to eat and sleeps when she is told it is bedtime. For the rest, time drifts past without her really noticing it; the people – whether kind and gentle, nervous, or resentful – meld into one.

Lien no longer goes to school and hardly ever sees other children. At first she misses Auntie, Kees, Ali and Marianne, and cries when she thinks of them, but quite soon they – like everything else – lose focus in her memory. They are shapes at the edge of her field of vision towards which she will not turn her gaze. Mrs Heroma, though, is still a presence. She is spoken of in whispers as a great personage by adults, and sometimes she even comes to a front room to collect Lien and take her onwards to a new house.

At one point Mrs Heroma takes Lien to her own home,

where she lives with her husband the doctor. It is bigger than the other houses Lien has been in, even though she sees it only very briefly from the outside – pressed, as she was the first time they met, into the folds of Mrs Heroma's coat. Lien stays in an empty room above the surgery, from where she hears the patients coming and going, the mums chatting on the pavement over the tops of their prams.

Dr Heroma is always busy. She hears his bass voice – but not the words he speaks – muffled through the floorboards every ten minutes as he opens the door to his consulting room and calls the next patient inside. Occasionally she hears the rattle of his keys as he closes the front door of the surgery, followed by his quick steps and the clunk of a car door. The engine trying to start sounds like a kind of laughter that won't get going: *he, he, he, he – he; he, he, he, he – he.* Then, at the third attempt it nearly catches, and on the fourth it does, turning almost straight away to a weak and then a strong *pitter patter, pitter patter, pitter patter.* For a short while it stays there while the engine establishes its rhythm, then the pitch of the *pitter patter* goes higher and moves off down the street and fades away.

Mrs Heroma is more strict during the time that Lien is staying with her. Lien has to be absolutely still on the sofa upstairs. Elsewhere in the house there are other people, but she never sees them. On the drying rack that stands in front of her there is laundry, women's clothing, which does not belong to Mrs Heroma. Sometimes in the night there is movement. The front door opens and then shuts with a tiny *click* that echoes in the silence. In the darkness Lien often lies awake with nothing but blackness in front of her eyes.

She keeps on being moved from one house to another. Whenever Lien feels sleep press in upon her, at night or on some empty afternoon while gazing at floorboards, she fills her mind with pictures and flies high over the buildings to the places where she used to play. She is Goeie Lientje (Good Lien) when she can do this flying and carries out little miracles in a world of familiar faces where the rules are not the same. She rescues animals and people and explains things to everyone without having to think at all about what to say. All the time there is that flying feeling, a kind of swimming through the air that she feels even when her feet are on the ground. Strange waves make her feel unsteady, but she knows that all will be well.

There is also a Kwaaie Lientje (Bad Lien or Angry Lien), who cannot fly and who seems to wade slowly through an invisible tar. Sometimes Kwaaie Lientje does not move forward at all and just drifts backwards on the stream of stickiness, however hard she tries. Kwaaie Lientje goes with Hans to the animal graveyard that they have made together. There they take the creatures that are dead or dying and carry them to graves so deep down in the earth that the bottom cannot be seen. As for the animals that are still living, Kwaaie Lientje helps them on their way, feeling the crack of their little bones as she holds them in her grip. Goeie Lientje or Kwaaie Lientje, she feels herself shifting from one to the other – from good to bad or angry – as she stares into the blankness while empty hours go by.

At last, the people who determine these things make a decision: Lien must go away from Dordt. So here she stands, dressed and ready, in another upstairs bedroom, waiting for another person to collect her and take her to a new place. The bell rings, but Lien knows not to answer and waits patiently behind the closed door. There are feet on the stairs and then – suddenly – a voice that is familiar, loud even when she is trying to whisper. It is Auntie. Lien does not rush out to embrace her but instead remains timidly where she is standing, one leg curled behind the other, waiting to be hugged. A familiar smell envelops her, the soft heaviness of arms pressing downwards, and a floating sensation, her feet dangling as she is pulled upwards towards Auntie's ruddy cheek. It is the first time that somebody has touched her in many weeks.

But there is no time for greetings and, anyway, this is not a reunion. Auntie will take her on the back of her bike to a new place where she will be safe. A few words are spoken that do not really register about everyone being well back at home in the Bilderdijkstraat, and moments later Lien is sitting side-saddle on the baggage rack of Auntie's bicycle, looking out in the early morning on the streets of Dordt. It is a Saturday, she thinks, or at least there are no schoolchildren, just a few men who walk with their heads down, stepping quickly on their way to work. At first it looks as if Auntie is heading to Granny and Grandpa's in Strien, because once they are out of the city there are the same dark, flat, empty fields decked with mist. But riding up on the silent dyke road, high above the land, they take the opposite direction, heading south-west.

After a while they ride beside the grey expanse of the Oude Maas river. A few barges that sit upon it struggle against the stream towards Dordrecht, creating small white waves around their bows and a yellowish wash behind. The barges are so heavily laden that their decks stand just a foot or so above the water, but they ride above the level of the land. Lien sits passively, looking outwards, while Auntie pedals without varying her pace. Auntie's legs move rhythmically upwards and downwards, upwards and downwards, just like the steam train that took Lien away from her home in The Hague. Spring sunshine clears the fog from the fields that stretch below to one side of them. The birds are singing. They pass through villages with tall red-brick houses where there are mothers queuing for bakeries and children playing in the street. Auntie cycles onwards. In her mind's eye, Lien magically begins to fly above the scene.

The journey is broken up when they cross the river on a ferry boat – a proper one like you get in books, with a funnel belching coal smoke that you can taste on your tongue, a deck with ventilation ports, and a real captain in a uniform on the bridge. It is almost like crossing an ocean, feeling the engine thump away below you as you run from one side of the boat to the other and then stand at the bow like a lookout, watching the approaching shore. There are two other children on the boat: a bigger girl of ten; and her brother, aged eight. Lien fits right in between them and soon they are Nile explorers, watching out for attackers, weapons at the ready. Here, out on the river, the breeze is stronger, blowing hair around your face and into your mouth. After weeks of solitary existence, in the sunshine Lien suddenly comes alive.

But now the sound from the engine changes and all too soon there is a squeak of wood against metal as the ferry bumps against a jetty and the mooring ropes are thrown. Almost at once the gates open and they cycle on, plunged again into the emptiness of the flatlands, which is disturbed only by the regular criss-cross of ditches and dykes. After the momentary animation of being with the other children, Lien drifts back to her dream world, hardly registering where they go. The day is warm, almost summery, and as time passes the air that surrounds them becomes heavy with the fragrant damp that rises from the earth. To Lien, who is sitting so uncomfortably with her legs dangling, it feels like a long journey, but it is still morning when Auntie finally stops.

IO

When Lien and Auntie step from the bicycle they are on top of a high dyke facing an even broader stretch of water than the one they crossed by ferry. This is the Nieuwe Maas, on the other side of which, a few miles downstream, lies Rotterdam. Lien has no idea where she is or where she is going, but this is the place where (according to the story that they told everyone in Dordrecht) her parents are supposed to have died. Three years ago, on 14 May 1940, German bombers smashed the heart of the old city, levelling 25,000 homes in a single raid. The destruction, and the threat that the same would happen to Utrecht if there was no surrender, broke the Dutch war effort. Without an air force, nothing could be done.

When Rotterdam was engulfed by this firestorm, the war meant almost nothing to Lien, who was only six, and even now she has never seen bombing, or shooting, or even anger from a uniformed man. A square mile of rubble that was once the centre of a Renaissance city lies just beyond the horizon. Yet, from where Lien stands on the great river, she sees only sunshine and newly cut grass.

In Rotterdam, though, in the spring of 1943, resistance is growing. This is the industrial base of the Netherlands, a place of union power where the now-banned Social Democratic Workers' Party (of which the Heromas and the van Esses are members) has deep roots. Across the river from the city is a landscape of farms, outhouses and small villages where it is easier for the resistance to hide. This, therefore, is the logical place to take a Jewish child now that the situation in Dordrecht has become too dangerous for her to remain.

Lien does not remember the moment of arrival in IJsselmonde. Following her departure from the van Esses' and the period of lonely isolation at short-stay addresses in Dordrecht, she has struggled more and more to engage with the outside world.

Once again Lien is passed from one adult to another, without a real explanation or a proper goodbye. It was the same when she was collected from the Pletterijstraat by Mrs Heroma just eight months ago. The Lien who is handed over this time, however, is a different creature: no list of funny street names could catch her attention now. You will not see her crying because she misses her parents or the van Esses, or reaching out to befriend a fresh set of children as she arrives at her new home. A curtain of self-protection has descended. Lien thinks little about the past or the future, and even the present has been reduced to just a small number of necessary things. When she later looks back at IJsselmonde, she will see it only in black and white. Almost all that registers in her memory is the cold stone floor and the lack of natural light.

The cottage where she stays is a single-storey whitewashed building, rather like a barn, that is half smothered by the dyke. There are ten people in this small building: a couple with six children, then Lien and another hideaway, Jo. The parents are teachers and, like Auntie and Uncle van Es, members of the Social Democratic Workers' Party. Mieneke, the mother, tells her children to make room for Lien at the kitchen table and afterwards shows her where she can sleep. There is a back room for the girls and the grown-up daughters. It is so full of bedding that you can barely see the floor. Lien should be able to squeeze in on the right, up against the wall, Mieneke tells her, and then checks in her bag that she has enough clothes to wear and points out where the chamber pot is kept.

Once Lien is hidden inside the dyke cottage, unable to return to the daylight, the heat within her turns cold and she barely speaks. The family – who are lively, friendly, and interested in her welfare – come into the house with flushed cheeks as if from a different world. Lien hardly sees them. She moves from the bedroom to the kitchen, doing a bit of cleaning, peeling potatoes and washing dishes. She is unused to housework, and the knife sits awkwardly in her hand as she cuts a still-muddy potato, revealing a thick clean slab of yellow beneath. She has to tell her fingers, as if they are somebody else's, to cut more gently so as not to waste the food. Mieneke gives her direction, standing behind her and guiding Lien with her hands.

Mieneke is there in the kitchen at mealtimes, but she often goes out straight after. It is only to Jo, with whom she is left in the house once the others have gone, that Lien ever feels close. Jo talks and she listens. He is eighteen and has escaped from a camp in Germany, but he is not Jewish. They are not just taking Jews now, he tells her: all men who are not in essential professions are being forced to go to work in Germany. If you are under thirty-five you can't get food stamps without a right-to-stay permit, and if you're caught without one they'll send you to an *Arbeitslager*, which is worse than prison. There's no way Jo's going to work again for the *Moffen*, as he calls them, and if things somehow work themselves out, he'll find a way to fight.

With his big frame, Jo is like a giant cooped up here under the rafters, looking almost straight across at the four small, square, strangely familiar windows below the roofline that let in a little light. Jo has a sense of the outside that doesn't need a window to see it. He laughs with the family, asks what they have been doing, has views on farming, teases the girls and remembers their names.

Weeks turn into months in IJsselmonde – light shines more brightly through the square windows and then, as July turns first to August and then to September, it gradually fades. Lien loses track of time amidst the sameness of the days. The house, which never got warm even at the height of summer, grows ever colder with the stove left unlit. There are itchy spots on her legs. She hardly noticed that she was scratching them at first, but as time passes more and more hard purple lumps appear that bleed when they are broken open, leaving gashes of black scab. She wants to hide them, but they call out with a thumping rhythm. They burn hot and sharp if she pulls her socks up over them, so she walks shivering with her bare feet swollen purple, feeling the eyes of the other girls as she steps.

At night Lien sleeps in the crowded room with the others, women and girls turning their weight in the darkness, thickening the air with their breath. She wraps herself tight under her cover, surrounded by the sense of the other bodies. Her legs, with their heat in the midst of the coldness, keep her awake. In the morning she stands up when the room stirs around her. It is hardly any brighter than it was during the night. Inside, she feels a numbness, keeping everything at a distance, not once having a sense of fear.

Then, one evening in the late months of 1943, another moment of crisis arrives, another knock at the door. Lien is doing the washing-up in the kitchen, and is told to go and hide. From the bedroom moments later, Lien hears excited talking, and then Mieneke comes in, telling Jo and her they must run because the police are on their way.

It is odd how shoes matter at these moments. When the men came to the Bilderdijkstraat she had to go out in the big boots that stood by the doorway, but now her feet are so swollen that nothing will fit.

Lien feels almost calm, but a charge runs through the rest of the household and before she knows it the freezing night air and the darkness are upon her and she is being jogged roughly on Jo's shoulder, one of his arms wrapped across her sore legs. He knows where he is going, and edges along the sides of barns and outbuildings in a crouching run. Then there is a thump to the ground and a feeling of wetness and the scratching of thorns around them as they lie hidden, Jo's chest quietly heaving against her, in a ditch.

There are invisible voices around them and they hear the barking of dogs. Not very far away there are lights on the road. The lights and voices grow stronger, come to a stop very near them, and then begin slightly to fade. Without warning, Jo grips her legs tightly again and pushes the two of them forward through the brambles at half pace. Though it ought to be hurting, she feels nothing but elation as she digs her fingers into the material of his coat. Jo jerks his head from left to right and then breaks into a second run, this time up the slope of the dyke. His feet slip beneath them, but he carries on scrabbling with a ferocious energy until they are for a moment high up on the road, where the wind hits them and where she sees the glimmer of the great river below in the dark. Then down again, sliding as the grass turns to mud at the weight of them. On the slope, they lie still with their faces against the wet. For an instant, Lien is reminded of the bank she used to climb down to fetch tadpoles with Kees back in Dordrecht, and her feeling of dread for the murky water below.

'It's going well,' whispers Jo encouragingly. After resting a moment he tells her to climb on to his back. Like this they move as fast as possible along the steep slippery surface. It is curfew time, so the occasional sound of movement on the path above them must come from the police. As Jo runs he has to loosen Lien's fingers, which she has gripped hard to his throat in her eagerness to hold on. After a bit, Jo turns to her in a whisper: they are getting near the village now and they'll need to go back over the dyke and then in amongst the houses. They will have to be deadly quiet.

Now that her eyes have adjusted she can see more by the moonlight, though right at this moment it's just Jo's broad and thinly bearded face that she can pick out in the darkness. That and the angle of the slope. She trusts Jo utterly. He is always kind.

On reaching the edge of the village, they move further up to the top of the dyke, with Jo again frantically glancing from left to right. All is clear and he darts up over the road with her, holding tight to her legs so that she notices again how much they hurt. But then, in the excitement of rapid movement, she feels nothing apart from a strange, wakeful, happy alertness that makes her see and hear everything more sharply than before. She registers the scrapes and bumps as they move between the buildings – the skin that is grazed off her knee against a wall; a twig that comes out of nowhere and strikes her in the eye. These injuries, though, come with no pain attached. They feel like they are happening to somebody else.

The two of them are in the thick of the streets now, and as Lien looks upwards she sees the outline of house fronts against the lighter grey of the sky. The houses flick by as Jo runs with her. One has a squared top with curved edges. Another is like two staircases coming together with a tower in the middle on top. Then, at the end of the street, she sees what must be a square and beyond that a church steeple. And across the darkness in the distance there are two lights moving about.

The lights mean danger, and when Jo spots them he crashes over a low wall into a garden, where they lie still for a long time next to a shed.

They hear nothing except the sounds of the night.

Eventually they dare to move again and go back over the wall and then left down a cobbled street with smaller buildings, where Jo's foot catches a pebble that goes bouncing across the stones. As they stand for a moment in the absolute stillness she watches the steam of his breath.

Then, as quickly as it started, it is over. Jo knocks on a door and they wait for agonizing seconds. It opens. There is a quick exchange of whispers and they tumble inside.

Where exactly they go after this is confusing. Everything is dark and constricted. A man she can barely see leads them first upstairs and then downstairs, through a corridor and then up a ladder. There is a movement of hinges; a heavy carpet rolled across the floor. Twists and turns lead them down a narrow passageway to a cupboard, which somehow moves forward to form the entrance to a room.

It is the dirtiest place that Lien has ever been in. The large central area makes her think of a tavern, although she has never been in a tavern and certainly not in one like this. There are a couple of chairs and sofas against the walls, and she can see people moving about. In the centre, half a dozen men sit at a table around an oil lamp, playing cards. A few sets of eyes turn towards them as they enter. She walks by herself now, her bare feet picking up grease from the carpeted floor. The smell of the place is incredible. She wonders if there is enough air to breathe. But still Lien is without fear and keeps everything at a distance, the heightened awareness and wakefulness of the night excursion starting to fade. The man who showed them the way did not come into the room and has shut up the cupboard behind them. Jo is now the only leader, and she waits, without impatience, to be told what to do.

Even with Jo, Lien feels no deep connection. As he moves to

talk to the men at the card table, she remains staring into the middle distance, aware of the dirt in the room around her and of the bodies shifting position from time to time on the furniture around the walls.

Her one thought is 'I ought not to be here', but this is not a cry of rebellion, just an observation that keeps running through her head.

After a bit, Jo returns and says that she should sleep upstairs, where there are bunk beds. He hunkers down and nervously puts his hand on her shoulder, so that she feels its weight and its warmth. They were pressed together all the while that he carried her, but now for the first time he is reaching out with affection, tentative as if fearful to hurt. He talks, in an embarrassed mumble, about how she should 'do her business' in the two buckets in the adjoining room. Lien nods as she listens. When she stands beside the buckets a moment later, her bare feet on the yellow wet of the tiles, she is nearly sick with the stench.

Then, having followed Jo up a ladder, she finds herself in the bedroom, in which all of the bunks are already occupied. Jo tells her to join the bottom one on the far left. The bedclothes feel damp as she lifts them to step under the covers. An old woman's face blinks up at her momentarily, says something in a dry-mouthed whisper, then rolls over to face another sleeper, who lies against the far wall. Lien has never shared a bed with anyone before, and it feels strange to sense the weight of the others pulling her to the centre of the mattress as she lies down beside them, fully clothed. She holds one hand to the cold metal of the bed frame and lies as straight as possible, facing outwards into the room. Below, where she can still hear him, Jo has joined the circle of card players and is telling them about the adventure of the raid and their escape. It must now be long past midnight and she has no idea what kind of place it is that she is in. As she lies there, sleep closes in upon her. When she shuts her eyes it feels like the room is swaying, and as she listens to Jo telling their story she can see herself again on his back, looking up at the outlines of the house fronts, black against the moonlit clouds. She loosens her grip on the bed frame and one foot moves across under the blanket towards the old woman, but when it touches she instinctively snaps it back. Nothing here is familiar except the regular throb of the sores on her legs.

The dirty dark house in IJsselmonde is Lien's home for just a few days. By the time she leaves, Jo has gone off in some other direction.

II

The afternoon has passed almost without our noticing it, and as we get to questions about the hideout in IJsselmonde it is already 6.30 p.m. Although the events themselves are traumatic, the process of reassembling them has a positive side to it. Lien has long since worked through her experiences, in part with a counsellor, and as I sit listening I find myself taken up with the practicalities, so that emotion takes a back seat. It is only as I think back that I am haunted by what has occurred.

Lien herself is almost euphoric. 'I didn't think I could talk for so long about all of it,' she says, as she stands up and begins to clear the tea things from the table. Only now, as an afterthought, does she mention that she may have a letter from Jo. I tell her that I would very much like to see it, and a few minutes later Lien returns from the adjoining room with a single sheet of lined A4 paper, folded to a sixth of its size. The enclosed photos, which Lien kept for a long time, are now lost.

While back in Oxford over Christmas I bought a digital recorder to use alongside my notes for our interviews. It is still running, so every word of our conversation is logged for me to listen to afterwards, as I write.

Lien unfolds the letter, pointing first to her own handwriting at the top. In neat, individually printed letters, Lien, by that point aged twelve, has written:

a letter that Lien must keep
"   "   from Jo

As she reads this out loud, Lien laughs at herself for having given this firm order to posterity. She continues on to the letter itself, occasionally stumbling as she tries to make sense of Jo's diction and spelling errors. It is dated 4 March 1946 and has come from Singapore:

Dear Lien

What a long time ago it is that we heard from each other. At about this time two years ago I had to leave unexpectedly and I didn't get to see you and we haven't written. When I heard from Mieneke that you were in good health and living in Dordrecht, I thought now really I must write to Lien. Lien, what a lot has happened in this time. Dear Lien, you have never been out of my thoughts. Not when I was in Amersfoort and not when I was in Germany and also not now, when I am so far away from Holland. Lien, if you have one you must send a photo of yourself. I will enclose a few of myself with this letter. Lien, now a few questions. How are you? Are you still at school, and in what sort of class? Lien, if I can do anything for you then you <u>must</u> write to me about it, if I can do it I will do anything to help you. You will have heard from Mieneke . . .

When she gets to the name Mieneke, for the second time Lien stops.

'I don't know who Mieneke is. Maybe the woman in IJsselmonde? I think it is the woman in IJsselmonde, but I don't know.'

The certainty only gradually grows. Then Lien continues:

You will have heard from Mieneke that I am serving in the Marines now, which is working out well. I was in England for three weeks, in America for six months, for the last two months now I've been in Malacca, and right at this moment I'm on the ship New

Amsterdam. *And the ship is currently in the harbour in Singapore –*
you'll have to look it up in an atlas! Any moment now we may
depart for Java. Lien, I don't know what other news to give you.
Pass on my warmest wishes to all our old friends, and also to your
adoptive parents, and, if you are writing to Mieneke, then do give
her my best. Lien, take from me the uttermost heartfelt wishes.
From your friend who will never forget you,

Jo Kleijne

P.S. Dear Lien, I don't know your address exactly. Now I will
enclose this letter in a letter to Mieneke. I think hope that Mieneke
will quickly send this letter on to you and that you will very soon
write back to me. Once again, all the very best from your friend. Jo.

At the bottom of the page, he writes his military ID number in block capitals:

CORPORAL OF THE MARINES, J. W. L. KLEIJNE. NL 4502759.

'He has written his address at the bottom,' Lien says in a voice that is full of cheerful reminiscence.

'And do you still know if you wrote back, and what you wrote?' I ask.

All at once the mood of the conversation changes. Lien's reply is thoughtful but not filled with any deep sense of regret.

'I have never . . . I have never done anything,' she says. 'I never wrote, I have never . . . I have never looked into anything. I never kept contact. No.'

She sighs.

'It's . . .'

There is a pause.

'And, for the rest, you never heard anything of him?'

'No, no. It stops then, doesn't it?'

'Yes.'

'It's, you know . . . I was in a different phase of my life then. The connection wasn't there.'

There is a long silence. Then the recording picks up the clicks from my camera as I take images of the letter from Jo.

'It's rather beautiful, the way he underlines his words for emphasis,' I say, as I begin reading it for the first time myself.

'Jo Kleijne,' she says and smiles, still reminiscing. 'I do still have a letter written by a friend of my mother, but that is . . . I don't know if you want that?'

'I want everything. I mean, if it can . . .'

Lien is smiling broadly now. 'You want everything!' she laughs.

And, after a bit more searching, she is holding the letter sent by Aunt Ellie for her birthday in September 1942.

'Aunt Ellie – I don't have much of a picture of her. Shall I read it out loud?'

Lien reads the letter to me, which we had missed before – the one about wanting to come and visit and about how Lien will now have a whole new set of uncles and aunts – and then, as Lien ponders, a few more details of the resistance hideout in IJsselmonde come to the fore. But of the journey onwards from there she still remembers nothing.

'I believe it was with Took,' she says, 'but I do not know.' Her emphasis is on the word 'believe', making this an act of faith rather than remembrance. So while the trip from The Hague to Dordrecht remains so vivid, this one, nearly a year and a half later, is a blank.

I am again reminded of what Lien said when we first talked together about her wartime memories. Without families you don't get stories. After all those months in the half-light, Lien did not really see other people, even if they were there, because she had no connection with them. As a result of her isolation, she stopped seeing the world.

'It was being that was just *being*,' she tells me, 'and where, and how, and with whom, that was all uncertain. Not concerning yourself with the past or the future, it brings a perspective with it. The "involvement" [Lien uses the English word] . . . the involvement was on a very low heat, if that makes sense to you. I believe, when I say it like that, I have got it right. Can you understand?'

The metaphor of 'low heat' strikes home to me, and I will use it more than once as I describe this phase of Lien's life. As I hear her speak about her feelings, both in IJsselmonde and afterwards, I begin to understand her better. I have never felt so strongly how a person is the product of the life they have led.

12

In the next few days I travel across Holland to visit archives and the other places of Lien's youth. At the NIOD (National Institute for War, Holocaust and Genocide Studies), amidst the studious murmur of academics and doctoral students in the grey light of the courtyard garden, I hold in my hand an index card that records my grandfather's imprisonment at Vught. He was sent there after the raid that Lien remembers. It is an innocuous piece of yellow paper, with his name (which, like his birthday, is the same as my father's) typed in uneven letters at the top.

Vught was the only SS concentration camp to be built in the Netherlands, constructed by the forced labour of its own prisoners in 1943. Behind its moat and barbed-wire fences stood the prison gallows, used for random executions in which at least 500 died. Others, packed too tightly in their cells, died simply of suffocation; there were constant dog attacks on the inmates; and there were clogs with spikes inside to cut the prisoners' feet. The camp was also used for the transit of over 1,000 Jewish children. With the yellow index card between my fingers, I wonder if my grandfather watched them and if he thought of Lien.

Other documents at the NIOD also connect with Lien's story, such as a printed letter on office stationery sent by a Dordrecht physician in 1941. In it, Dr Cahen explains to his patients that his medical diploma, hard-earned nearly thirty years ago, is now invalid and that he must ask them to switch their loyalty to another practitioner who is not a Jew. He suggests Jan Heroma, Took's husband, whom he calls 'a man with a golden heart'. If they join his practice, he explains, then Jan Heroma will transfer any earnings back to Dr Cahen, so as to help him through this difficult time. The patients may know him already, the letter tells us, this man with a golden heart, because he is famous as the hero who tended the wounded under fire in the battle for Dordrecht, which raged a year ago, when the Germans first came.

Finally, in the archives there is also confirmation of the fate of Lien's parents, something of which, of course, she already knew. A brief police report documents their arrest on 9 October 1942 at ten in the evening. The note of their capture, written out neatly in longhand, is dwarfed by the account of a minor bicycle collision, which takes up the bulk of the same page. It is striking to see how the police reporter, who went to the trouble of visiting the hospital to check on the condition of an injured bicyclist, could record the capture and deportation of a Jewish couple without apparent concern.

Having left their registered address, Charles and Catharine had travelled to Leiden to go into hiding, where it seems they were betrayed. I imagine them – he at thirty-five, she just twenty-eight – hand in hand, facing their captors, who were led by a Dutch policeman, Ulrich Koenrad Hoffman, who was the same age as Charles.

Koenrad Hoffman was in some ways the opposite of the Dordrecht policeman Harry Evers. A committed NSB man, Hoffman made no denials when he faced his trial in 1949. As is clear from the files put together for his prosecution, he was a sickly and nervous fascist, endlessly busy over details such as reporting on schoolteachers who expressed anti-German views. Koenrad collected the anonymous letters that were sent to him, addressed to 'Stinky Hoffman, Gestapo', and forwarded these, demanding action, to the Chief of Police. His correspondence was always headed with the logo of the sword and swastika and signed with the Dutch fascist salute, *HOU SEE!* Prone to attacks of anxiety, he fussed over ineffective measures, such as the installation of bugging devices in cells. But he was punctilious in carrying out his duties, which included the 'clearing' of a Jewish orphanage that housed 150 boys and girls. After the verdict at his post-war trial, he complained about his 'very harsh' five-and-a-quarter-year sentence, telling the judge that, as an empowered officer, he was guilty 'in no legal sense'. Hoffman told the court that, in retrospect, he had a few moral scruples about his actions, but these were 'on very minor points'.

Lien's mother, Catharine, was murdered at Auschwitz exactly a month after her arrest by Hoffman. She died alongside her own mother, which is of some comfort to Lien. Charles was killed a few months later, on 6 February 1943.

On 7 January 2015, after several days of working in libraries and archives, I am on my way to IJsselmonde, the place where Lien lay hidden with Mieneke and her family for around eight months. I am going because I hope to locate the house that she stayed in and also to retrace the route that she and Jo Kleijne took from there to get to the resistance hideout after the raid.

Once remote, IJsselmonde is today held in a knot of motorways and train lines running to Rotterdam and its enormous harbour, which stretches out along the Maas estuary to the sea. The scale of the development that has swallowed the village since the war is difficult to imagine. By 1962 the Europort, which lies to its west, had become the world's largest harbour, a position that it held until 2004. It is still by far the biggest port in Europe, well over twice the size of its nearest rival, and it delivers around a ton of material for every citizen of the European Union each year.

I have borrowed a little white Peugeot 108 from my aunt and uncle, with whom I have been staying. By mid-afternoon I am driving alongside the Waalhaven, stunned by the expanse of docks, storage depots and processing plants that stretches to my left. For twenty miles there has been a regular succession of container stacks and oil tanks. I have passed a string of refineries, each a mangrove of metal tubing, and, between them, have glimpsed the dull iron walls of the ships. With its constant flow of containers, which sit around me on trucks, the port of Rotterdam feeds the continent like some enormous mouth.

For anyone unfamiliar with the route, the journey to IJsselmonde demands a lot of concentration because the motorway wants to lead you onwards, either to the docks or to distant cities where the trucks can distribute their loads. Hemmed in by lorries, I manage only just to take the right exit, which leads me, through a corkscrew of roundabouts, to the old village, which now stands in the shadow of a concrete flyover that carries twelve lanes of traffic to a double-arched bridge. The village itself, though, is surprisingly untouched and tranquil. It is made up of pretty gabled houses, some with dates on them: '1889', '1905', '1929'. By the time I pull the little Peugeot into the car park on the outskirts of the old centre it is 3.30 p.m. and the sun is already low on the skyline, which is dominated by the bridge and flyover to the west.

Lien has almost no memory of the exterior of the house where she hid in IJsselmonde. Although she lived here for over half a year, she saw the building from the outside only once, on the day she came. She does know that it stood on the outskirts of the village, was rather farm-like, and was built against the dyke.

From the car park I climb up to the Nieuwe Maas river, which is busy with trade. Great flat barges plough their way through the water, laden with coal and iron ore. On the opposite bank, 300 yards away, there are four matching office blocks, each a sculpted triangle of glass, like a slice of cake on its side.

In search of a building that might match Lien's description, I walk along the top of the dyke towards the flyover and soon its humming concrete hangs high above me, like the ceiling of a cathedral. The fat pillars that stretch up on all sides carry a quarter of a million vehicles each day. In other countries a place like this would be threatening, but here everything is clean and well maintained. There is a set of neat recycling bins and, in the distance, still under the concrete, I can see a dog walker. Then a girl cycles past me in a bright blue Gore-tex jacket while checking her phone. Village life continues almost untroubled by the industrial sprawl.

For about two hours I scan the surroundings, mostly walking through the post-war housing developments that now abut the old buildings, but sometimes still finding patches of rural land. It is on one of these, towards dusk, that I see something that fits with Lien's memory: a white single-storey house that stands a little beyond the eastern edge. It has a barn door at one end, with four little square windows looking out from what is now a converted loft. A hedge of brambles and bushes shields it from the roadside, and it is built against the dyke.

This all fits with how I envisaged the farmhouse and, as darkness falls around me, I can imagine Lien and Jo clambering up the heavy slope on which I stand. Through the bushes I peer into the black windows and take some photos. Then I move upwards again towards the river, looking down on the roof tiles from above. I can see how Lien and Jo would move on from here towards the centre, keeping to the dyke edge near the river before crossing back again and heading inland. With growing certainty I begin to trace a possible route.

But then, twenty minutes later on the south side of the

village, I see a house that leans against a second, lower, dyke that might qualify almost as easily. It is also single storey and it is also surrounded by a hedge. Taking another set of pictures, this time with glowing street lights in the foreground, my faith in my imagination begins to ebb.

With whose memory am I connecting? Lien's or my own?

A year later, when I show Lien the account I have written of her escape from IJsselmonde she will be troubled by it, not because it is untruthful but because – unlike all the earlier parts of her childhood experience – there are so many blanks that she cannot fill. She remembers Jo carrying her in the darkness; she remembers the dyke; she remembers moving amongst the houses, then the resistance hideout, how it was very dirty and how it made her think of a drinking den. Upstairs there were beds and she lay in one with other people. There was a terrible smell. But how big it was, how long they walked to get there, whether they ran? None of this is clear. To her it seems somehow too active in my description. She was a spectator who barely registered what was going on.

'You have written it as it could have been,' Lien tells me. 'I can live with it,' she eventually says.

It is fully dark now, and my phone is out of battery so I can take no more pictures. A little downhearted, I make my way back to the car, which now stands in empty space. As I sit at the wheel, planning my journey, the warm red and white of the dials on the dashboard is oddly comforting. After a bit, the heater clears the condensation from the windows and the interior begins to warm up. Without my phone's satnav I worry a bit about the route to my aunt and uncle's house in Bennekom, in the centre of the country. All the same, I drive up the ramp to join the motorway, edging my way in amongst the lorries, and head towards the bridge. The traffic is almost stationary. It will be a long time before I reach any junctions at which I need to make decisions, so I turn on Dutch radio for the first time today.

Two men are in conversation, the programme's host and a guest. It takes me a little while to work out the subject, which is the culture of satirical cartoons in France. They mention what seems to be a magazine based in Paris. It is called *Charlie Hebdo*.

'This was an editorial meeting . . . generally cartoonists work at home.'

'Did you know the cartoonists?'

'Not personally, but I was familiar with their work.'

Something significant has happened. There is mention of depictions of the Prophet Muhammad and of the possible consequences for free speech.

At seven o'clock there is a news summary. Eleven people have been gunned down in the offices of a satirical weekly, which has a tradition of mocking religion, including Islam. A car has been hijacked and a policeman (himself a Muslim) has been shot dead on the street. The perpetrators – who brandished guns and said they had enacted vengeance – are still on the run. It emerges that they left an identity card behind them and that they are terrorists linked to a branch of al-Qaeda based in Yemen. Huge crowds are gathering in public places around Europe. Tens of thousands stand in silence and carry home-made placards all bearing the same slogan· *Je suis Charlie*.

As I inch forward with the little car in the red of the tail-lights, news anchors discuss the situation. They canvass the opinion of pundits and hold conversations with reporters on the ground. Few further details emerge in the course of the evening so the talk becomes more historical in its perspective and, at eight thirty, there is an interview with the former mayor of Amsterdam, Job Cohen. He describes his reaction, ten years earlier, to the murder of the Dutch film-maker Theo van Gogh.

Van Gogh (a descendant of the famous painter's family) was an award-winning film director and free-speech activist who made a point of pushing all possible boundaries. He made graphic jokes about the Holocaust, for example, and called Jesus 'the rotten fish of Nazareth'. Then, in 2004, he made the film *Submission*, whose title played on one possible translation of the Arabic word for Islam. It showed the bodies of Muslim women who had been violently abused by their husbands and families, and on those bodies van Gogh painted Koranic verses pertaining to the treatment of wives. The film was shown on national television by the VPRO, by origin a Protestant Christian broadcaster, and, three months later, while cycling to his office at nine in the morning, van Gogh was shot eight times and then had his throat cut in the street. His murderer, a Muslim extremist who also wounded two bystanders, left a message of vengeance addressed to the film's author (Ayaan Hirsi Ali) pinned to van Gogh's chest with a knife.

The radio plays a section of the speech that Job Cohen delivered as mayor that evening to a crowd very similar to those in Paris and elsewhere now. In it he speaks of 'the Dam, the symbol of our freedom' and of how progress is to be made 'through discussion, through the pen, and – as a last resort – through the courts, but not by taking the law into our own hands'. His words are tolerant and inclusive, and they are cheered by the crowd.

Yet even in November 2004 they were idealistic. The norms around freedom of expression that Cohen called upon at that moment were far from universally shared.

At one time the Netherlands really was a country where even the Prime Minister cycled to work in the morning unprotected. But then, on 6 May 2002, came the assassination of Pim

Fortuyn. He was, like van Gogh, a kind of extremist: a peculiarly Dutch combination of the left and the far right. Fortuyn was an openly gay man who was against political correctness, against immigration, and above all against Islam, which he called 'backward' and incompatible with modern life. As a candidate for a localist movement, he achieved 37.4 per cent of the vote in Rotterdam. After this he set up his own political party: the List Pim Fortuyn. Then, riding high in the polls, on the eve of the general election, as he left the national media centre at Hilversum, Fortuyn was shot five times in the back of the head. As it happens his murderer was not a jihadi but instead a fanatical opponent of factory farming, who considered Fortuyn's views on such subjects as Islam and immigration a threat to societal norms. But this detail (like the shooting of the Muslim policeman in Paris) is easily lost.

Gradually the traffic clears and I follow the signs for Utrecht. The interview with the former mayor of Amsterdam closes and the radio shifts to a panel discussion in which the phrase 'Islamic fascism' recurs. Tomorrow there will be new developments in Paris: a siege at a kosher supermarket that ends in more killings, this time directly targeting Jews. As I pick up speed in the darkness, I am struck again by the obvious overlap between the present epoch and the last one: absurd conspiracy theories, economic recession, and a loss of faith in moderate politicians, who seem to many people to be irrelevant and corrupt. The little car pulls past container lorries that carry goods into Europe: fridges, televisions, furniture, plastic shoes. From the look of these roads nothing is left of the old Europe, but its ghost remains.

13

It is warm in the church. Bright light comes in from the arched windows and the circle of stained glass above the pulpit shines yellow and blue. There is a clean mothball smell from the people around her, all in their Sunday best, standing and sitting in unison, half-singing the same words:

'Our Father, who art in heaven, hallowed be thy name; thy kingdom come; thy will be done; on earth as it is in heaven.'

Lien says the words with the others. Occasionally, when she is a little too quick or too slow, she catches the sound of her own voice, which feels unfamiliar in this space. It is nice here with so many people around you, making the same movements and saying the same things.

Her legs do not hurt now. Though the memory is fading, she can still picture the top of the doctor's head, with just a thin down of hair upon it, as he bent, dabbing her with something sharp, when she first came here a few months ago. It was very clean in the surgery. On the wall there was a diagram of a person opened up so that you could see their insides.

The visiting preacher is climbing the stairs now to go up to the pulpit. He has come from Arnhem this morning on his bicycle to speak. But first it is the turn of the lay reader:

'And Jesus said unto him, I must work the works of him that sent me . . .'

His voice is deep and the words have the rhythm of a poem.

'. . . the night cometh, when no man can work . . .'

They are doing poems now at school, including the Psalms, which they learn by heart.

'. . . he spat on the ground, and made clay of the spittle, and he anointed the eyes of the blind man with the clay . . .'

Will they have mashed potatoes again like they did last Sunday? She did not like them. They tasted of soap.

'. . . but the Jews did not believe concerning him, that he had been blind, and received his sight . . .'

Now that the reading is over the preacher looks down at them from the pulpit, fixing her interest with his silence and his serious face. Beside her, Mother van Laar shifts her position, tilting her head up further, hands locked together, all attention for what will come.

'Jesus spits,' the preacher says. 'He spits on the dry earth and he makes mud of that earth and he puts that mud into the eyes of a blind man . . .'

He makes you think about it, and she can imagine the scene. The dust of the desert and the crowd of people wearing rough cloaks and the white disc of the sun burning down. She likes the images of the sermons. It is the same when she reads from the Bible to the family after dinner. She enjoys the sense of togetherness and the sing-song rhythm of each line.

Lien has always been a dreamer and at night the pleasures and frustrations of the day come back to her, made strange by her imagination, as she lies there beneath the stiff laundered sheets. In school she is not allowed to run at playtime. This is because she has been unwell and needs rest. When she is dreaming, Lien kicks out at this rule with impatience, wanting to move, but she still floats there, unable to catch up. As she sleeps, she does the sums and the spelling tests that she is so good at and tries to connect with the girl who is sitting on the school bench next to her, but that doesn't quite work.

Then comes the part of the dream that is fearful. She can feel it happening but she is unable to make it stop. Walking down the school corridors with their high ceilings, through the bustle of other children, the urge becomes stronger with each step. She needs to pee. Finally, when she is safe in the cubicle, she lets go. There is a warm wetness, which is pleasant at first. But now it grows cold.

Heavy with drowsiness, she calls out.

It is completely dark and then suddenly very bright as she steps, dizzily, eyes scrunched, away from the bed.

There is a fuss around her. Sheets are pulled free from their corners and then bundled on to the floor. Arms up, her night-dress is lifted, trailing on her skin as it goes. For a second she is tented, and then, straight after, there is the scent of soap and the touch of a flannel, wetted, cold, at the sink. She awakens in full to self-awareness, standing naked in the light. While Mother van Laar is efficient and says nothing to blame her, there is still the pain of embarrassment. There is no blame, but also no word of comfort or gentleness of touch.

Ten minutes later she is in bed again, clean in the absolute blackness, and scared now of sleep.

On the photo in Lien's album she stands with the van Laar family in their garden amongst wintry flowerbeds that are marked out with white painted stones. The house behind them, number 33 Algemeer, is new, attractive and semi-detached. It stands on the edge of Bennekom, a village in the centre of the Netherlands, and looks out over a field and, beyond this, a wood. The gathering in the picture is rather formal: all five people (the fifth, behind Lien, is unknown to me) stand with their arms at their sides in the same pose, as if ready for inspection. Father van Laar and his son, Jaap, on the

left, look neat with their neckties, close-shorn haircuts and gleaming shoes. In the middle of the picture stands Mother van Laar, who, from the look of it, is their leader, with her high collar, tightly buttoned jacket and firm, assured smile. All of the family face the camera. It is only Lien who looks downwards and a little to the side. Her short-sleeved dress appears too light for the weather and it is blown by a wind that nobody else in the picture seems to feel.

The Protestant Reformed church (or *Hervormde kerk*), which the van Laars in the photograph look dressed to attend, stands half a mile away at the centre of the village: a solid red-brick building that was begun in the eleventh century, with a square tower and smallish clear windows near to the ground. Its walls were long ago stripped of their statues and frescoes and now resound to plain sermons that are delivered to an audience of the elect. Theirs is the Calvinist denomination that has its origins in the Synod of Dordt. It is the great national institution that once buried Baruch Spinoza in splendour and then demolished his grave for non-payment of fees. Practical and worldly, the Reformed Church has played its part in giving the Dutch their national character: direct, house-proud, and determined to offer a respectable exterior to the outside world.

With some notable exceptions, the Reformed Church has not been quick to come to the aid of its Jewish neighbours. While its elders, of course, disapprove of the occupation and are loyal to the House of Orange, they also have a dislike of grandstanding, activism and making a fuss. Law and order are the mainstays of their civic values, and that belief sits uneasily with any resistance to Nazi plans.

Back in July 1942 there had been a plan to read out a clear statement of disapproval in all Christian churches about the mass deportation of Jews. A joint text, agreed with the Catholics, was even prepared. In the end, however, the elders at the Reformed Church Synod retreated, persuaded by a promise that if no objection was made in public, Jews who had converted to the Protestant faith would be spared. Rather than expressing outrage at the deportations, the Synod instead issued a declaration describing the 'bitter trials' that God set for the 'folk of Israel' who stood out against conversion to the Christian truth.

There had been a real choice here. When the Catholics went ahead and read out the original statement of opposition, over 200 Jewish members of their congregation were arrested as a consequence and sent straight to the camps, where, amongst others, the philosopher-nun Edith Stein met her death. Even in the face of this action, the Catholic archbishop had chosen to stick to his position, thereafter diverting thousands of guilders of collection money to the resistance cause. The Protestant Reformed Church, in contrast, still refused to speak out.

Looking back, the retreat of the Reformed Church Synod in

July 1942 stands out as a defining moment in the history of the Netherlands. Seyss-Inquart, the Reichskommissar in charge of the country, had been genuinely worried about the prospect of church opposition, because in occupied Norway protest from the Lutherans had galvanized resistance on a significant scale. If a collective statement had been issued, more Dutch families might well have sheltered their fellow citizens, they might well have sabotaged the running of the railways to Poland, and they might well have been less cooperative, as policemen, in arresting and imprisoning Jews. H. C. Touw, the Reformed Church's great historian, would be unsparing in his verdict on the Synod. Their conduct was 'deeply shaming' and 'unprincipled'. There was 'a fear of being burned by cold water'. In summation, 'we must speak of enormous collective guilt'.

By the time that Lien was brought to the village of Bennekom in late 1943, things had changed for the Protestant Reformed Church, which now backed active resistance and told its members to protect their fellow citizens, even at personal cost. It was this alteration in the national picture, of which she herself knew nothing, that brought her to this rural and therefore safer part of the Netherlands.

The Lien who stands in a thin white dress on the right of the photograph is an altered creature. In the house that stands behind her she is more a housemaid than a daughter, even though she must say 'Mother' and 'Father' to Mr and Mrs van Laar. Every morning it is her job to clear out and then light the wood-burning stove in the kitchen and then to clean and polish the shoes. Straight back from school she sees to the furniture, holding a cloth in each hand so as not to leave marks. The Delft blue plates on display in the cupboard in the front room need to be lifted, one after the other, while the surface below them is first dusted and then wiped. Lien finds this difficult – she is unpractised and also unwilling – so it takes a very long time.

They are opposites, she and Mother van Laar. Even their pictures in the photo album could hardly be more different. Lien looks sideways, distracted, waiflike with her curls, and already a beauty – she has dark and perfect features that bespeak another world. In contrast, Mother van Laar has a direct countenance and a boyish side parting in her flat, close-cut hair. She is not easily pleased with Lien's efforts and, to the girl's hot fury, is dismissive about them when neighbours ask. As Lien sits at the kitchen table, she overhears comments about her slowness. They make her fingers tremble while she cuts and stacks the ration stamps, another of her jobs. Once at a low heat while in hiding in IJsselmonde, there is a fire now within her, only just under control. While Lien cuts, Mother van Laar holds forth about Sunday's sermon and recommends a method for keeping net curtains white. Each time she ends a sentence, to Lien's irritation, she rests her teeth on her bottom lip.

Heading upstairs to her bedroom, the girl leaves a pile of bent coupons on the table, improperly stacked. In her mind she is already half in the adventure of the book she is reading. It is called *Patriots and Liegemen* and forms part of a series that sits on the shelves in the living room, the gold and red of their spines all perfectly aligned. Lien loves them. Three cheers for the Liegemen! True to God and the Prince of Orange! Right at this moment young Maurits is stowed in the luggage rack of a stagecoach that is rattling along the cobbles to Paris, and beneath him, swigging wine from a bottle, is Marshal Soult. If Soult discovers the boy he will surely cut his heart out. But Maurits is brave and must find his way to the hidden French plans.

Lien spends her spare hours absorbed in this world of schooners, sword fights, and moonlit escapes over castle walls. The Patriots are the villains (and so not really patriots at all). They are in league with the French invaders and take their orders directly from Napoleon himself. The emperor has put his weak younger brother, Lodewick, on the Dutch throne and he has designs on Holland's riches, its freedom and its church. Meanwhile, the Liegemen fight him by bringing help from England, crossing the Channel under cover of fog and night. Beneath their cloaks there are daggers and silvery pistols and noble beating hearts. Lien sits in bed, half under the covers, at one with a princess imprisoned in a tower, or with a hero who climbs to reach her, knowing that any minute the rope may snap.

From the winter of 1943 to the spring of 1944, Lien works to the rhythms of the van Laar household: the morning fire-lighting, the polishing, the kitchen tasks, and the reading aloud from the Bible at night. She takes pleasure in stories and in her success at school, where she stands out as clever, but, all the same, resentment slowly builds within her. She dislikes the rules, the criticism and the cleaning, and the way that the van Laar boy Jaap tells tales on her, for example if she ever tries to run in the playground at school, which is not allowed because of her health. The van Laars, from her perspective, are concerned only with outward appearances, while she herself lives so passionately within.

The earth is warming, yet food is becoming harder to find even here in the countryside, and for this reason a new task is added to Lien's duties. It is called 'carrying from the farm'. The 'carrying' is really 'begging', and the girl, with her prettiness and her thinness, does this task exceptionally well. There are walks along hedgerows, through woods and over heaths to farmyards where she will stand at the open door of a barn. 'Do you have any eggs or milk for Mother?' she must ask. Almost always she comes back with something, such as a brown paper package with bacon inside it, a clutch of spring onions or a thin yellow triangle of cheese.

In this way Lien ranges through the landscape of Gelderland, a fairy-tale figure with a basket in her hand. This is a different kind of Holland from the square fields, canals, windmills and poplars of the west. Here the birches clasp their roots to dips and ridges, the dappled floor beneath their branches covered with blueberry bushes that have tiny dark leaves. Mixed in with the patches of wood there is heather, which shines pale purple amidst the white of dry grass. The farms are small and ancient, low wooden barns with mossy thatch that shelter a few goats and chickens and a cow. In some of the clearings there are holi-day chalets and campsites where German soldiers hang out their washing or sit at tables, smoking and playing cards.

One time, as Lien walks along a sandy track with broad, bright fields on either side of it, a horse and cart comes up behind her and slowly overtakes. The back of the cart is open and carries half a dozen boyish soldiers, propped up on sacks, sunning themselves. As she recedes, they notice her and wave and she waves back. And then they stop and call to her, all smiling, to claim her as a prize. A young man with a face full of freckles jumps down with his bare feet in the sand and in one easy movement he squats and lifts her on to the hot wooden boards above him in the sun.

It feels high up there. '*Sprechen Sie Deutsch?*' the young men ask. She shakes her head and looks a little to the side. To win a smile they offer words in their language for her to practise, and search their pockets for gifts, and so she eats the *Knäcke-brot* and imitation chocolate that they place, with laughter and entreaties, into her hand. The boys show Lien photos of their loved ones. They talk to each other in German while they fix her with sparkling eyes. In this way they ride for maybe half an hour through the fields and woodlands, with Lien a captive and a princess at the same time. Then, when they reach the edge of the village, she points to where her house is, and the soldiers lift her down.

Lien, as she walks on without turning her head, does not reflect on her encounter with the soldiers. Like everything else, it just happens. She does not think about the war or about friends or enemies. Nor does she ever think about her parents, or indeed about anyone else connected to her who might still be out there in the great wide world.

May 1944 becomes June, and the early heat that promised summer is replaced by rain. Four hundred miles away in Normandy an Allied landing is successful, but this barely registers with Lien. The main event is that the van Laar family are off on a short holiday, which means that she must stay with the neighbours at number 31. It is quite a change.

Corrie de Bond, the girl next door, is a few years older – a chatty, motherly type with a strong country accent and rosy cheeks. She envelops Lien with teenage gossip and advice. Though Corrie still wears a Peter Pan collar she is almost a woman and, to Lien's nervous excitement, she delivers home truths about Mother van Laar. Corrie's parents, Toon and Jansje, are a jolly couple. Jansje is tiny, always smiling, and round-faced – an adult, but shorter than Lien, with a very quiet and soft-toned voice. Illness when she was young has made her fragile, so she spends a lot of time resting in bed. This makes Corrie a kind of chief in the family: cleaning the kitchen, helping with dinner, and sometimes even scolding her father if he is late home. There are always people moving in and out of the household, and it is Corrie who tells them the rules.

A few days into Lien's visit Corrie's father comes in even later than usual. Though a giant, towering more than two feet above them, he bends meekly, with a smile of contrition, when his daughter points to the clock on the wall. Instead of a jacket and tie, he wears paint-spattered braces and an open-necked shirt. For a moment he stands there, waiting in silence, with a smile playing on his features and his hands behind his back, and then, with a wink, he reveals a sack of potatoes, edged with heavy soil, and puts them in triumph on the table, where they thunder to a point of rest. His little wife is delighted, but before anything can be said the youngest, Maartje, runs in, trailing a doll, desperate to be lifted up high. Corrie warns her father to be careful. So, gently, allowing just the checked bow in Maartje's hair to touch the plaster, he lifts her against the ceiling, which is only a little higher than the top of his own bald head. After, they sit together eating, with giggles and conversation instead of prayers. Lien is quiet, but she enjoys the togetherness and the pudding that they have at the end.

That night, lying alongside the older girl, she whispers that she would rather live here with Corrie and Maartje because she would fit in right between them, the little sister to one and the big sister to the other. But, as Corrie tells her with adult wisdom, it would be too dangerous to change. And so, three days later, Lien moves back to her familiar bedroom at number 33 with the van Laars.

It is unfair to make the van Laars the villains. They have been brave to take in a hideaway and they have ideals and standards of their own. It is not easy to take another person into a family. No doubt Mother van Laar wants to teach Lien to do better, and the child, with her dreamy distance from others and her sometimes sulky demeanour, is not a model of the modest, homely, God-fearing girl that she admires.

Still, the nightly prayers about being truly grateful feel to Lien like an accusation and, as the nights darken in September, her angry conviction that the values around her are crooked ripens to an open secret that can be read in her every gaze. Tension lies coiled in the household, and unsatisfied stomachs and rain do nothing to lift the mood. At table she scowls at Jaap as he reports, with all the detail that he can muster, that he saw her doing hopscotch in the playground at school. After dinner, as Lien reads aloud as always from the Bible, there is an edge to her voice.

The rain has stopped momentarily, so the parents decide on a walk before curfew and Jaap goes out to play. Lien hovers in the kitchen, uncertain. Maybe she could go and talk to Corrie, now that the dishes are done? Then a wicked idea steals upon her, and, almost before she is aware of it, she is in the hall. Here, under the stairs, is the doorway that leads to the cellar. She is still hungry. There is enough time.

She turns the handle and sees the wooden steps and clicks on the light. Her ears are singing with the rushing thump of her own heart. It is now or never. Bending in, she hovers at the open hatch. There are sugar cubes, she knows it for certain, in the yellow enamel container on the top shelf. Quickly, she backs down the stairway on to the brick floor, watching the grey square above her grow smaller as she goes. It is there on the highest shelf, just as she expected: the yellow tin. With stretched fingers, Lien tips it towards her, catching the weight with her thumbs. There is a slight rattle from the lumps inside.

'What are you doing?' says the voice of Mother van Laar.

It cuts through the girl like an electric charge.

She looks up into the greyness above her head, an animal trapped, and her blush spreads sharp as a knife. And then the heat that has been for so long inside her, like a peat fire burning beneath the grass, bursts out into the light.

'You're a rotten woman,' she mumbles, too soft to be confident but loud enough to be heard.

There is a long silence and then a reply.

'These are your Jewish tricks,' says Mother van Laar.

14

Bennekom, the place where Lien lived in hiding with the van Laars, is my mother's home village. This is the place I know best in the Netherlands, and it is in Bennekom that I have, for the most part, been staying with my aunt and uncle since I began these weeks of research. It is a coincidence that Lien should have spent years in this familiar location, because her connection is with my father's family and not at all with my mother's.

Lien stops talking, but, like last time, the recorder on the table continues to run. It is Sunday at 1 p.m. and I am back at her Amsterdam apartment. This has been our first session of interviewing for over a week.

Lien moves the photo album with the pictures of the van Laars off the table and sets out the plates and cutlery for lunch. We continue to talk as we eat.

The metaphor of a fire that burns beneath the surface, like the earlier image of a 'low heat' when she was hidden at the farm in IJsselmonde, is important to Lien and she returns to it now as we discuss her feelings. Resentment had been building for months, and once it burst out into the open it was impossible to contain. There would be fierce rows with the van Laars, with all-out shouting, and Lien herself would say terrible things.

'I think I was very unkind to them,' says Lien gently, 'and they also to me.'

In families, she observes, a pattern is often established where everyone's behaviour is fixed in advance. You know what one person will do and what the other will say long before anything actually happens. With her and the van Laars it became a pattern of unkindness. There was no respect, no validation; they did not say nice things to each other.

'But,' Lien adds, speaking slowly, 'I think it was also very decent of them, I think it was exceptionally moral, that, with the difficult behaviour I had – and I certainly had that – they did not give me up.'

'Give me up': the phrase means several things.

I ask Lien if she felt angry.

She pauses before answering.

'I think my main feeling was of having lost anything to hold on to. There were no borders . . . There were no fences . . . The biggest feeling, the most important feeling, was that I was free-falling and that nobody could hold me. You need somebody who can draw a line that you must not cross, and I did not have that.'

Lien explains that later, in her professional life as a social worker, it was because of this experience that she could identify so strongly with children who had a problem with authority. They also had no sense of a line that could not be crossed and, because of this, there was nothing that stopped them from entering the criminal world. She thinks, given the wildness and sense of abandonment that entered her, she could have gone that way herself.

Before resuming our interview Lien and I take a short walk in the Vondelpark, which lies just a few minutes from her front door. In spite of her age, Lien is quick on her feet and, as we cross the road, she chivvies me to pick up my pace.

The paths in the park are thronged with speeding bicyclists and crowds of other walkers. In the winter sunshine, people are sitting outside the park's restaurants and teahouses, drinking coffee or sipping from tall thin glasses of beer. From the three boys on the path ahead of us comes a strong whiff of marijuana.

It makes me think of the 1970s when this park was famous the world over as a 'magic centre', with thousands of hippies singing beneath the trees and by the lakes, spending their nights here in sleeping bags, celebrating peace and love. Apparently only 10 per cent of the hippies actually came from Amsterdam, the bulk of the numbers making the trip from elsewhere in Holland and from France, Germany and the US. Then, as now, the city was a haven of toleration that drew those who wished to experiment, even if only for the length of a mini-break. It is all the more haunting to think that during the war this place was a German military camp, surrounded by barbed wire, with concrete bunkers plumbed deep into the ground.

Back in the flat we brew tea. It is a bit of an effort to return to work after our outing and for a while my questions feel vague and forced. I try to get a picture of Lien's life that autumn, but little colour comes through. In spite of the quarrels and the tension, things continued as normal. She still did the cleaning, they ate their awkward dinners together, and she continued to flourish at school. In the evening she always read out loud from the Bible, and while this might seem, for a Jewish girl, an imposition, for her it remained a pleasure.

'I have always been one for stories. That's why the church was a joy to me. Learning psalms, hearing sermons, talking about the lesson – it gave such a sense of togetherness. It was the same as when I was a girl in the Pletterijstraat, when they would say, during a story, "She just sits there and stares." I was totally in that world.'

I remind Lien of the way that she entertained my aunt, little Marianne, in the van Es family, and her eyes light up.

'Yes, that's true,' she says, and then, in an instant, the balance of the conversation changes, the stiffness is gone and Lien begins to tell me about Sunday 17 September 1944.

15

Lien stands on a road at the edge of a wheat field and watches them: half-circles, some in bright colours – blue, red, yellow, green – drifting down.

Parachutes, right here in the sunlight now that there is a break in the clouds!

There are children around her, pointing. These are the English soldiers landing. She scans the uncountable silhouettes. And above them are planes in their hundreds that move as if they are locked together, sliding like a stencil across the sky.

It makes her laugh to see them, like the way you laugh at an accident when you know it is serious but you cannot make a serious face. It is silly how many there are. Thousands and thousands. It cannot be real.

Her neck hurts with watching. She follows one parachute from the moment it hatches. First comes a little mushroom of cloth and then the strings and then a lump that is really a man. They tumble downwards, the lump going first and the mushroom racing after, getting bigger as it goes. It fills up and then opens and slows right down. You can't see them landing. They just vanish in the distance behind the trees. When one is gone she looks up for another to follow. They pour from the backs of the planes, one after another, like dominoes on a run.

Sometimes it is not soldiers but packages that hang from the guy ropes. Adults who join the group tell her about the difference: some carry Jeeps and some carry cannons. And then, later, there are planes that are towed by others. These are gliders that cannot fly by themselves. She watches as the rope is cut and the pulling plane moves away from the towed one, which noses downwards so quickly that it looks like a crash.

These really are the English! Everyone keeps saying the same thing!

So many keep coming that it ought to be boring except that the excitement around her grows bigger all the time. A tall man explains things to a boy who hops up and down beside him, repeating strange words like 'Allies', 'Dakotas' and 'flak'. She watches out for the colours – blue, red, yellow, green.

Then suddenly there is a thump behind them and the crowd turns to see fire spread in the sky and then, after this, a worm of black smoke that boils up from the ground. It is all at a distance, so it feels pretend.

After a while a group of men races past on bicycles without tyres, the metal rims cutting into the sand. They are wearing orange banners and, around her, people begin a wild rendition of the song 'Long Live the Queen'.

In the distance there are rattles and rhythmic bangs.

Then, right above them, frozen it seems for a moment, there are two planes so close that she can see the rivets on their grey striped bellies as well as their hanging bombs. The propellers are just shiny circles of air. In a few seconds the planes have vanished, but the noise from their engines sings on for a very long time.

By the time that she gets home to Algemeer there is a siren wailing, filling the street with long, low, pitiful howls. As soon as she opens the front door she hears the voice of Mother van Laar calling, asking who it is, which is not what usually happens. When she answers, Lien is ordered to come straight into the cellar, where the whole family is squeezed in. Mother van Laar, her face all glossy, says with a frantic edge that two children have been killed on the Diedenweg, hit by a bomb. Father van Laar sits on a crate beside her, his hair standing sideways in a tuft. 'The English are coming,' says Jaap, as if this is news to Lien. Then, after a minute, the electricity cuts out.

Three miles away, on the large flat expanse of heather and grass that is the Ginkelse Heide, British paratroopers are moving towards Arnhem. They are part of Operation Market Garden, the plan to defeat Germany by cutting straight through Holland to the industrial heartland of the Ruhr. Altogether there are 10,000 of them and they need to move quickly across enemy territory to capture and then hold the final bridge of a sequence, which stretches – eight miles in the distance – across the Rhine.

In the morning it is clear that school has been cancelled because there are children playing in the street. Freed by an odd kind of holiday spirit, Lien goes out to join them and finds that boys are collecting trophies. One has a whole collection spread out before him on the grass. Lien edges in to join the group that has fanned out around him, and hears that the various bits of green canvas with straps and buckles are parachute cords. The boy also has cartridge cases: small shiny copper-coloured tubes. She is allowed to hold one and stares into the blackness of the inside. 'Smell the top of it,' he instructs her, and, without thinking about it, she takes a deep lungful of sulphurous air. She coughs and her eyes sparkle, a response that he clearly enjoys. The boy has chosen her now for special attention and he hands her, with reverence, the painted fin of a British bomb. Their fingers touch as she takes it with a shy smile.

There is a romance to those early days after the landings.

Often there is rapid fire in the distance or even the whistle of a bullet nearby. The trophy collections of the boys in the street get bigger, and girls are to be seen in colourful nylon dresses that have been made by their mothers out of parachute cloth. Lien would like one herself.

After a while, though, the announcement comes that school is restarting and the mood around her alters. The weather, which had been bright momentarily, turns to fog and then rain. War still continues in the sky above them and on the ground beyond the horizon, with low-flying planes, the rumble of artillery, and the occasional smell of oily smoke in the air. Sometimes there is news of a bomb that has hit a house. Within the bounds of the village itself, however, everything seems almost as it was.

Then Bennekom gradually fills with people: first a few families with stacks of luggage, who settle into houses and barns in the neighbourhood; but, after this, hundreds at a time, refugees who stop only for a few hours before they move on. One morning on the way to school she sees a long motley procession of bewildered faces, exhausted people standing still in the road so that no one can pass. There are walkers, horse-drawn wagons, and bicyclists, all awkwardly loaded, waiting to head out of the village. The wagons have white flags at their corners that hang down, heavy, against the rakes and broom handles that make do for poles. In front of her an old gentleman has a built-up wheelbarrow with planks sticking out of it on which a lot of packing cases have been hammered in place. Beside him stands a girl who is pushing a bicycle. Lien turns to see what is hanging from the handlebars and is shocked to find that they are rabbits, a whole set of them, dead, tied there with string by their legs. Above, feeling close, there is a constant drone of Allied bombers, but you cannot see these because of the cloud.

That afternoon, when Lien gets home to Algemeer, she is told that she must pack her things.

Between 17 September and 20 October 1944, the fate of the village of Bennekom hung in the balance. The landings nearby on the Ginkelse Heide were at the utmost edge of Operation Market Garden and British paratroopers had come down there, more than sixty miles into enemy territory, expecting reinforcement from Allied tanks that were intended to race to their rescue across six captured bridges connected by a single road. Those bridges all needed to be captured by separate landings of airborne forces. It was the seizure of these bridges and the rapid movement of tanks along the road between them that would create a narrow corridor from the old front line to the German frontier.

Day one had been fairly successful. In spite of heavy resistance, a small detachment had sped westwards to Arnhem and had captured the northern end of the sixth and final bridge, from which Germany could be reached. But enormous problems were already apparent: their Jeeps had failed to land safely; bad weather had delayed Polish reinforcements; and Allied radios did not work. The worst, however, was still to come.

Frederick Browning, the Airborne Corps' overall commander, could have spotted the two SS Panzer divisions that defended Arnhem, but, in the rush to get the operation going, signs of their presence had been ignored. These were full, battle-hardened, armoured combat divisions with thousands of soldiers. They had tanks, long-range guns, and far more ammunition than the lightly armed paratroopers. Even so, the small British detachment held out for nine days. In the end, however, on 25 September, with no prospect of relief from the Allied ground army (whose crossings were delayed at Son and at Nijmegen), they were forced to concede defeat. By that point, 1,500 paratroopers lay dead in and around Arnhem and over 6,000 more had been captured, many with very serious wounds. Their struggle would be remembered as 'a bridge too far'.

For the bulk of September, Bennekom lay outside the immediate zone of conflict and, as the situation worsened, it took in refugees from neighbouring towns. In the wake of the eventual liberation of Nijmegen, however, the front lines shifted, and Allied forces were now less than five miles away from the village. Allied artillery strikes were hitting the edges of Bennekom, as were German V-1s when these misfired. By mid October, SS units were moving through the streets, requisitioning houses, and on the 20th the German authorities ordered the inhabitants to evacuate, at the latest by midday on the 22nd. Bennekom was becoming a military zone. Lien, who had once lain hidden in a rural backwater, now stood at a pivot of the entire war.

On the morning of Sunday 22 October at Algemeer 33 there is tense order. An old pram blocks the hallway, its shape barely visible under a blanket that has been tied on with rope. In the kitchen, Mother van Laar is filling a suitcase with jars of food. Upstairs the house has a strange echo and is lighter than usual because the curtains have been taken down. Lien's little package of things is added to the jumble of objects on the landing, which Father van Laar ties up in another blanket and then carries to the front room. Lien is told to sit beside it with Jaap and so they wait there in silence, staring at the empty shelves while thuds and scrapes echo through the half-empty rooms of the house.

After what feels like a long time they head outside into a light drizzle, the sky bright in spite of the cloud. Lien is wearing three dresses so that they will not need to be carried, and she can feel the fabric cutting into the skin on the underside of her arms. They shut the door but do not lock it because it is likely that German soldiers will come to live here in a few hours.

All along the street there are similar groups emerging from doorways, calling to each other, testing the weight of the bags they will carry. The men (there are not many) stand together for a moment, then movement begins and they all take their place in a kind of line. Suitcases are dropped, awkward objects are left on the roadway, but fairly quickly a rhythm is established and they make their way up the street that normally takes her to school. In the village centre there are some wagons with white flags at their corners and here the line of people is split into smaller groups.

For a while everything is familiar: the bakery, the greengrocer's, the butcher's shop. Then the village peters out into more widely spaced houses and finally they are in woodland and unknown fields. It is important to stay close to the wagons, because if they do not, there is a danger that they will be attacked by planes. So they clump together with a few dozen neighbours, who, like them, are mostly silent as they walk. Father van Laar keeps Jaap close beside him. Lien has her eyes fixed on the rubber wheels of the cart that leads the procession and watches as wet leaves are picked up by its tyres. Sometimes the leaves stick on and are carried all the way over and sometimes they just drop.

It is slow progress, with a lot of breaks. At one point they pass a dead horse on the roadside, its hooves pointing upwards, the body covered with a shivering carpet of flies. It is interesting to look at and she stands there for a moment before the moving mass explodes into a buzz of flight.

The walk is not hard, though Lien feels sticky under her layers of clothing. It is mid-afternoon by the time they approach their destination, the town of Ede, a place she has never been. The first thing that she sees, before they reach any buildings, is a bomb crater at the edge of the road. She and Jaap, allies for a moment, step away from the group to stare at it. The crater is an almost perfect circle, like a kitchen bowl cut into the sand, and Lien wonders what it would feel like to be down there inside it, looking up at the high heaped sides.

Amongst the first of the buildings, they see rubble. Great hills of tangled metal, brick and concrete thrown up alongside houses that look perfectly fine. On the one in front of them it is just a corner that is missing: the room up there is cut open, with a door, a bed and half a ceiling surrounded by grey sky. A mess of wall and window lies beside them in the street.

Now that they have reached the town their group is merging with others. The road ahead is blocked, people are saying, because the Germans are conducting a search. So they stand and wait in the grey afternoon light. At first people arch their necks to see what is happening, but as time passes they begin to stare in nervous agitation at the ground. Men in uniform are walking slowly along the line of families, stopping now and then to ask questions or to shout orders that no one fully understands. Ten steps ahead, a young man holds out a bundle of papers, but in spite of this he is pulled all of a sudden, by his collar, to the side of the road. Father van Laar, beside her, clutches a cardboard folder and mumbles to his wife. The soldiers' helmets are close now. The helmets have small white shields on them with two lightning bolts side by side.

And then the soldiers are right next to them and taking papers from Father van Laar, who keeps repeating 'I am essential labour', which to Lien is just meaningless sound. Meanwhile, the young man who was pulled aside a moment earlier is being marched up the line of people by a soldier who is shouting and pointing a gun. Everywhere, now, from all the soldiers, there is shouting. But while Lien's heart beats quickly she does not shiver and she continues to look around. The world that she sees is strange and distant, almost a kind of play. She feels that she could be flying now, like the Good Lientje of her dreams.

*

If Lien could fly above the road on which she is waiting with so many others then she would see Ede spread out below her, a fortress town. The trees have been felled to give clean lines of fire, and young men, like the boy who was pulled out of line ahead of her, are now digging trenches at the point of a gun. The town has been gouged by Allied air strikes and everywhere, pointing upwards, there are the long steel barrels of Flak anti-aircraft guns. Strung along the roads that lead to Ede there are the bodies of forty resistance fighters, left as a warning, with signs that read 'Terrorist' pinned to their chests. And in the woods there are hundreds of tanks and tens of thousands of soldiers: the might of the two SS Panzer divisions, with more arriving all the time.

For the winter of 1944–5, which is known to the Dutch as the Hunger Winter, the front lines of Europe lay frozen. In the east the Russian army had entered Poland but stopped short of Warsaw. In the south the Allies faced the Apennine Mountains, impassable until March. And in the west a huge counter-attack, the Battle of the Bulge, would leave the Americans entrenched in the snow-covered forests of the Ardennes. North of this, the Netherlands lies divided. In the wake of Operation Market Garden, British and Canadian tanks have moved up to the Waal and Rhine, freeing Middelburg, Breda, Nijmegen, and 's-Hertogenbosch. But the big cities – Amsterdam, The Hague, Rotterdam, Dordrecht, Utrecht and the shell of Arnhem – remain under German rule.

In Amsterdam in January 2015 it is dark outside and it has begun to rain. Lien and I face each other across her table in the light of a single lamp. Her memories are not as clear as I have made them. She remembers scraps – the landings, the sirens, crouching down in the cellar, the girls in their dresses of parachute cloth, the dead bodies of soldiers in the streets of

Ede – but some of the rest I must patch together from other sources, such as history books and diaries, and the witness accounts that I will get from other people whom I have yet to meet. The gaps in Lien's memory are getting bigger as her contact with others grew less. Of the journey to Ede, which is still so vividly recounted by hundreds of others (who tell, for example, of the bomb crater or the dead horse with flies on it), she can picture nothing at all.

Lien gets up to fetch us something to eat. When she opens the fridge the light that it casts is harsh on her face amidst all the darkness. I move around unprompted, at home here already, and switch on a few lamps. The silence that we share is now the silence of friendship, comfortable though also sad. It feels as though we too, like the Lien of wartime, have been on a journey. We stretch our aching limbs.

Somehow the meal has the character of a roadside stop. Tomorrow I will visit Algemeer to see what the house is like and I will walk from there to the church. Lien nods. The van Laars' house is still vivid to her: a point of light, though not of happiness. We stand, the remains of our dinner spread out on the table.

Outside, I rush to the car through the rainstorm and then sit for a moment, wiping my glasses, as the engine warms up. After a bit I reverse and pull out on to the highway, listening to nothing but the engine, the swish of the wipers, and the rain on the windows and the roof. A little way into the journey, out on the empty flatlands, I stop for fuel. As I stand there filling the tank, I am struck by the petrol station's unusual beauty: its clean lines of illuminated colour against the dark of the night. Inside I browse the backlit fridges for a moment before paying with my card. Then I am on the road again, following the signs for Ede, the town where I was born.

16

In Bennekom the next morning, I wake up to an empty house. My aunt and uncle, Jan Willem and Sabrina, must have left for work hours earlier. Even their dogs are missing. A note on the kitchen worktop tells me that the neighbour will collect them at eight, which means that they must have left more than an hour ago. I sit with the newspaper, eating breakfast. At the far end of the sunlit room a large window stretches up to the ceiling, which follows the triangular pitch of the roof. It frames a cluster of pines across the lawn.

The house, a spacious low-rise, was built by my maternal grandparents immediately after the war and embodies their faith in the modern: clean-lined and inspired by the American architecture of Frank Lloyd Wright, it sits on a wooded hill just outside the village. A privileged child, I spent my summers here in the 1970s and 1980s, enjoying the huge garden and the swimming pool with my brother and my cousins. The place feels different now, after hearing Lien's story last night.

The newspaper that I am reading is the *NRC* for 14 January 2015. Its front cover shows a long line of people in Paris, the Arc de Triomphe right behind them, queuing for copies of the magazine *Charlie Hebdo*. From a circulation of less than 100,000 it has run to 5 million copies for its first edition since the attacks. Inside the paper there are photographs of the Empire State Building and the National Gallery in London, both lit up in the colours of the French flag, and, under the headline 'Terror in Europe', the shooting in Paris is described as an 'act of war'. Articles and opinion pieces set out the threat to Jewish life in many countries, with synagogues closed as a precaution in case of attack. There is talk of mass emigration. More than 7,000 Jews left France for Israel just last year, one of the reports in the newspaper tells me, and numbers are on the rise.

Lien's history and these recent terror attacks sit so strangely alongside the familiar house that surrounds me: the parquet flooring; the stylish modern and antique furniture; and the huge speakers of the Quad stereo system on which classical music was always playing when I was a child. On the wall by the door there is a little pencil sketch of a duck in a pond with some reeds around it, perhaps ten centimetres across. A few nights ago I learnt that this picture was given to my uncle's great-aunt by her Jewish neighbours just before they were transported to the east. Like almost all of the 107,000 Dutch Jews who went through the transit camp at Westerbork, the neighbours never came back. That is why the little sketch is now in my family's possession.

As I look at the picture I am reminded of Lien's first observation about stories and families. This square of pencil lines is not even a scrap of information – without the family story it could end up in a junk shop if there was nobody left to tell. I reflect that, for me, Bennekom has never really had history: it always felt so modern and has had associations only with a happy youth. It feels different now.

Before visiting the van Laars' old house at Algemeer, I decide to go for a run. Soon I am jogging through woodland and then into winter stubble, heading towards the level crossing over the railway line. I had not planned this, but it strikes me, while I scan the horizon, that it is through these fields that Lien remembers being carried on a wagon by German soldiers. And then, as I cut into the Ginkelse Heide, I am on the broad expanse of yellow grass and purple heather where British soldiers landed in September 1944.

It feels somehow orchestrated, this encounter with history, and that sense grows as, looping back, I see the familiar hillocks that are prehistoric burial mounds. There are lots of them, earth lozenges, obscured now through tree growth, almost at one with the undulations of the land. Brown tourist signs mark out the different phases: Neolithic into Bronze Age, hunter-gatherers replaced by farmers who scraped a living on the fertile sandbanks of the Rhine. Bennekom, just like The Hague and Dordrecht, can be seen as a birthplace for the Netherlands. It was one of the earliest regions to be cleared, drained and put to use, and then, when the Romans came, these lands stood at the edge of an empire, overlooked by watchtowers and forts. And then, in the winter of 1944, it was once again a front line.

Ten minutes later I reach a little heath that has what as children we called 'the climbing tree' on it, where I spot two familiar dogs. The neighbour who picked them up at eight this morning has taken the pair for a walk. Although he has not always lived here, he has spent time in Bennekom on and off since he was a boy, so we vaguely know each other, and as I reach him I come to a stop. We exchange the usual questions, and after a bit he asks what brings me to Holland.

Even now, I find this an awkward question to answer. The right reply is too lengthy, too intimate and serious. Also, I'm still uneasy about what I'm really doing, not clear if I have a plan. Still, I can't help answering and, when I do so, I find, as elsewhere, that the story opens an exchange. Like almost everyone of his age here, the neighbour remembers the time of the landings. He describes how, in the weeks that followed 17 September, he and other boys collected spent ammunition, scraps of uniform, and military equipment, which they found around the woods. What he also recalls – one of those details that sticks with me – is the carcass of a cow that he and his friends came across, right here in these woods, butchered by British soldiers, all hollowed out, and reduced to leather and bone.

It is two o'clock by the time I set out on my uncle's bicycle to visit the house of the van Laars, and in less than five minutes I reach Algemeer, a leafy residential street that extends right up into the woods. Sizeable properties, mostly detached, are set back from the tree-lined pavement, surrounded by clipped hedges. Further in towards the village centre, the houses become a bit smaller. Number 33 is an extended semi with a pretty front garden and a neat brick drive. I park my bicycle against a lamp post and head straight to the door.

A woman of around my own age answers. Practised now at these introductions, I begin to tell her about Lien and her time here, but I have not got far with my explanation when she interrupts, smiling, to ask if I mean at the time of Mrs van Laar?

'Yes,' I say, 'do you have a personal connection?'

'Not directly, but we found a little book of hers when we extended the cellar – we still have it somewhere.'

A moment later I am seated in a pleasant open-plan sitting room and kitchen, which has fitted wooden floors, uncurtained windows, and walls that are decorated with modern art. Even the wood-burning stove (which reminds me of Lien and her morning duties) is new.

The woman, whose name is Marianne, comes to sit with me while her teenage son searches for the little book, which is soon discovered and brought downstairs in a small Perspex box of the kind that might once have contained a pack of playing cards.

'We kept it because it felt important,' Marianne explains, 'because it was linked to the war.'

It is rather exciting. Lifting the lid with the air of an expert, I am reminded of the National Archives in The Hague. There is a frisson because the book dates from exactly the time when Lien was here, and it looks impressively time-worn, mouse-eaten and spotted with damp. On inspection, it is a housekeeping notebook, full of shopping expenses, like gherkins bought at thirty-five cents. This makes my pose as an expert a bit comic-al. It reminds me of Jane Austen's heroine, Catherine Morland, in *Northanger Abbey*, who builds a plot in her imagination from the discovery of some old laundry lists. Mrs van Laar's book really does list the household washing – the sheets, the vests, the tablecloths – with precise dates for each wash. All the same, it has a kind of magic to it. You can see the daily staples (mustard, for example) and the moments of celebration (where cakes and lemonade, but never alcohol, are bought in at great expense).

After the little book, there is a tour of the house, including the cellar. The original wooden steps are still there, as is the old shelving, which is now stacked with little-used kitchen items, such as an electric deep-fat fryer still in its box. I think of Lien here, stealing sugar lumps. Upstairs, Marianne points out the period features, like the doors with their top panels of frosted glass. There are football boots drying on a sheet of newspaper by the radiator on the landing. How strange that, seventy years ago, this was a house under occupation, full of the soldiers of the SS.

As I thank Marianne on her doorstep, she mentions her neighbour.

'He was born right after the war ended – you should speak to him,' she suggests.

I'm reluctant. Knocking unannounced is never easy and here there is not even a direct link. All the same, because Mari-anne still stands there looking, I cross the drive to a blue door that has a ribbed window in it with a sticker stating that cold callers are unwelcome. I press the bell and inside I hear the barking of dogs. The face of a woman appears, blurred by the glass. As I struggle to explain who I am, two Alsatians come to the high steel side gate beside me and I see a stocky man in his late sixties striding behind.

My Dutch feels awkwardly formal. 'I'm sorry, your neighbour, Marianne, suggested I call on you. I'm looking into the life of my aunt, who lived in hiding at number 33 as a child –'

Before I can say anything else, he interrupts me. The expression on his face has utterly changed.

'Lientje!' he says. 'She is the reason that I was born.'

17

Moments later I am in another living room as someone searches for a book. A large television is on at a low volume and there is the warm smell of oven chips. The floor is strewn with children's toys. 'I'm sorry, the grandkids have been here all morning,' says the man, whose name is Wout de Bond. Thus far he has explained very little, but he has said one thing that comes as a revelation. During the war, Lien stayed for a time in this house.

This news disorients me. Lien herself has no recall of the neighbours. Right now, Wout is too busy to offer further explanation; he has his back to me and is rummaging through a chest of drawers. Occasionally he pulls out documents and photographs, which are placed on a growing pile. I sit a little awkwardly, full of questions. When could Lien have been here? Why does she not remember it? And how could this man have been born because of her?

Eventually, the book that Wout was looking for is found and handed over, but he has other things that he wants to show me, so he heads out to the kitchen, calling out a question to his wife about a red folder, which he thought was in the drawers.

I am left alone, seated on the sofa. The book that he has left with me is called *Bennekom: Jewish Refuge* and it has been opened on page 142. There, I see a picture that is familiar to me, of Lien aged eleven. Beside it is a small paragraph of text:

> At Algemeer 33 with Gijs van Laar there was a Jewish girl, Lientje, in hiding. Lientje belonged to the family and was a

total part of it. She attended the Reformed School. She survived the war.

There is nothing else.

I turn back a page and see that the previous entry is devoted to Algemeer 31, the house where I am now. Here there is much more text as well as two photographs. One shows a three-year-old girl with a checked bow in her hair labelled 'Maartje'. The other is of a woman in her twenties who is called Hester Rubens. Both were Jewish and they lived here during the war. 'There were many more people in hiding at number 31,' the book tells me, 'but their identities are unknown.'

As with the earlier news that Lien stayed with the neighbours, this information comes as a shock. So there were other Jews in hiding right where Lien lived on Algemeer. When she met Maartje or Hester Rubens, as Lien must have done if she stayed here in this house, she could have had no idea of who they really were. The notion that Bennekom was a Jewish refuge comes as a total surprise to me. I have spent a lifetime visiting this village and, even now, though I have talked to my mother and her family about the work that I am doing, no one has ever mentioned this past.

Still waiting for Wout's return, I scan page 140, which is devoted to the house across the street. Here too, I learn, there were Jews hidden. A man and a woman, not a couple, lived concealed in an attic space, which could be accessed only through a ladder that ran behind the false wall of a bedroom on the first floor.

Skipping back a few pages, I start the entry at the beginning and read about Bertha Ruurds, a local woman who often visited Algemeer during the war and who even lived for a while on this street. Through small tokens, Bertha signalled her loyalty to the resistance. She planted orange marigolds in her front garden, sold portraits and little tiles that featured the royal family, and distributed copies of the Protestant underground newspaper, *Trouw*. In this way, she became a point of contact, a distributor of information, always quick to help. Only after the war had ended and the relevant files were gone through was it discovered that Bertha was, in reality, an informer, employed by the Political Police. It was thanks to her that, on 4 September 1943, officers raided number 32 Algemeer, right across the street from the van Laars. The homeowner went to prison and Solomon Micheels and Wilhelmina Labzowski, discovered hiding in the attic, were sent straight to Auschwitz as 'punishment cases', both dead before the end of the month.

Two hideout addresses within a few metres of where Lien lived. Another six on the adjoining street. My sense of the one village in the Netherlands that I thought I knew has suddenly changed.

It was, it turns out, not just Algemeer and the adjoining street that had secrets. At least 166 Jews spent time in hiding in Bennekom, a village of just 5,000, and more than 80 per cent of them survived. This is the opposite of the national picture. So why here, a place in which, in 1940, there were virtually no Jews?

The answer is really twofold. It is the achievement of remarkable people, but it is also the product of history, of connections and of land. Bennekom is a place of hills, woods and simple farmyards, which, in terms of landscape, makes it un-Dutch. In the 1930s the place was known as a holiday resort to Jewish visitors from the cities and, when the war came, it was a natural location to seek out. There was room here for disappearance, and its rental villas, campsites, hotels and leisure clubs were points of contact through which rescuers might be found.

Help itself, of course, came not from land but from people. For example, from Piet and Anna Schoorl. This couple, who enjoyed sport and motorcycling, owned a food-testing laboratory in the centre of the village. In July 1942 Piet got a call from an old acquaintance, a businessman from Rotterdam named Leo van Leeuwen. A few years earlier, before the war started, Leo and his family had come to the village for a vacation, and he and Piet had played tennis together at the local country club. They were hardly close, but Leo was now desperate. He and his family had just received their summons for transport to Poland, and so, with no other options available, he asked if Piet and Anna might be willing to help them by saving the life of their little girl.

It was the decision of a moment. Piet, who was away on business in the big city, could not even consult his wife. She later described the sudden arrival of a stranger on her doorstep who brought 'a pretty little blonde girl with a tear on her cheek'. Anna knew nothing of the situation, had in fact never knowingly met a Jewish person, but she could imagine what had happened. So little Eline, aged just three, was tucked into bed next to the Schoorls' own daughter, who was four, and hidden from view.

And once contact was established, the connection deepened. Eline's older brother, Karel, also came over and, sometime later, so too did their parents, Leo himself and his wife Pauline. Then, on top of this, as the crisis deepened, Leo's cousin and his family joined the group. The pressure on Piet and Anna was almost unbearable, but, in spite of this, they decided that it was possible to do more. So they rigged up the laboratory in the village as a safe house and, through Piet's business connections, put out the call that sanctuary might be found. Families and unaccompanied children now made their way to Bennekom, often to stay only for a while beneath the laboratory before being brought, with the help of the village doctor, Wim Kan, to a permanent address. In this way over fifty people owed their lives to the Schoorls.

And then there was a raid. Police from the big city had heard, through their interrogations, about what the Schoorls were doing and they descended on the house. Amazingly, the hiding place proved effective and no one was discovered, but Piet was arrested soon afterwards and spent seven months detained by the SS. By this time a whole network was active: food suppliers, couriers, and locations throughout the village to keep the hideaways safe. Piet kept his secrets and, when released in May 1944, simply resumed his work.

Finally, after the failed Allied landings, while the SS patrolled the streets and requisitioned the houses, the Schoorls took a dozen Jewish children – white-faced from their months in hiding – one by one, by bicycle, to safety in a forester's shed on the Keijenbergseweg. From there they were collected a day later, concealed on a wagon amongst bales of straw. The children survived, as did all the others who relied on the Schoorls.

One might think that Piet and Anna would today be remembered through a street name or a statue, that their names would be famous, but this is not the case. After the war, Piet's business, which was ill-equipped for the modern food industry, went under. He got a job at the agricultural college, which to him was a comedown in life. In his declining years he was plagued by depression. When he died in 1980, Anna applied for a war pension, but her request was declined.

As I read about Anna's disappointment, I am struck by the contrast with the case of the widow of Wim Henneicke, the head of the Search Division of the *Hausraterfassung*, the Jew-hunting operation that sent around 9,000 to their deaths. In the final stages of the war, Henneicke was shot by the resistance and, afterwards, in compensation, his wife was granted a pension of 200 guilders a month.

Wout returns, having found the red folder and, as we look through it, he tells me about his father and mother and the work that they did during the war. Right underneath me, he explains, below the sofa where I am sitting, there is a wooden panel, which is lined up with the grooves of the floorboards and therefore difficult to spot. To get to it you would need to move the furniture and then lift the carpet. Once opened, this trapdoor leads to a dug-out space beneath the house. It looks empty and innocuous. To a searching policeman it is supposed to look like space for ventilation, preventing damp. But, if you crawl flat in the darkness on your stomach, this shallow passage will take you to a wall of sand and behind that to a room, with furniture and electric light, where a Jewish family lived in hiding during the war.

To me, seated on Wout's sofa with the TV still on in the background, the world suddenly seems different. To think that this secret life existed, unmentioned, right below Lien's feet. I look again at the book and see that, alongside Lien's entry for number 33 Algemeer, there is mention of another woman, Bets Engers, who also hid with the van Laars. Who was Bets Engers? Lien remembers nothing of her. Was this before her arrival? If so, how long did she stay? On my phone I look back at the photograph of the van Laar family, remembering now that there was another figure standing with the group. There she is, a curly-haired young woman, to one side, directly behind Lien. Is this Bets? Wout does not know. Memory is selective and not always reliable. So many facts are irretrievably lost.

Wout and I talk for a while about his parents, looking over

old photographs as we speak. He writes down a series of email addresses, listing people in the local history society who might be able to help me with my research. Then, with the light outside already fading, I ask what he meant when he said that he was born because of Lien. This part of the story is still unclear.

'Oh,' he smiles, 'it's best to hear about that from my sister. She lives in Ede now.'

Together we look at a picture of a teenage girl with a Peter Pan collar who holds out a doll-like baby in a christening gown. Printed with ruffled edges, it looks staged and formal. The girl's smile, though, is real enough.

'That's Corrie with me just after the war,' Wout tells me.

In neat printed letters he writes down her full name, telephone number and address, and attaches his card, which bears the head of an Alsatian.

'Keep in touch,' he says.

Back on the bike, I head through the woods to my aunt and uncle's house, riding alongside the big trunk road that was, during the war, still just a forest track. It was somewhere along here that the Schoorls hid the group of Jewish children in a forester's shed.

This morning I was running through the landing fields of the Allied Airborne and then, straight after, past burial mounds that date from more than 4,000 years back. These woods are no longer simply a childhood playground. Even the trees are not quite what I thought.

During the war there was one small pine very close to here, on the edge of the village, in the grounds of the Keltenwoud Hotel. It looked no different from the others, but, all the same, it was regularly uprooted by its owner and replaced. Below the ground, this tree fitted into a wooden, box-like structure, which formed the entrance to a secret room.

It took until 1995 for Leo Durlacher, by then in his seventies, to describe it in writing. He and his family spent time hidden in a shed at the back of the hotel. A warning system, which was driven by a sewing-machine motor, told them when police were on their way. If the alarm was raised, the four would then run to the tree that was really a secret entrance and seal themselves into the darkness below ground. Breathing by means of a hand pump connected to the surface, they would listen in silence as heavy boots moved around above their heads.

When I get in I call Wout's sister, Corrie. She would be happy to talk, she says, and adds, only half joking, that I had better hurry: she is well into her eighties, after all.

They all feel rushed, these meetings – Marianne at number 33, Wout at 31, and now this with his sister, whose home, it turns out, is right behind the office where my uncle works.

I suggest ten the next morning.

'That,' says Corrie, 'should be quick enough.'

18

The next morning, having got a lift into Ede from my uncle, I walk up to a substantial complex, made up of new, well-built retirement flats with balconies and large, wheelchair-accessible lifts. After crossing the car park I come to a courtyard of patterned brick paving and huge flowerpots from which pansies shine in the January sun. Several groups of residents are sitting outside at metal tables in their hats and coats, chatting. Signs show me the way to the gardens, to the medical centre, and to a stylish communal eatery called The Grand Café. This place is a snapshot of wellbeing in the Netherlands, which is near the top of global league tables when it comes to quality of life in old age.

Corrie's flat is warm, and crowded with an assortment of objects. She is tall, like her father was, and despite her warning that I had better come quickly she looks in good health. It is not difficult to match her with the young woman who held her baby brother in the photo from nearly seventy years ago that Wout had shown me. There are pictures of children and grandchildren around the apartment and right behind her as she sits is a large photograph of her late husband, who worked at the cement factory for most of his life. As she pours sweetish condensed milk into our coffees I realize that Corrie reminds me of someone. It is my grandmother, Ma van Es.

I show Corrie a current picture of Lien, as well as some other photographs.

'She became a beautiful woman,' she says with a kind of pride.

'Lientje had it hard there,' Corrie continues. 'They only had her for the cleaning. It was no kind of life.'

Corrie's verdict on Mrs van Laar is not favourable: 'She was one only for outside appearances and she did nothing if it could done by somebody else.'

Lien, in her memory, was very thin, warm-hearted and put-upon – always working, always criticized and hardly ever allowed out.

'What she really wanted was to live with us. I remember her saying so very often as we lay in bed at night when she stayed with us, and we all wanted the same thing, but we had to keep on good terms with the van Laars, so it was too dangerous and could not be done.'

Corrie tells me of the time when Lien came to lodge with them for over a week while the van Laars went off on holiday.

'Two chatty girls in one bedroom, you can imagine how that was,' she laughs.

And yet Lien remembers nothing of this.

Corrie's was a happy youth in 1930s Bennekom, with a lot of strong uncles who would carry her about on their shoulders and play with her.

'I was like a ball to them – so thrown about!'

We look at a photograph of Corrie's parents with her as a baby. The three of them sit together in a vegetable garden with beanstalks growing tall behind them on neat, interlocking canes. Her father's long legs stretch right up to the camera. He wears braces and a somewhat scruffy open-necked shirt. Her mother, in a flowery dress, is holding her daughter's hand, squinting a little in the bright sun.

Toon de Bond worked as a house painter. His wife, Jansje, was frail in contrast, having contracted TB in her youth. After the birth of their daughter, the two of them were told by the doctors that they should have no more children, because

Jansje was not well enough to cope with pregnancy a second time. This was a great loss for the couple and also, as she grew up, for Corrie, for whom a little brother or sister was always a dream.

Then the war came. In 1939 Toon enlisted in the army and his wife and child moved to Rotterdam for a spell. Corrie still recalls the bombing of that city. She remembers being huddled in a barge on the great river, with sheets of flaming bitumen hissing into the water around her, as they escaped the docks.

She and her mother came back to Bennekom straight after the national surrender. One afternoon a few weeks later, Toon returned, unannounced, appearing in the garden in uniform, his head shaved bare. He had walked from Germany following his release as a prisoner of war. The first thing that they did as a family was to go to town to buy him a hat.

It was over two years later that the first hideaways came to Algemeer. Nothing was said to Corrie, but she remembers people in the house. She thought they stood too close to the windows, and one time she saw them running downstairs from the bedroom through the kitchen and into the woods. It was sometime after this that her father began digging and laying cables underneath the house.

And then Maartje was there. A girl of three. She was rescued, they heard, by the maid in a big household, who snatched her to safety when the rest of the family was already lined up, under arrest. On Maartje's photo she still has the round cherub face of a baby, framed by a triangle of black curls. The checked bow in her hair sits right up above her in the style of Minnie Mouse. Her puffed-sleeve dress is also like Minnie's and she has dark, rather sad-looking eyes.

The de Bonds loved her from the first instant. Toon carried her around on his shoulders and his wife, Jansje, sang the little girl to sleep at night. This was the sister Corrie had always wanted. The family recorded her as Maartje de Bond at the register office, so it was safe for her to run around outside.

During the evacuation they all lived together in a chicken hutch in Ede, cold and hungry. They made sure, though, that Maartje had enough to eat. Then, after the liberation, the family returned to a smashed-up house in Bennekom, but it did not really matter. They had a summer of rebuilding and playing.

And then, all of a sudden, a woman came. It was Maartje's mother, who had survived the war.

Of course, they should have been happy. They gave Maartje, whose real name was Sari Simons, a little silver bracelet when she left.

The de Bonds went to see her once, in Leiden. There were still no trams or trains running, so the journey took a very long time. Corrie hardly recognized her. The curls of Maartje's hair were done in pigtails that Corrie thought went too tight against the girl's head.

And then, for her birthday, they bought a bicycle, which Toon brought all the way to Leiden, even though there were still no trams or trains.

But when Toon got there Maartje and her mother were no longer living at the same address. They had gone to Israel, the neighbours said.

From her chair in the apartment, Corrie looks at me, her voice constricted.

'Without a word of goodbye. I can't understand that, can you?' she says.

I am silent. Looking around the apartment, I can see now why she reminds me of my grandmother. There is the same mixture of ornaments and practical furniture, kept nicely clean, that I remember from Dordt. The two of them even look similar: robust and maternal, with strong voices and ruddy cheeks. Their histories – a rural upbringing followed by life as working-class mothers to large families – are much the same. And there is also, at this moment, a familiar edge of sadness when it comes to the past.

Can I understand it? A woman, whose husband and parents have been murdered in the gas chambers, returning to find her child hidden in a strange little country village, wanting to leave the Netherlands as soon as possible, without a trace? Yes, I can.

But then I have been listening for a long time now to Lien.

After Maartje's sudden departure, Toon and Jansje wrote letters and made enquiries to find out what had happened to her, but no answer came back. The red folder that Wout showed me at the house on Algemeer is a record of those efforts and the years of silence that followed in their wake.

Finally, long after Jansje had passed away, a letter arrived one Christmas. It was sent from Jerusalem and dated 18 December 1983:

Dear Mr De-Bond

I am very sorry it took me so long to answer your letter. I simply didn't know where to begin, at first I tried to write in Dutch, but now I feel that goes better in English. I hope your friend can read it, although it is in handwriting . . .

Maartje tells Mr de Bond that she works in a pharmaceuticals laboratory, has a religious life with her husband, and has five children – four boys, aged between twelve and seventeen, and a girl of eight.

I have a photograph. I think it is from you, your late wife, and daughter. I remember almost nothing of those years, but I remember I had always a good time. I don't remember that I ever had been

hungry, or afraid, and that is thanks to you. I remember I had
many beautiful toys, like dolls, and I still have with me the bracelet
of 'dubbletjes' you gave me when my mother took me home . . .

There is an account of her mother's remarriage, of new brothers and sisters, and of the Yad Vashem memorial ceremony,
which, it is hoped, Mr de Bond might attend. They would be
honoured to have him as their guest. This is the least that they
could offer, after all he has done. Then the letter closes:

Strange we came to Israel very lonely, but thank to god we are now
a large family. Maybe that is some of a reaction of what happened.
I hope that you understand something of my English and receive
this in good health. I hope to hear your news from you as soon as
possible.
Best regards from Haim, and with hope we meet soon. With a
lot of affection.

Yours
Maartje

Corrie feels awkward about this letter. Though the invita-
tion is warmly given, it came too late for her father to visit and
she herself is barely mentioned. There is just a brief question
that recalls her existence:

Have you one daughter or more?

The question is kindly meant, but Maartje cannot know how
hard it is to answer or the sadness that it brings.

We sit in silence for a moment and then I ask what Wout
meant when he told me that he was born because of Lien. Corrie smiles a little weakly. Well, perhaps it was more because of

Maartje than because of Lien, but, in their absence, the two girls grew together in the minds of the de Bonds. The life that these hideaways had brought to them was missing. Each girl had been imagined as a daughter or a sister, only to vanish without so much as a farewell. They could not have known it, but these cut out girls left holes behind. It was because of this that, though the doctors told them it was dangerous, Toon and Jansje took the risk of trying for another child.

I look again at the photo of Corrie holding her baby brother. She looks elated.

'My mother spent nine months in bed, pretty much, she was that sick,' Corrie tells me, 'but then we had Wout.'

After leaving Corrie's place I stop off at my uncle's office, a solo legal practice that stands around the corner from the end of her street. The plan is to have lunch with him before heading off to Amsterdam to see Lien. The building – a low-rise 1970s construction with long strip windows and interior divisions of curved glass – was once a small public library. Inside there is antique furniture, a grandfather clock and a heavy oak table, which contrasts with the bright simplicity of the walls. The place is not big but it is spacious, and, as I take the tour with Jan Willem, I am struck by the Dutchness of its layout. Natural light slants down across textured plaster to mark out a desk, a painting or a chair. It makes me think of Vermeer. Engraved on the glass divisions there are excerpted texts from the country's constitution, which tell me that 'all those who find themselves in the Netherlands will be treated equally in equal circumstances' and that 'discrimination on grounds of religion, belief, political opinion, race, gender or on any other grounds whatsoever is not permitted'. In style and substance, the office is a quiet expression of the country's ideals.

That is a selective vision, though, and, as we sit having lunch together, Jan Willem and I discuss the curious split personality of the Dutch state. On the one hand, at least from the early nineteenth century, when the constitution was written, the Dutch were able to picture themselves as an ideal community: classless, peaceful, prosperous, and governed by equal rights. In 1864 the romantic poet W. J. Hofdijk vaunted the nation's mission to become 'the most virtuous people on the earth'. Yet, while equality reigned at home, abroad the country remained a ruthless colonial power, deriving more than half of its tax income from the exploitation of Indonesia, the Dutch Antilles and Surinam.

The sense of entitlement to those colonial possessions was still evident in the years immediately after the Second World War, when the Dutch government's primary focus was not on internal matters but on Indonesia, which had been lost to the Japanese. Though Holland had been reduced to rubble at home, it raised an army for the reconquest of its oil wells, mines and plantations using surplus military hardware bought from the Canadians. The Dutch Marines were sent into action. Jo Kleijne, the young man who carried Lien to the resistance hideout in IJsselmonde and who afterwards wrote to her from Singapore, was a part of this force.

Tanks that had once faced the Germans now rolled into Java and this strange mirror image of Holland's recent history extended still further when, on the island of Celebes, suspects were taken out of prison cells, lined up in town squares and killed by firing squads. The young Dutch commander Raymond Westerling warned his soldiers that their mission would require them to 'walk up to their ankles in blood'. On 1 February 1947 Dutch troops began what was called the 'cleansing' of villages by selecting 364 unarmed men more or less at random, shooting them, removing their watches and jewellery, and dumping their bodies into a mass grave. Their villages were then burned to the ground.

Jan Willem cites these facts from memory. In post-war Holland, however, they were never mentioned and not a single soldier ever faced trial. For the country to recover from such actions, which saw the deaths of least 4,000 civilians, would require an act of collective amnesia, which left many stories like that of Jo Kleijne untold.

A little over an hour later, having borrowed Jan Willem's car again, I am back in Amsterdam with Lien. I tell her about my discoveries in Bennekom, especially about the village's wider resistance network and the fact that there were people in hiding right next door and also across the street from where she lived. To my surprise, what excites Lien most is not the unexpected news about the neighbours but rather the confirmation of her own memories when it comes to her time with the van Laars.

'It makes a big difference that she confirms that I had it hard there. I have always worried that the problems came only from me or that I was being unjust.'

While we clear the table, I fret a little about the kind of book that might grow out of our work together. There are so many books already out there about the war. Lien smiles and tells me that repetition is no bad thing. 'There are also so many songs about love.'

19

In other places Lien recalls front rooms, but of the house in Ede, where she hid from October 1944, she remembers only a flight of stairs. They are steep and carpeted and there is a glass door at the foot of them, which shuts you off from the rest of the house. It is possible to stand there, undetected, while listening and looking out. If need be, she can race up to a bedroom, her footfall deadened, leaving no one aware of her presence.

The atmosphere in this house is nicer than it was in Bennekom, even though there is little food and she is stuck inside all day. There is almost a holiday atmosphere. The family is camping, sort of, and making do with less cleaning and fewer rules. Father van Laar's brother, Uncle Evert, who is the man of the house here, helps with that feeling. He keeps everyone jolly even when things are hard. Mother smiles and blushes when she hears his jokes.

'What's the difference between the Germans and a bucket of shit?' he asks loudly, his red face beaming.

'I don't know and I don't want to know,' she answers, but still stays to listen.

'The bucket! The only difference is the bucket!' comes his thundering reply.

He is fearless. You feel his presence in a room. Father van Laar is almost like a boy when he is with him. They have games, like playing catch with a teacup or flicking each other with the wet ends of towels. Jaap, who is less annoying here than he was in Algemeer, is included in their battles. He giggles when he is bundled, struggling, to the floor.

'We have ways of making you talk!' says Uncle Evert as he tickles his ribs.

She is Uncle Evert's favourite. When they are all huddled around the stove, which is lit for just an hour every evening, he takes her on his lap and calls her his little friend. They play dominoes together. Uncle Evert gets furious if he loses, but this is only a joke.

'You have painted extra spots on to yours,' he tells her, bringing the suspect piece right up to his nose.

He even starts to lick the domino to see if the paint will come off. It is all a bit childish, but still quite fun.

He has a warm way of touching people. For her it is squeezes and tickles. She laughs so much that she loses her breath.

In the evenings there is talk amongst the adults and dominoes for the children, but for most of the day nothing much happens. She gets up, changes into her day clothes (snatching a moment alone in the bedroom), then she heads down to breakfast, which is usually two slices of dry bread. After this she simply drifts around the house.

Upstairs, a little away from the window, is a good spot for reading, with a pillow wedged between the wall and the bed. There are not many books, but the ones that she loves she can read over and over without getting bored. Their words become a rhythm and Lien enters completely into the adventure: the companionship and beauty of a world. Days drift by from grey dawn to the darkness that comes by mid-afternoon.

When everyone is away, the house has its own sound to it, unheard until you listen. There is the tick of the alarm clock on the washstand, the murmur of pipes, and the light scrabbling of birds' feet above her head on the tiles of the roof. In the stillness she sometimes picks up the sounds of her own body and is embarrassed even though there is no one to hear.

Today she is not alone in the house, because Uncle Evert is moving things about in the kitchen. There is the scrape of furniture, the stacking of metal on metal, and the creak of his weight on the floorboards. Once she is absorbed in her book these sounds vanish completely. She hears them again only when they change.

The glass pane in the door at the foot of the stairs gives a faint rattle. The latch clicks back into its slot. Then, beneath the carpet, the wood sighs a little with each step. A moment later the door to the bedroom, which was already half open, swings wider, and the face of Uncle Evert appears.

'Still reading, my little friend the bookworm?' he smiles.

Walking in, he seats himself on the bed and gestures to his lap. This, she knows immediately, is not quite normal, but she moves without thinking. As she settles, his body arches towards hers. He says something about her liking this and how this makes her a naughty girl.

She is flustered and confused.

Lien has no words for what Uncle Evert is doing. No ideas even. She is shivering in a cold sweat. It is tickling but different. His hands do not stop. She is not sure, even, if she has said no to him. Her body is rigid but he unlocks her legs. Then his fingers are inside her, inside her underwear, and it hurts and there is blood.

Afterwards he says that she wanted it herself.

Now the fear grows within her each time that the house empties. Once the last has left, she must go with him to the space between the door and the foot of the stairs. There, after the glass clicks shut behind them, she must stand, her dress up, half naked, while he unbuckles his belt. It hurts so much as he pushes his penis inside her. Sometimes there is blood on her legs.

'You wanted this yourself,' he always tells her, and eventually she almost believes him. The rapes are a secret, hard and poisonous, that she swaddles within.

Evert van Laar has an unseen power. It is a mystery how it works. How is it that the house is empty so often? Why is her place now always on his lap? He is a jovial bully, expert at bending others to his will. With the women of the house he is flirtatious, full of cheeky suggestions, while with his nephew and brother there is a charming, cajoling menace. He deals out thumps that are friendly but just a little too hard. Lien is right in the middle, between the boys and the women, courted as a princess and then tumbled like a pet.

Grey days, weeks and months blur into each other. Lien sees almost nothing and grows familiar only with the space between the door and the foot of the stairs. Meanwhile, twenty miles away in Nijmegen, an army of half a million men stands waiting. When the spring comes 1,000 heavy guns will fire into enemy territory around the clock. Smoke will clothe the rivers in preparation. Already now, thousands of bombers swarm and darken the land beneath them. They will rain down half a million tons of ordnance in these last few months of the war.

Amidst all this there is still the edge of carnival in the evenings at the house in Ede: a restless, random celebration that Uncle Evert drives. He insists that they all have pancakes (even though there are no eggs, milk or butter) and somehow they get them: gritty and paper-thin. At the table he sits triumphant. Lien, as his little friend, must have some, so he slides a sharp-edged wafer on to her plate.

Cold hungry days pass, but then one day, unannounced, it is over: 17 April. First there is gunfire, then silence, and then, in the distance, the crazy rumble of cheering and what sounds like a marching band. From the top-floor window, through which she has never looked till now, Lien gazes down on small groups of men and women who are emerging, full of caution, from their doors. Right below her, down on the pavement, a woman starts shouting – a drawn-out, high-pitched, uncontrolled squeal. The woman stands and bellows at the buildings, an orange flag held up with both hands.

Now everyone rushes out, Lien with them, and crowds jostle her as she steps on to the pavement for the first time in half a year. It is dizzying to feel the sun and the sky again. In the cloudy brightness everything is overwhelming: the letters of a shop sign, the flecks of gravel on a pathway, the dark leaves of a hedge. Her ears ring with the sound of a moving, shouting, crying multitude, and in her mouth she can taste the fresh air.

Lien runs with a group of children, leaping over rubble, finding her balance on crumbling walls. In an alley they come across the body of a German soldier. It lies face down on the cobbles, one arm pointing upwards, the helmet still attached with a strap. For a while they just stare at it in wonder – frightened, not sure if it might suddenly move – but then a girl steps forward and softly kicks the side of the head. With shrieks they back off in horror, but then they edge back. Now a boy, and then others, dare to give the body a kick. When she has a go, Lien is surprised at how heavy the dead soldier feels against her foot.

Out on the main road it is almost a frenzy. Men sing loudly into the warm, grey afternoon air. Then the line of troops comes through. They are from Canada, the Allied soldiers, it seems. Lien sees them in snatches through the limbs of the thronging crowd. She watches as girls climb to sit on the tanks, their skirts flying up. The air is thick with smoke and diesel. Finally, as Lien walks back from the high street, she locks eyes with a woman who stands on the pavement, her head newly shaven with spots of bright red.

And all through this, though she is part of the madness of the celebration, though she runs and joins in with everything,

Lien has not understood it. The liberation has no meaning. It is a party, people are cheering, and that is all.

It was 5 May 1945 when the Canadian General Charles Foulkes and the German Commander-in-Chief Johannes Blaskowitz reached agreement on the capitulation of German forces in the Netherlands. The surrender was signed in Wageningen, just three miles from Bennekom. Adolf Hitler had already shot himself at the end of April, and on 8 May the war in Europe was officially over when Allied victory was declared. After a few days of celebration, however, the mood in the Netherlands was at best one of grim resignation about the work of rebuilding that lay ahead. Nineteen thousand civilians had been killed during the combat, 8,000 non-Jews had died in prison camps, and a further 25,000 had starved to death. Calorie consumption per person had more than halved in the last year of the conflict, 8 per cent of the landmass lay under water, having been flooded by the German army in the course of its retreat, and systematic looting meant that economic destruction was greater in the Netherlands than in any other occupied country in the West.

This national devastation does go some way towards explaining the poor treatment of the nation's surviving Jews. Sixteen thousand of them emerged from hiding and, in the east, a further 5,000 were left alive in the camps. Other countries, such as France and Belgium, already liberated for the most part in 1944, were much quicker to send aid and transport to help the return of survivors. The Dutch, with a repatriation force that consisted of two hired motorbikes and four small lorries, could do almost nothing. Most of their citizens had to struggle home by themselves.

With nearly half a million Dutch men stuck beyond the borders (most in German labour camps) and another third of a million internal refugees, the government that returned from exile in London would always, even with the best intentions, have struggled to provide sufficient help for the surviving Jews.

There were, however, no signs of best intentions. Not even a statement, let alone any special arrangement, was made. When the issue came up, Dutch ministers insisted that Jews should expect to be treated the same as others. They saw no contradiction between this and the substantial orders that they placed for hymnals, prayer books, Bibles and even communion chalices which would be waiting to give spiritual comfort to the refugees.

The vast majority of Jewish survivors who made it back to the Netherlands found arrival a traumatic experience. When they reached the borders they were met by a large, though disorganized, defence force made up of men wearing clogs and mismatched uniforms, because the government was frightened about an influx of foreigners, above all communists, who might destabilize the state.

Dirk de Loos described afterwards how he arrived on a bus with other Jews from Dachau that was stopped at the border, where, in spite of their authentic Dutch accents, the authorities were unimpressed by their lack of papers and placed them under arrest. They were dusted with DDT powder and then sent to an internment camp in Nijmegen, a place from which, after ten days, Dirk managed to escape. When he reached his home in Leiden, however, he was re-arrested and sent back by the Dutch police, who were, as ever, all too quick to follow orders from above.

Dirk's experience was not unusual. In Westerbork, the transit camp from which more than 100,000 had been transported to Auschwitz, over 500 remaining Jews who had been destined for extermination were kept prisoner for months after the war had ended. They were held there alongside 10,000 newly arrested Dutch fascists, the very people who had wanted to send them to their deaths. When they were eventually released the situation barely improved. Jewish property had been robbed, there were new people living in their old houses, and in some cases there were even tax demands to cover the years they had spent in the camps.

To an extent, such experiences could be blamed on the chaos of the immediate post-war situation, but in those first months after the liberation there were also signs that anti-Semitism in the Dutch population played a part. At one time Holland had stood out as a haven of toleration. Yosef Kaplan, a historian of Jewish life in the Netherlands, could find no significant incident of anti-Semitic persecution during the entire history of the Dutch Republic, stretching from 1581 to 1795. During the nineteenth century, however, a new stereotype of the grubby, heavily accented, Jewish swindler did emerge in the national culture, an image fuelled by immigration from the east. Partly also thanks to the rise of international Zionism, the notion surfaced that Jews were not entirely Dutch. Then, in the wake of the Nazi takeover in Germany, 35,000 foreign Jews escaped to the Netherlands, to which the government responded by restricting immigration and putting people in camps. There was widespread talk of Jewish communists, of Jewish moneymen, and of how Jews might bring down the tone of a good restaurant or a good club.

Though the fascist vote in the Netherlands never got beyond 4 per cent, there had been something there for the wartime Nazi propagandists to work on, and this was evident in 1945. The nationalism of some resistance news-sheets was far from tolerant. *Het Parool*, for example, warned Jews not to draw attention to themselves after the liberation, and it also criticized Dutch Jews for leaving their posts in the face of the German threat. Another news-sheet, *The Patriot*, wrote of the need for Jews to be grateful given that the Dutch resistance had saved them when 'quite possibly better people had died'. There were Jew jokes in popular magazines. On the letters pages of various newspapers readers complained that, now that the war was finished, the Jews were again on the rise. One government office even decided not to re-employ Jewish workers on the grounds that the feeling against them in business was so negative that such people could not possibly be effective in their jobs. Meanwhile, the Minister of Justice wrote to the Jewish religious union (which had just been excluded from the National Church Council on grounds of their diminished numbers) to ask if they could please make an effort to help reintegrate the more than 120,000 detained Dutch collaborators, who were rapidly being released. In the media the fact of the Holocaust was briefly acknowledged, but it was then passed over as too horrible to contemplate at length. Unsurprisingly, Jewish emigration from the Netherlands in the post-war decade ran at far higher levels than it did in Belgium and France.

In Ede in April 1945 Lien has no great sense of the war having ended. She simply awaits the decisions of others. It is an enormous relief, though, to escape from Uncle Evert once the family sets off for Bennekom after a few days. The old road is now full of dirty green lorries, which roll towards them filled with soldiers who signal 'V' for victory with their fingers. When they get to number 33 they find it undamaged. While the de Bonds' house next door has been ransacked, the floorboards torn up, in theirs the jars of pickles are still lined up, just as before, on the cellar shelves. Mother van Laar is soon directing the cleaning. Lien is put to work again with cloths and dusters, and, as she shines the wood of the front-room cupboard, life reasserts its familiar grain.

Nowhere are questions asked or answered: not at home, not in church and not at school. Not a word is spoken of what happened to her parents, neither now nor in the months ahead, but somewhere, somehow, the permanence of their absence is lodged in her consciousness. The whole world of Mamma and Pappa and grandmothers and grandfathers and aunts and uncles and cousins and friends in The Hague has vanished, and there is no turning back, not even in her mind.

Lien is re-established in her little bedroom, with its pane of glass above the door. On Sundays there is preaching and Bible study and each evening, after dinner, she reads aloud once more about the acts of the Apostles and the struggles of the Old Testament kings. She returns to school, where the teachers notice she is behind with her studies. She gets extra maths and history homework, which she completes, in the late afternoon, half under the covers, sitting up in bed. Outside she hears Maartje in next door's garden. Lien goes to the de Bonds now more often, is somewhat freer, and has Corrie as a kind of friend. A month passes and down the street towards the village a few planks of wood are laid out as men begin to repair the damaged houses. Their cement mixer stands there unused in readiness, its mouth caked with a rim of brittle rock.

In Bennekom, life continues in its old regular pattern and it is already early summer when Lien hears the sound of a motorbike out in the street. Working up in her room she doesn't even think about it, but she does notice a moment later when the bell rings and Mother van Laar answers the door.

'Lientje,' she calls, 'it's for you.' Her voice is neutral, and Mother van Laar has already retreated to the kitchen, with the door shut behind her, by the time that Lien comes out of her room.

It is only when Lien reaches the lower stairs that she sees who it is from the shoes and the trousers. Her heart stops, because it is Evert van Laar. There is no one to call on, even supposing she dared, and her whole body feels suddenly frozen and passive. Stepping forward, Uncle Evert looks up at her, eyes a-glitter, and he gestures, through the open door, at the road and at the bike.

If you close your eyes then maybe it is not happening. She grips her fingers to the steel of the handlebars and feels the heat radiating from the engine against her bare legs. Once they reach the woods the ground is uneven and the seat hammers against her, the motor whining as he drives at speed. She strives to make herself numb to it, but the numbness that she felt a moment earlier will not come.

Deep in the undergrowth there is an old Jeep, wedged into bushes, overhung with a canopy of trees. He drives straight to it. He has planned this, she can tell. He pushes the motorbike up against a stack of abandoned tyres. She, still seated, squeezing her eyes closed, picks up the tang of engine oil that has mixed with wet fungus and leaves. When her eyes flick open for a moment she sees the Jeep's windscreen, which is slicked with a mossy sheen. There is a step just behind the wheel arch, and Uncle Evert speaks slowly. He says to her, 'You wanted this yourself.'

Again there are no questions asked or answered, and after this his visits on the motorbike turn into a regular fixture, like school or like church. Uncle Evert and Lien have a 'special friendship', according to Mother and Father van Laar. They don't seem to find it odd that he comes to collect her, or, if they do, then it is an oddness that they attribute to Lien herself.

The season runs from summer to autumn and she turns twelve. Without their thick green cover the woods are brighter. It is cold and wet underfoot. The old Jeep, which they always visit, begins to rust like the leaves that surround it. Its headlamps are now milky grey with fog. Lien's sense of herself grows smaller with the fading seasonal light. Ever more silent, she is fearful, like an animal that has been hurt.

And then, in mid September, there is suddenly a very different caller for her. From the top of the stairs Lien looks down, almost unbelieving. Mrs Heroma has come back!

The moment Took Heroma sees Lien, she steps forward, unprompted, past Mother van Laar, into the house. From the foot of the stairs she stretches out to touch the girl's shoulders.

'Lientje, I am so happy to see you!' she says.

An hour later the two of them sit on a bench in the watery sunshine, looking out over the heath. They are going to do some serious talking and Lien should say what she herself thinks is best.

First, there are questions about her health and her school studies. Each time that she answers there is a pause as Mrs Heroma writes things down in her book. Sometimes she sits still for a moment, thinking, pen in hand. Then, after all the questions have finished, Mrs Heroma places the notebook beside her, looks out at the treeline and turns with a thoughtful expression to Lien.

The van Laars, Mrs Heroma says, have looked after Lien for a long while now. It is not a big family and there is a spare bedroom and Jaap must be almost like a brother by now. Of course brothers can be annoying and we all have arguments sometimes, but Bennekom is a nice village, and the van Laars would like her to stay. She could earn her keep as a maid, doing chores for the household. She could carry on with her schooling, which seems to be going well. What does Lien think about that?

The girl stares down through the slats of the bench at the ground beneath them.

What does Lien think?

She is not used to being asked this. Lien keeps her eyes fixed on the thin strip of soil and yellow grass.

'I don't want to stay here,' she says, almost to herself.

'Then what would you like instead?'

The answer comes to her only at this instant.

'I want to go to the van Esses,' Lien answers with firmness, and looks up, her eyes squinting against the low afternoon sun.

Now that the words have been spoken Lien can see it: the house in the Bilderdijkstraat with Kees, who is her friend, and Ali and Marianne and Auntie's kitchen. It is the only place that she can imagine where she could, once again, be a child.

These things cannot, of course, be sorted out quickly. Mrs Heroma must go back to Dordrecht to see how matters can be arranged. There is a long week of waiting, during which the Bilderdijkstraat grows in her mind. She thinks of going swimming with Annie Mookhoek, as she used to, or of seeing Fau Buyne, the neighbour across the street. As the days pass, the presence of that world grows more and more urgent. She fears the arrival of Uncle Evert in a way that she has not feared it for a very long time.

And then at last it is Saturday and Mrs Heroma is coming. Lien cannot eat her breakfast and when the bell rings it sends a current to her heart. Mrs Heroma stands there on the doorstep, locked in conversation with Mother van Laar. She smiles and waves at Lien, but she does not talk to her and after this she moves to the front room to speak in private with the adults while Lien must go back upstairs. Up in her bedroom, her stomach burns with waiting, but at last she is called down.

'Right, now, Lientje and I will go for a walk,' says Mrs Heroma, briskly, and she takes her hand.

Then they are walking down the street and Mrs Heroma is talking. It takes Lien a little while to connect with her words. The van Esses are well and they send Lien their warmest wishes. Things are very busy for them at the moment because Auntie is having a new baby and the family have just moved to a new house. Uncle Henk has a different job now. He is in charge of housing for the whole city. This is a very important job and lots of people need his help. Also, he is still not very well because of what happened to him in prison, where he was sent for fighting the Germans during the war. Also Dordrecht is not a good place to be right now because of the damage from the bombing. There are no bridges and the people are still hungry and there is often no heating. Quite often the electricity does not work. And all of this means that it is not possible for Lien to come to live with the van Esses right now.

This makes no sense to her, and as Lien tries to understand it her breathing stops. Took Heroma shoots out a hand in comfort, but it is already too late. In Lien's mind a chasm has opened and she stares out blankly in panic, her mouth contorted. It is as if she is falling to the centre of the earth.

Took Heroma is truly frightened.

'Lientje, I will ask again,' she says, but Lien, for a long time, can hear nothing, so overwhelmed is she by shock and grief.

Back in the apartment in Amsterdam it is now just after seven. On the recording, Lien stumbles a little as she speaks of this moment, but her struggle comes not so much from emotion as from a desire to get things right.

'The news came that they did not want me . . . She came

back and she told me it couldn't happen, that it wasn't allowed . . . And I was dazed by it.'

There is a very long pause.

'I could not believe it. I had so totally counted on it, had set all my will upon it. I had seen it as the only way out.'

In the silence I ask myself what could have made my grandparents give their answer. After Lien left, the family had sheltered two other Jewish children and these had gone back to their families. Perhaps my grandparents felt that something like this should be done for Lien? They were themselves under enormous pressure, and they had already done so much. It is also true that, at this distance, I cannot know what exactly was asked of them or what exact answer was given. When Took asked for a second time they said yes, and they did so with grace.

All the same, that first answer damaged something precious. It damaged the confident sense of belonging that had been, perhaps, my grandparents' greatest gift to Lien.

Not long afterwards Lien stands for the last time on the doorstep of number 33 Algemeer. Out on the road a spluttering car awaits her, with Mr and Mrs Heroma inside. It is an awkward farewell.

When she has said her quiet thank-you and begins moving, the girl is handed something, a white unsealed envelope that has four photographs inside.

''To remember us by,' says Mother van Laar.

While the car idles, Lien looks briefly through the uneven little stack.

The first is of herself. It is a studio photograph taken in Ede a few months earlier and it shows a pretty young woman with a beautiful curving staircase spiralling upwards behind her. In white knee socks and a dark sailor-suit dress, Lien looks straight at the camera, a half-smile on her lips and a girlish

checked bow in her hair. The image on the picture is not real though. If you look down at the floor you can see the edge of the photographer's backcloth. The marble and wrought-iron stairway is just an illusion that can be replaced by something different simply by pulling a cord.

The second photograph is the one of her with the van Laars in front of the house, which was taken almost two years ago, when she first came to Bennekom. She looks much younger in it than she does now.

And then there are two passport snaps, one of Father and one of Mother van Laar. They both gaze over the photographer's left shoulder. With his high Brylcreemed hair and five o'clock shadow, Father van Laar appears uncomfortable in his tight formal clothing. His wife, looking plain, rests her teeth on her lower lip.

They do not seem happy.

Now that Lien is leaving there is something almost pitiful about these people, averting their eyes as instructed, and doing their best to conform.

For Lien the backdrop is about to change from country to city and from old-style religion to new socialist ideals. It is a long journey, but Dr Heroma, who is driving, makes an adventure of it. Each misleading road sign or broken ferry is a challenge. On the map he shows her the route they are taking and he includes her in the discussion when the way is suddenly blocked. Sheltered in the little car with rain spotting the windscreen, she and the Heromas stop in a lay-by at lunchtime to eat corned beef sandwiches. Then they are on the road again. There is little traffic as they cross the country, mainly just struggling cyclists. Outside, through the mist, Lien sees the stumps of bridges, which – Dr Heroma tells her – were cut up for steel and transported to Germany in the final months of the war.

It is dusk by the time they get to Dordrecht. Her first glimpse of the van Esses' new house in the Frederikstraat will always stay fixed in her mind. There are so many people crowded around the door. They either want help with their housing or they are journalists asking for comment from Uncle Henk. Mrs Heroma, with her usual self-assurance, cuts right through the crowd. Then, there in the hallway, in the warm light, stands Auntie, round and ruddy, looking tired but well. As Lien steps through the front door into the trusted smell of cooking, laundry, cigarette smoke, and people, Auntie surrounds her with softness. 'Lientje,' she says, 'you are home!'

Then the whole house pours out its embrace to her. She is petted and praised. 'Lien!', 'Lienepien!', 'Lien is here!' Kees stands a head taller, embarrassed and wide-eyed, while Marianne crumples with momentary shyness into her big sister, Ali, before turning, quite boldly, to ask, 'Where are you going to sleep?' Even Uncle comes towards her, lean and intense with rolled-up sleeves and a loosened tie.

'We are all so pleased to have you,' he says, fixing her with his gaze.

The house, though only a little bigger than the van Laars', is more than twice the size of the one in the Bilderdijkstraat. There is a sun porch, closed off with heavy curtains, a steep curling staircase, and a balcony on the first floor that looks out on to the street. Auntie works away in the galley kitchen while Uncle Henk returns at once to his discussion, surrounded by men and papers, in the high-ceilinged front room. It is all so different and yet familiar. Neighbours drop round to gossip while children of all ages run about.

At dinner Ali ladles out pea soup as Auntie follows after, holding a chopping board with sliced sausage on it. Using her knife, she flicks a few pieces into each bowl. It is obvious that there is still not much food to go around but, on reaching Lien, Auntie asks if she would like some sausage and when Lien nods she is given twice as much as anyone else. Then there is pudding, a rarity, provided specially with Lien in mind.

After dinner Lien goes outside into the sharp-aired darkness where there are children playing. She does not join them. Instead, she only walks a little, keeping the house in her sight. The Bilderdijkstraat, the street where she first arrived in Dordrecht over three years ago, is less than ten minutes' walk away but it already lies beyond her imagination. She will not see her old best friend Annie Mookhoek again.

Tomorrow there will be a new school and new neighbours. It is strange, this half-connection with Dordrecht, part familiar and part new. She feels a little dizzy with it, just as if she were very tired.

Back inside, the house is winding down for the evening. The electricity has stopped working, which happens often in Dordrecht at the moment, and there are only a few points of light. In the halo of an oil lamp Uncle is bent over a pile of papers. From Auntie, who sits knitting beside him, there is the old word for goodnight, *'trusten*, which was once so strange to Lien but is comforting now.

Ali goes upstairs ahead of her, shielding a candle, and steps into the room that they now share. It looks cosy in the weak yellow of the flame. Double doors lead out to the balcony and three beds stand close together.

'That's yours,' says Ali, pointing to the furthest, 'though we can swap if you like.'

But Lien is quite happy. Placed on her blanket there is a small pile of the things that she left behind over two years ago: some books, pens and pencils, a cuddly toy. Long forgotten, they feel like new gifts to her now. All the same, each item sparks a memory when she touches it, like a brief fire. And then she sees it: her poesie album, with the forget-me-nots of its cover blue-grey in the faint light. Lien stands and holds it for a moment and then places the little book, unopened, on her bedside shelf.

In Amsterdam in 2015 the digital recorder has run uninterrupted for nearly two hours.

'Shall we eat something?' asks Lien.

I nod and shift from my seat. It is already quite late.

In the kitchen, steam soon rises in the light of the cooker hood as Lien sets to work, and twenty minutes later we are seated at the table again, this time with plates of food. There is a pitcher of water with slices of lemon in it, coated in silver bubbles of air, and as we sit under the lamplight I feel just as I do with my parents or with my aunts and uncles, comfortable and entirely at home. It is strange, though, because our talk at this moment is not of family connection but of its opposite, of the break between Lien and the van Esses that came in the early 1980s.

After we have cleared the dishes Lien proposes that we watch the recording of her testimony to the Shoah Foundation. We watch on her computer, sitting at her desk. Lien clicks the icon, and a second later we see her twenty years ago in her house in Eindhoven, seated in the red chair that now stands in her front room.

Although younger, the woman on the screen looks less vibrant than Lien as I know her. There is a heaviness about her and a tired look in her eyes. She addresses the camera in a flat, cautious, matter-of-fact tone. Starting with her name and then the names of her parents, she answers the interviewer's questions and in this way the narrative plays out over the course of an hour. But there are no stories, there is no family, there is no life.

Lien, as she sits beside me, quarrels a little with her former self. She interrupts with small adjustments and even laughs at what she feels are moments of excessive grandness. She is like a child making comments from the back of the class.

The DVD stops and we are left looking at the frozen image of the last frame of the interview. It is past midnight and the room and the city outside it are quiet.

'I had better get going,' I say. 'Tomorrow I want to go to Dordrecht again.'

In the darkness a few minutes later I feel an intense clarity of vision. Never before, it seems to me, have I understood someone so completely, from their earliest memories, through the small, intimate details of an inner life. Lien, as she returned, aged twelve, to my grandparents in the Frederikstraat, is real to me. I feel I know her better than I know myself.

But then I also know that this is an illusion, the kind of illusion that only a story can bring. How could I, brought up as I was in a world of privilege and stability, understand the experience of a young girl during the Second World War? How could I understand what it feels like to live as a child in utter isolation, to lose all sense of myself? How deep can any sense of another person's experience really go?

Then, as I drive the little car through the night air towards Bennekom, I am suddenly struck by a perplexing and nonsensical moment of recognition. It hits me as a tremor, exactly like the shock I once felt when I lost my young son in a crowded space. I see my own stepdaughter (though I've never called her that), Josie, at the age of twelve, from the inside – fractious, cut out and difficult – at the same instant that I see the badly damaged twelve-year-old Lien.

This is not rational, their situations were quite different, but flashes of the past – in which Josie was free-falling, furious, desperate, and without boundaries – come at me like blows to the head.

As I hold my course on the motorway I see Josie, aged sixteen, on the gravel of our driveway, leaving the house, it seemed for good. Then I remember the series of dismal rooms that she lived in, with dirty communal kitchens and windows that looked out on to brick walls.

Self-justification rises inside me: she wanted to leave, said she hated the family, was impossible to control. Surely I was not unreasonable? I was not unkind. Each time, at a new address, I constructed the same bits of shelving for her and watched as the same few photos (one of her best friend from childhood in Cambridge) came out of a cardboard box. We transferred money, monthly. We met in restaurants. I left the occasional unanswered phone message or text.

But the truth is that I did not want her home and did not understand her. The truth is that there were moments when I wanted her out of my life.

In those terrible days when our daughter seemed lost to us, my wife, Anne Marie, would sleep fitfully with a phone beside her pillow. Sometimes she would head out in the dead of night. Every day she would ring our daughter, even if the call went unanswered. It was important, Anne Marie said, that Josie knew she was loved. I, on the other hand, rarely called her myself and often did not see or hear from her for months on end.

And then I think of the fact that my grandmother sent Lien a letter that cut her out of the family and that after this the two of them never set eyes on each other again. Could I have sent Josie such a letter? When I think of how we sat together in a car on this same motorway only weeks ago that seems impossible to imagine. We felt so close then, the family enclosed together, soothed by the buzz of the road. I remember that on that journey I tried to tell Josie the beginning of Lien's story and that my throat froze and I could not speak. Is it possible that the two of us could have lost each other? I have to admit that it is.

The house in Bennekom is silent when I reach it. The dogs pad over softly, touching their tongues to my outstretched hand. In bed I lie awake for several hours and at 3 a.m. I reach for my phone. I send Josie a text message. 'I love you' is all that it says.

20

On the train to Dordrecht early the next morning I study a dossier that describes Lien's life with my grandparents from the time of her return in late September 1945 to the time when the report was completed, 25 November 1947. It was put together by an organization called Le-Ezrath Ha-Jeled, which promoted the welfare of Jewish orphans after the war. Lien gave me the bundle as I left last night. In the quiet railway carriage I spread its loose sheets – about thirty in all – on the speckled blue plastic table and place them in order. There are reports of meetings, accounts of correspondence, descriptions of the rooms in the household, and summaries of the people involved. There are also various letters in an appendix, including one from Mr van Laar, who believes that Lien is now living in England or Palestine. He is asking to be reimbursed for some dental expenses that he incurred on her behalf.

Le-Ezrath Ha-Jeled (meaning 'for the help of the child' in Hebrew) was formed in response to the situation facing child Holocaust survivors in the Netherlands in 1945. After the war had ended, Jewish children who had been rescued by the resistance were being stopped from returning to their families, not simply through personal action, but through policies supported by the Dutch state. As early as September 1944, Gesina van der Molen, a Calvinist resistance leader, had begun printing leaflets that instructed members of her network, which had saved around eighty children, to keep hold of their charges in the event that a mother or father should return to reclaim their child. By handing their children to the resistance, she argued,

Jewish parents had renounced their parental rights. Then, on 13 August 1945, when the government established a Commission for War Foster Children (known as the OPK), Gesina van der Molen was appointed as its chair.

The OPK, which had only a minority of Jewish members, pursued what it called a child-centred policy. This meant that the cases of around 4,000 Jewish children who had survived the war in hiding would be dealt with on an individual basis. If, in the view of the commission, their best interests would be served by remaining with their foster-parents, this should happen, even where family members, potentially including parents, were still alive.

Seventeen days after the commission was established, Abraham de Jong, who had himself survived the war in hiding, founded Le-Ezrath Ha-Jeled. Its aim was to combat the OPK's power.

Thanks to funding from the American Jewish Joint Distribution Committee, de Jong's Le-Ezrath Ha-Jeled quickly established itself as a serious and professional organization. By April 1946 it had thirty staff members, and by September fifty-two. These included social workers, investigators, carers and campaigners. In spite of fierce opposition from Gesina van der Molen's OPK, the staff of Le-Ezrath Ha-Jeled soon began to conduct research into the circumstances of Jewish children. The report on Lien was one product of its work.

In contrast to the OPK, Le-Ezrath Ha-Jeled wanted, if possible (and even against an orphan's wishes), to return a child to the culture into which it had been born. To do this they would track down surviving relatives or, where this failed, suggest Jewish couples who might be willing to adopt. In Lien's case both options were considered. She had been part of a large extended family, but, as the dossier tells us, only two adult members of that family were left alive in 1945.

It is perhaps natural to assume that there would be a specific moment at which Lien discovered that her parents had been murdered. The realization, however, had been more gradual and it stretched back a very long time. Already in December 1942, when she rolled her two rings between her hands until they fell under the floorboards of the house in the Bilderdijk-straat, Lien had said a kind of farewell to her mother and father. After this, she shut off her mind to their memory. In a way, for the nine-year-old girl, they ceased to exist as real people, either in the present or in the past. When, after the war ended, her parents continued not to be mentioned, this confirmed that they must have been murdered, but this fact remained somehow distant and abstract, too awful to contemplate as an actual event. It was impossible to visualize that horror. It would be decades before Lien could even see them in her imagination as they had been. When, eventually, she was again able to picture her parents, the shock to her psyche would prove profound.

The person who last saw Lien's mother alive (at the moment before she stepped with Lien's grandmother on to the cattle truck that was bound for Poland) was Aunt Roza, who features in the report by Le-Ezrath Ha-Jeled. Aunt Roza was the widow of a maternal uncle. She came to see her niece almost immediately after Lien returned to Dordrecht, and (during a day trip to The Hague) she contributed a poem to Lien's poesie album, which is dated 24 November 1945. It is the first entry for over two and a half years:

Dear Lientje,

> *I hope that in your life you'll meet*
> *Health, prosperity, and all that's sweet,*
> *And of all the people that there are*

I wish this most for you, by far.
And if you're always dear and true
I know these things will come to you
For she who's good is sure to find
That others in return are kind.
So always trust in your good luck
Then from yourself you cannot be unstuck.

With much love,
Aunt Roza

The handwriting is a little blotted and uneven, but, other than this, I wonder whether there is much that is personal in this poem. It is hard to think so. The wishes for her niece are heartwarming, but surely, for Aunt Roza, there had been nothing in the last five years to back up the view that 'others in return are kind'. It had been her 'luck' to survive Auschwitz, but only at the cost of years of medical experimentation at the hands of Josef Mengele, which had left her infertile amongst many other terrible things. In the group photo of Lien's family that was taken on the beach at Scheveningen in the 1930s it is Aunt Roza who stands there at the centre, in a white bathing costume, holding a volleyball. A decade later, of the twenty-three healthy young men and women in the picture, she is the only one left alive.

By 1947, when the dossier was completed, Roza Spiero had already left the country, first for Indonesia and then later for the US. Lien remembers her as a force of nature, full of glamour and strong opinions. When they first re-met, Aunt Roza disapproved of the Socialist Youth Club uniform that her niece was wearing and took her shopping for something that had what she called 'allure'. Lien followed meekly. In the almost empty department store, she remembers how her aunt knocked over a display stand, scattering and smashing little bottles all over the floor. The scent was overwhelming. But, rather than being embarrassed, as Lien was, Aunt Roza rounded on the serving staff, raging that they ought to be more careful when setting out their wares. The Le-Ezrath Ha-Jeled report is heartless in its verdict on this traumatized woman, who is labelled a 'shallow bohemian'. Still, their conclusion that she was unsuited to the care of children was probably right.

There was no more optimism from the committee about Lien's other adult relative, Uncle Eddie. He is missing from the photo of the beach party in Scheveningen, because, even then, he was regarded as the family's black sheep. Aunt Roza had once lent him an expensive camera that was not returned, and there was also the matter of some missing suitcases, which resulted in enquiries from the police. By the time that the war broke out Eddie was abroad, in irregular contact.

Unsurprisingly, he was not considered a suitable guardian for a teenage girl.

He was charming though. Lien remembers his sudden arrival in the summer of 1946 at the door in the Frederikstraat, a man in his late twenties in a sergeant's uniform, full of stories about his travels. He had brought a pair of shoes for her, high-heeled and pretty but too small to wear. There is a photo of the two of them together: he in his military formals; she, bright-eyed, her whole face transformed by a triangular smile. Of course Uncle Eddie wanted to write something in her album. Sadly, there were no more empty pages, so he used a separate sheet of paper, which she tucked, next to Aunt Roza's, into the back of the book. It is dated 10 July 1946.

Uncle Eddie worked hard on his entry, and he no doubt meant what he wrote about 'meeting together again as friends before long', just as he meant to send her the promised sweets and bicycle from England, but promises, for Uncle Eddie, were always difficult to keep. She waited in for him once, on a day when he said he would visit, but there was a problem with transport. He would send some photographs of his new wife and daughter in London, but she never saw him again.

With neither Aunt Roza nor Uncle Eddie an option, Le-Ezrath Ha-Jeled did consider whether a Jewish family might be able to adopt her. A couple from Gouda came over to the Frederikstraat to visit. All went well and they invited Lien to their house to stay for a weekend. She was collected by a chauffeur in a Bentley, which smelled of wood and polish, as did the great house with its tennis court and marble floors. But Lien did not like it. All she had ever wanted was to stay with the van Esses, and in the end even Le-Ezrath Ha-Jeled agreed.

Though they were, in general, very far from easy to persuade on these matters, the committee agreed that family relations at the Frederikstraat were exceptionally good:

> Mrs van Es makes no distinction between the children. There is great harmony. The ideals of humanism are put into practice here. The children get on delightfully. Have always had many Jewish friends. During the occupation had other Jews in hiding . . . The foster-parents are warm and kind. They bring Lien up with care and good sense and regard her as their own daughter . . . The van Esses are truly very remarkable people. The whole family bears their stamp.

'She is with us now,' my grandmother is quoted as saying, intending this to be the final word. As for Lien, she already feels part of the family. The interviewer reports as follows:

> She dearly loves her foster-sisters and -brothers. Her dearest friend is her six-year-old foster-sister and when asked 'Who else are your friends?' she answered, 'This little brother' (a boy of one and a half).

That boy is my own father, who was born just two weeks after Lien returned.

*

In the end Le-Ezrath Ha-Jeled defeated Gesina van der Molen, whose OPK was abolished on 1 September 1949. This meant that, by and large, child hideaways went back to a Jewish environment, especially where it could be shown that their home background had been religious. Around half were reunited with one or both parents. Others, who were not so lucky, were sent out for adoption or were transferred to orphanages, in quite a few cases forced to leave a caring rescue family with whom they had wanted to stay. The large-scale rescue of children separated from parents had been a phenomenon unique to the Netherlands. Many thousands had been saved, but the emotional repercussions of survival would play out over the decades to come. Lien, in staying with the van Esses, was an exception. Out of more than 4,000 children nationally, she was one of only 358 who remained, at the end of the process, with non-Jews.

My train pulls into Dordrecht station. From there I take the short walk to the city library, which sits at the centre of the old town. Here I hope to learn more about the public life of my grandfather, who is heralded as such a remarkable person in the report by Le-Ezrath Ha-Jeled. The picture they paint of him is of a serious, intensely hard-working man of principle. His large bookcase, which they describe, is filled with socialist literature and with history books and journals on the latest developments in technology and science. Largely self-taught, he had a prodigious appetite for learning and a faith in the potential for human progress. During the war he had risked everything for the resistance, and afterwards, to my grandmother's concern, he took a big drop in salary to run for political office. Things continued to be financially precarious for him each time elections came around.

In Dordrecht's central library, upstairs on a steel mezzanine amongst sections on travel and teenage fiction, there are some shelves devoted to local government. Here I read about my grandfather's role in the city's development after the war. It does not take long before I come across a photo of him. Resting his chin on his fist, he sits as one of the five burgesses at a raised table addressing a meeting of the council, a clerk taking shorthand at a desk directly in front. Behind him, on the wall, huge maps show plans for the city's transformation. He looks lean, businesslike, confident, and a little bored by the questioning, which, according to the record, kept on for fourteen hours.

The picture was taken in January 1962, a high point of optimism, both for my grandfather and for the town. Like almost all of the country, Dordrecht saw spectacular growth in the post-war decades. Once Marshall Plan aid came on stream in 1948, the bridges, ferries, rail lines, power stations and factories that had been destroyed or stolen were quickly rebuilt. The city stands as a model for the national effort of reconstruction (the so-called *wederopbouw*) that was driven by investment in infrastructure. My grandfather, who also spoke at national conferences about what was called 'gas and water socialism' (aimed at improving living standards through practical interventions), played a big part in that.

By the mid 1950s, the city, which had been a relative economic backwater, was a booming industrial centre. It assembled ships and aircraft, turned coal into coal gas, and manufactured biscuits, leather goods and cigarettes. The Electrical Motors Factory, where my grandfather had worked, was expanded. Meanwhile, the iron-working company Tomado launched a range of iconic products that were inspired by the abstract art of Piet Mondrian. They made shelving units, bookcases, draining racks, bottle scrapers, and later mixers, coffee grinders and kettles, all in a range of primary colours. From the early 1960s, new factories came to make vacuum cleaners, paint and ovens. Then DuPont chose the city to manufacture its miraculous substances: Orlon, Lycra and Teflon, each on a separate site. To meet demand, workers were bussed in from as far as Belgium, more than two hours away.

For my grandfather, the new prosperity would be the engine for a socialist future. New housing was needed: clean high-rise flats with fitted bathrooms and kitchens, and elevators that carried you, almost soundlessly, into the sky. He pushed through the development of new estates of affordable public housing: thousands of reprints of the same sensible design. There were new parks, libraries and leisure centres; new health clinics and new schools. The invention of 'grain concrete', in which cement was made from the crushed stone and brick of demolished buildings, speeded the process still further. With this magic, the dust of history was transformed into the clean, the bright and the new. Some complained when the old neo-Renaissance post office, with its fairy-tale turrets and towers, was knocked down and replaced by concrete shopfronts, but my grandfather's faith in progress was boundless. For him and his fellow burgesses, fourteen hours of debate at a council meeting was a waste of precious rebuilding time.

I look again at the photo of my grandfather, framed by maps three times his size. Given his experiences before and during the war, the answers were obvious: central planning, a clean slate, education, cars and car parks, more train lines and bigger roads. Such improvements would bring shared prosperity and decent provision for the sick and the old. And it could all be paid for from the profits of the factories. The war, for all its horrors, had shown what government and industry, working in partnership, were able to achieve.

*

At lunchtime I head out for a sandwich. The town centre outside the library was left almost untouched by 1960s renewal, although there had been plans for demolition even here. Leaning on some wrought-iron railings, I gaze at the medieval city hall, which is built, with gorgeous lopsidedness, half of brick and half of stone, across a low-arched bridge. On either side there are Renaissance merchants' houses with stepped gables glinting in the sun. This, though, is just an island in a sea of modern construction. Two hundred yards away, down the street, I can see the discoloured grey-brown brick of the C&A building, the white panelling on which has buckled over the years.

Before this morning I never understood how town planners, here and throughout Europe, could have demolished ancient tenements to construct such buildings, but their actions can be traced, at least in part, to the confidence in improvement, the wish to be rid of the old history, that came in those frantic decades of reconstruction after the war. When I think of my grandfather and his wartime experiences I start to see how all this could have come about.

Returning to the library in the afternoon, I read on into Dordrecht's history in the next decade when, almost overnight, the good news disappeared. On 1 January 1970 the metalware factory Bekkers shut its doors, with the loss of 220 jobs, and a few months later the pharmaceuticals company Chefaro also announced it would close. All of a sudden there was competition from Asia; the US undid the link between gold and the dollar, making Dutch exports more expensive; and then the oil crisis hit. Dordrecht, which for a short time had been so new and full of promise, was now old-fashioned, polluted, and too small to pull its weight. Its great companies – Tomado, the steelworks, the leather factory, Victoria Biscuits, the shipbuilders, the brewery – went bust or moved production elsewhere. Steadily, from 1975 onwards, the city, whose population was still only 100,000, lost 2,700 jobs a year. Unemployment brought crime and drug addiction, and also a degree of racial tension with the Moroccan guest workers who had been invited to come to Dordrecht at precisely the moment when the job losses began. By that point my grandfather was no longer on the city council, having been elected to parliament's First Chamber (the rough equivalent of Britain's House of Lords). The family moved for a while to Brill, a small town in the west, where he served as mayor, but his bid to get a seat in the Second Chamber (the main national parliament) did not meet with success. He had been an impassioned modernizer, and the troubles of his city must have hit him hard.

That night I stay in a dockside hotel, a converted building that once housed the offices of the Electrical Motors Factory, the place where my grandfather used to work.

The EMF went bankrupt in the 1970s. A colour photo of it taken a decade after the closure shows a steel skeleton surrounded by piles of rubbish and stagnant pools. By this time the whole docks area, once thronging with labourers, was derelict, and to the thousands of men who had worked here since their school days the place must have felt like a grave. Once in my room, which looks out on to a smokers' terrace with rubber matting, I think back to my grandfather, who spent so many years here and who did so much to shape this town.

I was seven when my grandfather died. I remember the news of his death with perfect clarity. My dad picked the phone up in the living room and after a few moments began to cry. Beyond this I have just two snatches of memory related to him: my grandfather's anger when I broke a window of his greenhouse; and his relentless, determined winning when we played a game of cards. In both cases I recall the sharp smell of cigar smoke (we collected the boxes that the cigars came in and these still carried a deep, sweet, leafy scent). I also remember the sharpness of his eyes. There was a sense of greatness about him, an aura of command that came from his heroic war years (which were never talked about) and from his decades of political work. My father recalls that in Dordrecht it was always quite something to be known as his son.

My grandmother, who died when I was twenty-three, is much more vivid to me. Love came from her especially through the kitchen, which she kept perfectly tidy with a small wall-mounted spice rack and a set of hanging stainless-steel pans. On the fridge there would be news from the Labour Party stuck on with magnets, and I also remember a few wise sayings (such as 'The days are what we make them') around the house, painted on wooden signs. She was great with young children. When we travelled on buses she could make pressing the stop button on the handrail an act of immense power. On current affairs, which we enjoyed discussing together as I grew older, she was pessimistic. People's lack of appreciation for the good things that the welfare state gave them made her angry, and this was especially true when she talked about women. They got up too late, served too many ready-made dinners, drank beer, and sunned themselves on foreign beaches, when they should have been thinking about their children. As she grew older I think my grandmother's life was coloured by a feeling of disappointment that the paradise that she and her husband had thought they were building proved unreal and unloved. My mother quotes a letter that Grandma wrote in the mid 1990s in which she mentions my brother and me:

> And then my two lovely grandsons. In dark moods I think 'it was all pointless', but then I see Bart and Joost in front of me and I think, yes, it did have purpose after all.

Children, especially her grandchildren, were a constant pleasure to her, and she loved Lien's children, when these arrived, as passionately as the rest. But those 'dark moods' were something that came, in later years, to haunt her. In the diary that she kept for some of the post-war years she mentions a 'long-lasting spiritual depression' that was connected in part to global politics and in part to problems closer to home. She writes of 'ungratefulness' from the children that she took in and rescued and of how 'the duty to care for children in addition to your own should be wished on no one because it is such a heavy burden to bear'.

On the desk in my hotel room lies a second sheath of papers. They were given to me by Lien last night, along with the dossier from Le-Ezrath Ha-Jeled. There are eleven typed pages of narrative, which she wrote as part of a set of therapy sessions in February 2001. They bear the title 'This Will Be for Once the Concrete Story of My Relations with the Van Es Family'. Lien's 'Concrete Story' will be an important source for how I understand the row between her and my grandparents.

In the middle of page 4 she begins a new section, dealing with her return to Dordrecht in 1945. It begins as follows, with her reception by Auntie van Es:

> The welcome was very warm. She embraced me, called me 'Lienepien' and said that it seemed as if I had never been away. But for me it was very different.

I read further into the document, which presents a picture of life in the van Es family from Lien's perspective in the post-war years.

21

Not long after returning to Dordrecht, Lien switches from saying 'Auntie' and 'Uncle' to saying 'Ma' and 'Pa' like everyone else. It first happens one evening as she sits at the table doing her homework, shading a map of Holland. 'Ma,' she calls out, and the word shocks her when it comes out of her mouth. But Ma just answers with 'Yes, Lienepien', which is the pet name that she always uses, and after that the change becomes fixed. No word is spoken – the family does not really talk about feelings – but it feels normal, which makes sense because Kees and Ali, who once had a different mother, must also at some point have said 'Ma' instead of 'Auntie' for the first time.

At least on the outside, life at the Frederikstraat is just as it was at the old house. After school she plays kick-the-can with children in the street. The tin can is put on the pavement at the corner where the field starts, and you can creep up to it in different ways. One is through the bushes, crouching amongst the prickles, inching forward, feeling the cold through the soles of your shoes. Or you can edge along the fence. You can also dodge in and out of the hedges on the Emmastraat, risking an angry word from Mrs Peters, who does not like you bending her plants.

If someone calls out your name and your position then you are out.

'I see you, Lientje, behind the postbox!'

'I see you, Kees, in the hedge on the Emmastraat!'

Kees is not really her friend now. He joins in with the big

street games but, alone together, he does not like to play with girls. She has plenty of friends though, such as Rieka Maasdam, who writes in her poesie album on one of a growing collection of loose sheets tucked in at the back:

11 March 1946

Dear Lientje

What shall I write on this page?
I have been thinking for an age!
Hey, Lientje, I know what,
Just be happy with what you've got!

For the remembrance
of your friend
Rieka Maasdam

Diagonally, at the bottom of the page, Rieka writes: 'the 29th of November, that's the day you must remember.' When that day comes Rieka will be twelve. Lien will be thirteen: she has gone back a year in school after all the lessons that she missed during the war.

Some friends, like Rieka, are from her class, and some are from the streets around them, and still others are from the Socialist Youth Club, the AJC, which is where she spends almost all of her weekends. Lien still remembers when the material arrived for her uniform: a rough, brown rectangle of Manchester cloth for the skirt and a blue cotton one for the blouse, plus a red neckerchief, all tied together as one packet with string. Ma cut and sewed it for her. Now, early on Saturday mornings, she, Kees and Ali will head out to a park, to town or to the station, collecting others on the way. At the AJC they play rounders, hold quizzes, practise dancing

or do gymnastics. There are also lectures with serious titles like 'Women in World History' or 'Life on a Collective Farm'.

The big event for the AJC is the annual gathering, where young people from all over the country join together. For this they travel to Vierhouten, four hours away by train. Lien's group is called the Migrant Birds, and they do sound like birds all squeezed together in one carriage, squealing and laughing, making promises about who will sleep where in the tent. The group leader tries to keep order by starting singing practice, but after a while she gives up. At Utrecht the train stops and, through the window, they see another youth group waiting in line on the platform, Catholic girls in velvet purple capes.

After two more hours the train stops at a station with no roof and a wooden platform. There the doors open on to a sea of brown, blue and red. She keeps an eye out for the Migrant Birds flag so as not to get lost in the crush of people as they worm their way through the crowd to find their camping field. Inside the big white tent the light is weirdly hazy and it smells of grass and earth. Lien puts her bag down next to her friend

Maartje's. Through the shining, moving canvas she can hear the camp announcements from the speakers, slightly deadened: there is news of the nature knowledge lecture, the forest hike, the campfire, and the arrival of a group of visitors from France.

In the morning, after a night of secret whispering, they eat their breakfast in the sun. It is porridge from an enormous pan. Seated on hay bales, cradling the hot metal of their bowls, they look across at the neighbouring group of boys. Then there is exercise, with long lines facing a big stage that has microphones on it and a woman in a kind of swimming costume who shows them what to do, such as bending, stretching and doing star jumps on the spot. Later, there are running races, which she loves. She glows with inner pride when she wins her heat.

There is a boy called Wim who likes her, Maartje says. By the third day they are exchanging nervous glances and then, on the evening of the fourth, during the maypole dancing, their fingers touch and stay in place. After this, on hikes, they often walk together. She likes the funny stories that he tells her and the way he wears his collar flipped right up against his neck. Wim is also from Dordrecht, so they plan to stay in touch.

The journey home feels shorter. She leans against the girl beside her as the carriage jolts along. For the final roll call at Dordt station they answer weakly through a fog of sleep. After this she, Kees and Ali trudge back to the Frederikstraat. Though Ma has dinner waiting, they are too tired to eat it and can barely speak.

In the morning the curtains shine bright orange. Downstairs, Marianne is running and calling out. Ali stretches in the bed beside her.

'I have slept soooooo well!' she yawns.

Lien points her toes and fingers, making her body as long as it will go.

Then they play the game that they call 'tickling, scratching, rubbing', which has a precise order to it. One girl lies flat on her stomach while the other tickles and then scratches, gently, down her back. And finally there is the rubbing, with hands flat and warm in circles, which is bliss.

At this point Marianne bounds in and orders them to breakfast.

'You must get *up!*' she chants, bouncing and repeating '*up*' with every bounce.

Tousle-haired, the two girls are shooed down to the table where Ma is seated with a stack of washing, sorting items into different piles. Their three blue shirts are already hanging in a line across the window, darkening the room.

'You girls have slept a hole in the day,' Ma tells them, smiling. 'What you need is a bit of healthy sunshine and then tonight you're off to roost with the chickens. It's school again tomorrow.'

Off to roost with the chickens. That means going to bed when it gets dark. Ma likes these funny expressions. It is one of those differences between the talk of the van Esses and what she was used to at the van Laars'.

'If we go to bed with the chickens then we can lay our own eggs in the morning!' Lien answers, but as she says this she knows all of a sudden that her joke has not fallen right. In Bennekom such farmyard language was common, whereas here the idea of people laying eggs is somehow dirty, and Lien feels she has caught this infection in her way of speaking and that, because of what she has said, the mood in the room has changed. Ali smiles in her loyal, kind way, but Lien senses an edge of pity. Ma continues sorting the laundry piles.

Feeling downcast in the silence, Lien adds this error to her secret mental list of mistakes. Last week, for example, Ma called her a fusspot for cleaning, as Mother van Laar taught her, with two separate cloths. And then there was the bike trip where she called out 'Hooray for the Liegemen!', which Ali told her afterwards was all wrong. The Liegemen, apparently, were the bad ones, not the goodies. The van Esses, the Labour Party, they were on the Patriot side, whereas the Liegemen, that was the side of the church, which was the side of the van Laars. So all her dreams of castles and towers and princes and princesses, which she got from those books that she read in Bennekom and Ede, were wrong.

Lien sits there scowling.

'Hey, Lienepien,' says Ma, not unkindly, 'enough now of those dirty looks!'

There is a group photo of the five children – Ali, Kees, Lien, Marianne and my father – that was taken around 1948. Lien, who is now fifteen and who sits to the far left of the picture, is, for the first time, too old to have a bow in her hair. My dad, the baby of the family, sits directly in front of her, his sister's arm holding him steady. Blond and smiling, he looks exactly like my own son did when he was that age. Ali, in an armchair with a wicker back, sits crosswise at the centre, already looking like a grown woman in her long skirt and white blouse with a brooch at her neck. By the time that I was old enough to remember Aunt Ali she was over fifty, but it is easy to recognize her sweet-natured, timid, serious expression.

Marianne, who is eight and stands behind her older sister, is still more familiar. She looks self-possessed and not at all childish in spite of the big white bow that she wears.

The van Esses are a good-looking family, but the most

striking is Kees, already dressed in a suit and tie, who smiles in a roguish, confident manner. You can see the man in him: the handsome and kindly big brother my father so fondly remembers, for whom everything seemed to come easy, and also the family patriarch of later years.

In the picture there is a big empty space between Kees and his foster-sister. The gap looks awkward, yet the two of them had first been such close friends. It is not just from him, though, that Lien seems to be separated. In spite of the physical closeness, she looks somehow set apart from her siblings, and this is not just on account of her darker complexion and differently textured hair. There is a brooding quality to her, at once dreamy and fierce, which matches with Lien's own account of her feelings at this time.

In the hotel room in Dordrecht, shifting from Lien's 'Concrete Story of My Relations with the Van Es Family', I look back at the report by Le-Ezrath Ha-Jeled, which I studied this morning. The report makes mention of 'a break in the girl's emotional engagement' and states that 'the child gives the impression of not having fully developed'. 'The delay in her spiritual growth,' it concludes, 'is noticeable.'

Maybe I am projecting too much on to a single photo, but I do sense this aura of separation in the picture. The light falls differently on her. Lien looks almost as though she has been taken from another photograph entirely and then pasted in.

Lien's 'Concrete Story' describes an incident that occurred around the time that the family portrait was taken:

I remember one time that I was darning socks by the stove. I thought it was really rather a fun little job. But at a certain moment I was sent directly to bed without my supper, something that was used as a punishment in the house. Ma's point was that I had been looking so angry and disagreeable and that I had to learn that sometimes I had to darn socks and that was that. It didn't matter that I said that I hadn't minded darning socks at all. The punishment went through.

Ma also said to me quite often, 'You are irritating me immeasurably, but I don't know why.'

As I write this, memories are triggered and I think that I must have been deaf and blind to the signals that my presence was too much for the family. And the question is, did they love me?

Even then, I always had the feeling that they didn't need me but I did need them. I was conscious that I probably loved them more than they loved me.

There are these moments when Lien feels separate from the family, when she stares into the distance and feels an oppressive sadness, but life is good, really, on the whole. The buzz of the house is a joy to her. There are always people at the door who need to speak to Pa. And over dinner there are heated conversations: big important topics with principles at stake. Ma and Pa are completely honest. Though the house that they rent is quite large, they own almost nothing, and what they have they share. Come 1953, when the great flood (the *Watersnood*) drowns much of the country, they will, without a moment's consideration, open their home to refugees.

As well as sisters and brothers, Lien has many friends around her. Girls still sometimes write in her poesie album. She has a special pad of yellow paper, which she now uses for these extra entries, like the following verse:

> *Two clear eyes, the prettiest I've seen*
> *I hope that you love me, my dearest Lien*

It is 'Lien' now instead of 'Lientje'. One day in school a teacher tells her that 'Lientje' sounds childish, and this moment marks the change.

School is a pleasure. Though a year behind, she is soon again near the top of the class. She enjoys the stillness of homework. Numbers line up and resolve themselves as her pencil moves from square to square. In Dutch, she likes the gentle unpicking of sentences: the subject, verb and object that are strung together on an invisible line. Best of all, there is geography, in which she traces the edges of continents, oceans, deserts, jungles and great sheets of ice.

There are friends at school, at the AJC, in the street, and also at home, where she can talk about Wim (whom she has seen quite a few times now) to Ali, do puzzles with Marianne or read stories to little Henk. It is only with Kees that she has lost her connection. There is a wildness about him, something she used to share but that now excludes her. He is always saying that she is odd. Lien wants him to like her again, and maybe it is because of this that one time, when walking through the fields in August, she tells him what happened in Ede and afterwards in the woods outside Bennekom.

They have just come back from an AJC meeting, and as Lien talks she looks down at her sandals and her grey woollen socks.

'You know, when I was away, in the wartime, a man did things to me that I didn't like.'

Kees slows his step.

'What kind of things?' he asks her, intrigued for once.

She hadn't planned this and doesn't have the language.

There is a word that has been whispered by wide-eyed girls in class.

Rape (*verkrachten*).

'He used to rape me,' she says.

The phrase feels awkward in her mouth.

Kees stands still.

'Did he take your clothes off?' he asks.

As she looks up at him, Kees suddenly looks childish in his red neckerchief and his khaki AJC shorts. Turning away, she starts to walk.

He lags behind and then strides towards her.

'Hey, if you can do it with some stranger you can do it with me,' he puffs.

'I could make you,' he adds after a moment, mumbling.

When he speaks like this she is suddenly frightened and she begins to run.

'You are odd!' he shouts after her, without trying to catch up.

It was an exchange that took just a few seconds and Kees, a fourteen-year-old with no understanding of his sexual feelings, perhaps hardly thought about it. Afterwards, he told his parents, who did their best to talk the matter over with Lien. But there was no language for what had happened to Lien in Ede and Bennekom. In that post-war half decade there was barely a language for emotions at all. So the rapes that

Lien suffered remained as a fenced-off part of her existence, never referred to but still sensed, perhaps by everyone, as a presence.

It is not long after this that Lien finds herself on the broad tree-lined gravel path through Orange Park that leads to the Higher Burgess School (the HBS), on her way to sit the entrance exam. This is the secondary school that teaches more difficult subjects such as Geometry, Sciences, Greek and Latin; from here students can go on to university, although Lien has not thought at all about that. Almost a year ago, after good reports in all of her subjects, the teachers told her that she should try for HBS admission. They even provided some extra lessons in preparation. Mostly, though, Lien feigned illness and did not turn up.

It is not the thought of the school itself that frightens her; it is the thought of what will happen at home. Once, when she brought an English book back from the library, Ma told her that she could not possibly understand it and she ought to be careful of showing off. That comment has stuck like an awkward piece of grit inside her. With Kees and Ali already at the MULO (the More Advanced Lower Education College, where the subjects are easier), how would it feel if she were suddenly one of those boastful HBS girls?

On all sides children are heading in the same direction, some with their parents beside them offering last-minute advice. The building is enormous: row upon row of high blank windows staring out across the park. The muted crowd is gathering around a side door, digging holes in the deep gravel with their shoes. After twenty minutes the door opens and a man with whiskers invites them in.

It smells of chalk, chlorine, packed lunches and damp clothes. Rows of wooden benches are lined up opposite a lectern and a clock. On them there are little stacks of printed sheets, face down, evenly spaced. These are the exam papers. The big room echoes with the squeaking and scraping of wood.

And now it is really happening. When the whiskered man calls out, there is a frantic rustle. Beside Lien, a girl starts writing immediately, her tongue edging in and out to the ridge of her teeth.

Part I is mental arithmetic, with no rough working allowed. Lien turns her paper:

    1. $88 - \ldots + 8 = 70$
    2. $3/\underline{125} = \ldots$

The girl beside her is working fast.

What would it be like to be here? Lien looks up above the panelling to the white wall and the clock.

    1. $88 - \ldots + 8 = 70$

Is it true that the girls who go here are mostly snobs?

    1. $88 - \ldots + 8 = 70$

If she gets in, how will the news be greeted back home? The thought gives Lien a shiver. In her imagination she can see Kees scoffing at some 'Burgess School expression' that she will pick up here, and Ali, though supportive, inwardly hurt, as if by an act of betrayal. And then Pa? Almost every evening he sits at the dinner table at his studies. What will happen if Lien brings home books about geometry, Greek and Latin? Thinking of Pa and Ma, the idea fills her with shame.

Lies decides that she does not want it. She does not want to stand out as an HBS girl. And so, after five more minutes, she starts to guess at the answers almost at random, her figures crossing the dotted lines.

A few weeks later, she gets the news of a disappointing performance in the examination. Admission, the letter says, is permissible, but it is not recommended in her case. The decision to go to the MULO instead comes to Lien as a relief.

And so life goes on as before in the household, with Lien in the class below Kees at the MULO, where he rises with distinction to become head boy. And life really is happy. After Henk there is another baby brother, Geert Jan. There are holidays to the seaside and long visits to the grandparents in Strijen. And there is Wim from the AJC, who becomes her fiancé, though, in the end, they break up.

Of course there are family tensions. Pa is, to be honest, a man with a temper, and Lien too has a passionate side. At rare moments Lien can boil over, hot with fury at some injustice, defiant of consequence, railing in her anger. On these occasions Pa will hit her, hard. This, though, also happens to Kees (with Ma just the same, screaming and desperate to stop the beating) and on the street these rages from fathers are far from unique. Lien has nothing to complain of. Her lot is far better than most.

When the time comes, Ali leaves home to go to nursing college, and Kees, the star of the MULO, goes on to train as a flight engineer and then to work for Fokker in aircraft design, quickly rising through the firm. And Lien? She would like to work with children. There is a place in Amsterdam that would suit her: a residential nursery. She can live there and get training and return to Dordrecht most weekends. Then, after a year, she would progress to Middeloo College in Amersfoort to complete a qualification in Social Educational Care.

So, in 1950, aged seventeen, she takes the train to the big city and then the tram to a grand villa with gates around it, where she gets her uniform: a white apron over a blue dress. The evenings are lonely because few of the other girls stay over, except to do the night shift, and she never goes out. But the work appeals to her. They take children with behavioural problems and work with them, giving them confidence, drawing them out. As she follows her course of studies, Lien takes a special interest in organizing little concerts, with the children playing their recorders all in a line.

On Fridays Lien will pack her bag and head out to the bus stop, looking forward to Ma's cooking and to seeing everyone at home. She will sleep in her old bedroom and chat, maybe, to Ali, if she is also back for the weekend. Downstairs Pa will be smoking and reading, first the work papers from his briefcase and then his books on politics and history and science. It is all so comforting and because of this it hurts her that Ma, feeling that the house gets crowded, says sometimes, 'You know, you don't have to come.'

At work they are developing new approaches. It is a matter of understanding the child as a whole person, with a specific background and a character of their own. The idea is to give children the freedom to develop not only as individuals but also as part of a social world. To help them with this, there are methods such as counselling, setting child protection guidelines, home visits and play therapy, which change the old routines.

After a year, Lien moves, as planned, to Amersfoort to continue her studies. Then, another year on, she must decide on a placement. The director asks Lien to come to his study to look at the options as to where she might go. There is a new children's home called Ellinchem that, he suggests, would suit her. The establishment is based on innovation. It is the first to mix boys and girls together, from babies to the age of twenty-one. With a humanist ethos, it sets out to tackle issues such as loneliness and bereavement. He has spoken to the management. Might Lien take up a position and continue her education there?

She considers for a moment. The place is quite near Benne-kom, which spooks her a little, but she agrees.

So in 1953 she is twenty and working in another villa, this time in a rural village rather than in a big town. Less than a decade back, Ellecom was the home of the Dutch SS training college, but to most people now that feels like a long time ago. And the director was right, it does suit Lien. She is expanding her contacts, becoming more of a leader, finding a mission in life. But still, like all young people, she wants a home to go to, and she feels the pull of the Frederikstraat.

It is on a Monday there in late autumn that she is dozing on the sofa at the end of a weekend visit, having been a bit off colour and planning to go back by train the next day. Rain slants across the window. The objects in the room are so familiar: the clock, the armchair, and the cabinet of polished wood with its china teapot and matching unused cups. For once, the house is peaceful. Even Ma is out. Only Pa is to be heard in the kitchen clinking crockery as he brews his coffee.

She drifts off, well now but still tired, and only wakes when the door opens and Pa asks if she's OK. It is not like him to ask. Lien lies there, confused and dozy for a moment, and then answers that she's fine.

Then something strange, frightening and unexpected happens. As an event it is fleeting and what actually occurs is open to interpretation, but the consequences will be profound. Pa is there beside her as she lies on the sofa, his breathing unsteady. Before she knows what is happening, he is kissing her and stroking her hair. This man, whom she thinks of as a father, seems excited by her as a woman.

Lien stands up and laughs a little, her heart running incredibly fast. He stands close by her, his hand touching her arm.

'I'm not so well, I'm going upstairs to bed' is what she thinks she says.

As she rushes up, her mind is scrambled, unsure what has happened. She paces and looks out on to the rain-slicked balcony, trying to calm down. Her hands are trembling, more from shock and confusion than from fear. After ten minutes of silence in which her hearing buzzes, she curls up on the bed and lies there under the covers, staring in the half-light at the door.

And then the handle turns and he is there again, to get something from the cupboard, he says. He's gone within a minute but then he's back and standing by her bed. Pa bends to kiss her and she hears that heavy breath.

Perhaps she screams? She really doesn't know.

And then he's gone and it's over and nothing happened. But, for Lien, the world has altered and it can never be the same. For her, Pa is no longer her father, he is just a man.

She writes a note to say that she needs to be alone for a while and then she leaves the house.

In my hotel room a sharp smell of cigarette smoke is pushing through the closed vent above the window from the terrace. I head through to the bathroom, where my skin looks blue in the mirror under the tile-reflected light.

Some might say that Lien, her perception distorted by the rapes she endured at the hands of Uncle Evert, imagined intentions that were never there. The circumstances – the empty house, the trusted older man who seems at first to comfort – have something in common. Perhaps they triggered an association that had long been latent in her mind?

In the end, though, I do not believe that what Lien experienced was a projection. Her testimony in the typescript 'The Concrete Story of My Relations with the Van Es Family' is straightforward:

Suddenly he came towards me, breathing very fast, and began to kiss me. I can still feel the shock and the fear of it. Pa, the stern father, the uncompromising moralist, who was suddenly so tactile and excited . . . He saw me as a woman.

Later, Lien and I will discuss her recollection of those moments. Aware of the danger of a false accusation, she has played the incident again and again in her memory, but her judgement has remained the same. In the end, I must write my account of these few minutes from her perspective, aware that it could colour my grandfather's reputation, and risk distorting the legacy of a life of courage and ideals.

Tomorrow I will go to the Frederikstraat, to look out on to the balcony and walk around those rooms. After that I will take the train to Amsterdam, where I am meeting Lien. She wants to show me the Portuguese Synagogue, the place where she got married.

22

Sunshine pours in through the windows of the Portuguese Synagogue in Amsterdam, and under my feet I feel the grains of the sand strewn on the floorboards to dampen sound. Above my head, golden chandeliers float against the dark timber of the vaulted ceiling while stone walls and columns rise all around me, massive and honey-white. It is all so simple and restrained. At the time of its completion in 1675 this was the world's largest synagogue and, aside from its temporary closure in the 1940s, it is still the oldest in continuous use. Even now, there is no electricity or heating. It is lit for the great services by nearly a thousand candles, which shine from holders on the plain wooden benches as well as high up from the three-tiered chandeliers.

Lien smiles proudly as she stands beside me. We are on a walk around Amsterdam's old Jewish Quarter and will head on to the Jewish Historical Museum after this. As we wander across the courtyards and peek into prim little rooms and offices, she tells me about her wedding, which took place here on 20 December 1959.

By that time her connection with the van Es family had been re-established. She stayed away for a year, living rather miserably in institutional accommodation, but then Pa came to see her. They met on neutral ground in the bar of a hotel in Arnhem, not far from where she worked. He told her that nothing had happened and that she had better come home.

That was not how Lien saw it, but because she missed Ma and her brothers and sisters she accepted the offer, resuming the old pattern of weekend visits. The incident and her year of absence were never discussed.

There was, though, a new sense of distance between Lien and her foster-parents, and perhaps it was partly this that made her choose to join the Jewish Student Society rather than the Socialist Union when she began to study in Amsterdam for an additional qualification in Social Work. It was in Amsterdam that she met her future husband, Albert Gomes de Mesquita, a scientist completing his PhD. Physically frail and soft-spoken, he nevertheless had a confidence about him.

'He *was* someone,' as Lien puts it. 'I remember that he told me it was easy to be happy. He knew how to live.'

Happiness, for Albert, flowed from the rules and the rhythms of Judaism, the age-old patterns that brought with them a sense of peace. He was himself a descendant of those who had built the great synagogue. His maternal grandfather, a prosperous banker, had been Chairman of the Board of the Portuguese Jewish Council and his great-grandfather had been the author of celebrated Ashkenazi books of prayer. Although, in contrast, his father's family were poor diamond cutters, they too were observant believers, their lives shaped by the Sabbath, the marking of feast days and the keeping of dietary laws.

Albert, of course, had his own story of survival. In August 1942, aged twelve, he had gone with his parents and sister to hide in a set of purpose-built safe rooms. Holed up in the hidden ground floor of an Amsterdam town house they had a large store of provisions, a secret escape route, a set of reliable friends to supply them, and a routine of exercise and mental occupation to keep their spirits up. They played Monopoly, whist, chess and bridge. Each week Albert completed the logic puzzles in a magazine supplied by their outside helper, who also brought in fresh food. Every Sabbath they performed the usual rituals and sang the usual prayers.

Yet, in spite of all their preparations, before the year was over they had been discovered. Very early in the morning there was banging on the blacked-out windows and then a burly figure charged in through their escape route, shouting for them to move to the back room. One by one he interrogated the family members, including Albert and his little sister, all of whom fully expected that outside there must be a police van waiting, which would take them to a concentration camp. Weirdly, however, at the end of a morning of questioning, they were left alone and unguarded, free to leave. The raider, it turned out, was a robber and not a policeman. The family had lost their possessions and their safe house, but, though friendless on the streets of Amsterdam in late December, they were still alive.

After this narrow escape, they went through a dozen different hiding places across the Netherlands, crouching behind panels in attics and escaping several raids. At times they were starved and flea-bitten, beyond hopelessness, but somehow they stayed together as a unit. They had stories to share and, come May 1945, their collective survival as mother, father and two children to celebrate. So, for Albert, the saddest moment came only after the liberation, when he discovered that of his large extended family of aunts, uncles and grandparents, just three people were left alive.

After the war, Albert's family resumed its old patterns of living, which they had tried to keep going even during the occupation. They rejoined their community, kept kosher, observed the Sabbath and celebrated the festival days. On 9 May, the same day as the overall German surrender, a service of thanksgiving was held in the Portuguese Synagogue. Across the whole of the Netherlands, however, Albert's family were now numbered amongst just 800 remaining Sephardic Jews.

*

The photographs of Lien's wedding at the synagogue have a golden quality to them. She and Albert stand, arm in arm, in a doorway, her head tipped down shyly in a Lady Di pose. In another shot they are seated in the back of a gleaming motor car, Lien looking as perfect as a 1950s film star, her Colgate smile framed by her veil and white dress.

Then there are the pictures of the reception: my grandfather in a pinstripe suit with a spray of flowers in his buttonhole and Ma, in a hat, both caught mid-conversation as they stand in a line to accept the congratulations of well-wishers, beside a resplendent Lien. My father sits smiling at a table with his brother and sisters. Aged fourteen at the time, he remembers it vividly: the brilliantly funny speech from Jan Heroma (Took's husband); the stage that collapsed as the rabbi

was speaking; and his little brother, caught short, having to pee against a wall in the street. Everyone was joyous and united. Even Ben, Lien's cousin (the baby who had sat beside her in those photos in the Pletterijstraat), was present. He had survived, also as a child in hiding, and Lien had found him only very recently, by searching through the records of war orphans kept by Le-Ezrath Ha-Jeled.

For Lien as well as for my father, the speech that Jan Heroma made towards the end of the evening was a highlight. The words that he spoke about her are the only element of her story that she has repeated to me more than once. Having given a brief and witty outline of her character, he turned to the subject of Albert and asked the audience, rhetorically, 'Now is this scrawny ginger-haired gentleman really good enough for *our Lien*?' Good enough for *our Lien* – it was a revelation to her: that she should be presented as something special, and that she should be thought of as *theirs*. Happiness shot through her. She felt completely united with the friends and family who had gathered to send them on their way. She felt at one with the van Esses and now a part of the Jewish community as well.

If one were looking for a simple happy conclusion to the cut out girl's story, then this would be the place to end it. Albert is proud of her, protective and gentle, and he knows so many things. Ma also loves him: he is so interested, hard-working and polite. In the morning, in the back of the shiny black wedding car, the honeymooners drive to the airport, where a gleaming Dakota awaits them for Lien's first ever journey by plane. As the flat, regular fields of the Netherlands recede below them, Good Lientje rises towards the sunlight on silver wings.

23

Leaving the Portuguese Synagogue behind us, Lien and I cross a busy road to get to the Jewish Historical Museum. Her hand, as always when we cross roads here, is on my elbow, not because she needs my support as an 82-year-old, but because she suspects I'm not to be trusted with the traffic. As was the case at the synagogue, it takes a little while to enter the building on account of the intense security. A white police box stands outside on stilts, presenting its blacked-out windows. Inside, we queue for airport-style searches before we can enter the museum itself. The people waiting around us are mainly American teenagers wearing headphones and carrying backpacks, part of organized tours. They sip from their water bottles, apply lip balm and check their phones as they chat about topics like the quality of the breakfast at their hotel. Mixed in with this, though, there is also serious talk about history. Most have been or are going to the Anne Frank house, and in their preppy New York accents the two girls who lean against the wall beside us are discussing the details of life here in the 1940s, specifically the idea of wearing a Jewish star. I wonder if Lien beside me is listening. If she is, then she must feel almost like an exhibit. Her husband, Albert, had Anne Frank as a classmate and once, in the playground, Anne offered to tell him about the facts of life.

The museum, which is housed in the old Great Synagogue (one of the four ancient synagogues that are clustered in this area), is divided into two display spaces: the first covers Dutch Judaism, mainly in its religious practice, until the end of the nineteenth century; the second takes us through the twentieth century up to the present time.

Lien sweeps through the first hall with all the focus of a ten-year-old. 'We don't have to worry about that,' she calls back, as I lag behind and peer at an ancient Torah scroll that sits on a lectern behind protective glass. I point to a historical painting, but pre-twentieth-century art does not especially interest her. 'I suppose I don't have the context to appreciate it,' she says, as she trips up the steps to the higher gallery, clearly having no intention of picking up that context now. Lien has inherited my grandparents' passion for the modern and will be reassured, a year later, when she visits my office and finds it (contrary to her expectations of Oxford) to consist of exposed concrete and walls of plate glass.

The space devoted to more recent Jewish history in the Netherlands is also part of the ancient synagogue, but it feels contemporary, thanks to its sleek aquarium-like display cases and the low blue light of its numerous screens. Subsections on topics such as 'Amsterdam's Jewish Quarter', 'The Diamond Industry' and 'Life in the Provinces' chart the gradual emancipation of poorer Jews as they joined unions and socialist parties, where many became prominent on a national scale. After this, a section on 'The Elite' shows how a small tranche of Jewish society flourished through the growth of big businesses such as the department stores De Bijenkorf and Maison de Bonneterie. Then there was also cultural influence: theatre, music, literature. As I stand looking at a display about famous music-hall acts and jazz players, Lien calls out to me with excitement in her voice.

'Look!' she says. 'This is exactly the material I remember my mother cutting at the kitchen table!'

And there it is – like some animal suspended by Damien Hirst in a tank of formaldehyde – a broad strip of yellow cloth on which stars are printed reading 'Jew', 'Jew', 'Jew', 'Jew'.

It is monstrous, yet also intimate. Lien stands beside it, half smiling, her face yellowed by the reflected light. Right behind her in another aquarium is a little girl's dress with a star stitched upon it and also a wooden sign with the printed message 'Forbidden for Jews'.

An hour later we are seated at a plastic table in the museum café. Lien wants me to try some of the kosher food that they serve here, and especially recommends *gefilte fisj* (chilled salty fishcakes) and *bolus* (hot, syrupy, ginger-filled doughnuts straight from the oven). Amid the white simplicity of the café, Lien tells me about preparing meals in the 1960s, when she and Albert lived in Eindhoven, where he worked for Philips Electronics. Every Thursday evening a pack of kosher meat would arrive from Amsterdam which, given that they had no freezer, needed to be cooked and processed before the lighting of the Sabbath candles the following day. Albert's mother, an imposing presence, was often there for the weekend with her husband, giving precise instructions on how to follow the dietary laws. An enormity of single-purpose saucepans simmered with separate dishes in them, and all focus was on the coming evening with its white-clothed table, candles and sung prayers.

Lien had no experience of this kind of existence: her family in The Hague kept up a few Jewish traditions, but nothing with this kind of formal weight. She did find the mechanics quite troublesome. Albert insisted that all this was necessary if his parents were to be able to visit. For him, keeping kosher was partly a social requirement rather than an absolute religious belief. At the same time, following the old customs was what made him happy, and for Lien too, in spite of the work it demanded, the orthodox life gave a sense of assurance that she was part of a group. She was, she thinks, someone without much sense of her own identity, so it was easy for her to follow where others led.

Lien and I talk about these customs. On the one hand they are a restriction, to me completely irrational, but there is also a magic to them, especially through the feeling of belonging that they confer. Nothing quite like this exists in Christianity and certainly not in my own atheist family, where even my parents are the children of non-believers who had no special rituals around mealtimes at all. Still, I can see their spiritual power. You can understand how Albert could say, 'It is easy to be happy.'

For a decade, pretty much, the patterns of the old Jewish life also helped to make Lien happy. There was a community around her, there were weddings and bar mitzvahs, there was comfort in being part of a tribe. Albert was mild and clever. He did well at his job and their children did well at school. And Lien? She was a busy mother and wife.

We leave the café and head back out into the sunshine. The ticket that we bought for the Portuguese Synagogue also covered the museum. In addition, the Hollandsche Schouwburg is part of the standard itinerary for the Jewish Cultural Quarter, although entry there is free, so Lien and I begin the half-mile walk towards it. She has never been.

Until the war, the Schouwburg was a popular theatre. In 1900, for example, it saw the premiere of *Op Hoop van Zegen* (*In the Hope of Blessing*), a play about the hard lives of North Sea fishermen, written by the Jewish playwright Herman Heijermans, which still attracts large audiences today. The Nazis briefly made it an official Jewish playhouse. Then, in August 1942, it became a kind of prison: the assembly point from which tens of thousands of Jews, who had first been concentrated in Amsterdam, were sent onwards to the transit camp of Westerbork in the north of the Netherlands and from there to the death camps in the east. For a year it was full of frightened, intensely thirsty men and women, who were often so tightly packed together that they struggled to breathe. Its task completed, the place was sold in 1944 and converted into a venue for parties, dances and weddings, which continued to be held there quite successfully even after the end of the war.

Lien and I spot the Schouwburg long before we reach it, because another white police box stands on stilts in the road guarding the entrance, its windows dull black in the bright sun. Since 1962 the Schouwburg has been a memorial. Beyond the temple-front façade, which is all that remains of the original building, there is a courtyard with benches in it and a dark stone column that sits on a base in the shape of the Star of David. On the wall to the left, as you enter, 6,700 family names look down on an eternal flame. They represent the 104,000 Dutch Jews who died.

The contrast between this and the sunny street where, a moment ago, we were chatting quite happily is absolute. A few figures in heavy coats stand alone in silence. Two people are whispering as they scan the list of names. It is a good thing that this is now a place of remembrance instead of a party venue, but the wall (from which the names shine green, back-lit, through darkened glass) has a clinical quality to it. The names of the dead run – long and then short and then long again – column after column, like a patient's cardiogram:

Jolis
Jolles
Jolofs
Jonas
Jong
Jong, de

Jong-van Lier, de
Jonge
Jonge, de

From a plastic trough we are handed a device like a mobile phone to point at the names of our choosing, but there are so many de Jongs that we have to scroll through to select the ones who lived at number 31 in the Pletterijstraat (an address that pops up in a little 'active map' in a square on the right):

Charles de Jong
Rotterdam, 10 December 1906 – Auschwitz, 6 February 1943

Catharina de Jong-Spiero
The Hague, 28 October 1913 – Auschwitz, 9 November 1942

On the memory bar of the touchscreen we are presented with various options, such as 'Print family', 'Add a family member', 'FAQ' and 'Donate!'

'I'm going home,' says Lien.

After hugging her goodbye at the exit and agreeing on a time for dinner at her apartment, I head upstairs, where there are still some scruffy rooms that are attached to the original façade. For an hour I stand hunched over old display cases that contain some intensely moving objects (a bundle of farewell letters, for example, and an infant's clog). Then I leave the old theatre, cross the road and head down a side street, with the gates of the city's zoo to my right.

Two minutes later I am at the doors of the Resistance Museum. The building, like the Hollandsche Schouwburg, was once a centre of Jewish culture, having been built for a choral society whose Star of David is still there on the gable facing the street. There is a fixed route through the collection, a kind of tunnel with plasterboard walls that takes you from invasion to liberation, past a series of windows that show things like official call-up papers and false identity cards. Over time, as you follow the route, the national mood shifts from reluctant acceptance to mass opposition, with violent reprisals from the Nazis becoming more common. Occasionally, the tunnel opens out on to a mocked-up interior, such as one where an illegal news-sheet is being produced.

Secret printing played a big part in the story of Dutch resistance. As well as providing information to those who were directly fighting the Germans, it helped to build a new national identity, which became all-important after the war. Even today, a substantial part of the national media (including newspapers such as *Trouw, Vrij Nederland* and *Het Parool* and the publisher De Bezige Bij) has its origins in the underground press.

Set against this, there was government propaganda. In an imitation town square I look up at billboards on walls and street hoardings. 'MUSSERT SPEAKS', announces a poster bearing the face of the Dutch fascist leader, who became a powerless head of state in December 1942. Mussert, a clownish version of the already clownish Mussolini, never got much of a following, but the other images that I see around me undoubtedly had some effect. Many feature cartoons of attractively vulnerable women, cast down amidst debris and blood. 'BOLSHEVISM IS MURDER' and 'THIS IS THE SECOND FRONT' they call out, while the women's modest dresses, in spite of all their best efforts, ride up to reveal curvaceous thighs. Alongside these posters of women there are others with muscled blond men, whose chins stand resolute in the face of great blasts of cold air. 'TOUGH GUYS FOR THE WAFFEN SS', 'BE BRAVE, BE A STORMER' and 'A NEW NETHERLANDS IN A NEW EUROPE, JOIN THE BATTLE WITH THE NSB' these announce. On one there is also a bearded, hooked-nosed villain, who clasps a little dagger and flaunts a six-pointed star.

*

I am the last to leave the museum. Having retrieved my suitcase, I walk through the centre of Amsterdam to Lien's apartment, crossing little humped-back bridges, looking into shops and cafés, and dodging bicycles all the way. When I get there Lien is busy in the kitchen. She sends me through to the seating area, where she puts out some bowls of snacks and a glass of beer. It will be our last evening together before I fly back to the UK.

After dinner, Lien fetches a letter. It is a long one, from Ma to her, dating from the early months of her marriage. It responds to Lien's worries about a growing distance between the affluent and orthodox religious world she has now entered and the more basic values of the family in Dordt:

> Dear Lien
>
> Oh, oh, sometimes a whole life does not make us any wiser I think. How uncertain and how vulnerable you are. And you so often take things differently from how they were meant! . . . You are worried, you say, about the distance between Albert's family and ours when it comes to atmosphere and life view and that this will always be there.
>
> Look, Lientje, I see it like this.
>
> When you came to us in those years as a child and a growing girl we were often so grateful that you were with us.
>
> Perhaps you remember one time, when you'd come back from Bennekom, I said, 'That Lien, now she is home again and luckily not at all changed.'
>
> And you said, 'Unchanged? I'm so happy!'
>
> You were amazed, I think, that I said you were the same.

Ma reflects on the war and its fear and hardships and also about her money worries. Then she says:

> Now I must tell you that our dear little Lord has blessed me very
> much in life in being unmissable for others. I was twenty-eight and
> had four children to look after and only one of them was my own.
> You had all been shaped by others and sometimes you looked very
> critically on what I was doing. When you have a child yourself you
> must in all honesty imagine for yourself for a moment what it would
> be like to have three more, all dependent on you for everything.

'But still,' she continues:

> I sometimes had this great feeling of joy because I felt so needed.
> What is there, I ask you, that a person could want in life more
> than that?

She writes about the marriages of Kees and Ali and about Pa:

> Pa also needs support and he comes off worst with me because
> somewhere (and I tell you this in confidence) I do have a sense of
> resentment that he has left the care of you all pretty much entirely
> to me. But still, everywhere we go we are met with great respect
> and admiration and that did not come out of nothing. That has cost
> Pa a lot of effort and it has also taken a lot of sacrifices from me.

She describes some of the pressures upon her: parents and a
sick sister to look after, her own children, and then grandchildren as well.

> And who is there to comfort me amidst all these troubles? Everyone
> expects something from me. It is nice to be unmissable, but it is also
> very tiring.

Ma paints a picture of a chaotic St Nicholas evening a few days
ago, where there were half a dozen children in her care:

Anne screaming, completely exhausted. Anneke and Geert Jan
fighting over a toy. A moment later, Anneke vomiting because she had
swallowed far too large a piece of bread. And then Gerard was insulted
because I dared to find it disgusting. Really it was like some comedy in
the cinema. It was all easy enough to manage eventually, but you have
to be used to it. Imagine your Albert in the midst of all that!

And because of this, my dear 'Pientje. For us you will always
belong to us, but we want to protect you from being closed off to the
outside world. You have to make choices in life. You will never lose
the things you left behind that were valuable to you. We did so
much in the past to make for happiness in life.

Ma worries about some of the choices she made as a mother,
that she sent her adopted or fostered children into the world
too soon, that she pushed them away with a sense of release.
Then she closes:

Now, 'Pien, I'm going to stop here, there is no more to say. Try to
come for Christmas for a few days. Maybe Albert can come and
collect you afterwards?

Bye, Lienepien. Love from Mum, who will always love you just
as much as the others.

This is a kind and loving letter, filled with a true and solid
wisdom. Ma understands Lien, and for all the trouble that
lay behind them it is hard to see how the bonds that tied
these women together could break. My grandmother could
sometimes be hard and judgemental, but she was also someone with a deep sense of duty, especially towards her children.
How could things go from such a letter to the one that severed
contact for good?

24

The newly-weds, Lien and Albert, buy their furniture from Bas van Pelt at number 24 Leidsestraat in Amsterdam. Its enormous front window, more than three times her height, reveals an almost empty interior: a grey stone floor, white walls and a white ceiling, all perfectly featureless and flat. For the first five metres beyond the glass there is nothing to look at. Then, set back at unconventional angles: a steel and glass table, a curving bright orange armchair and an inverted standard lamp. The shop smells of polished wood and leather and there is music playing. As they enter they receive a smile from the sales assistant, who wears a purple tie. Lien and Albert move freely, her heels clipping on the steps as they climb to the showrooms upstairs. The two of them lounge back on a sofa to try out its feel.

They already have a flat in Eindhoven, assigned to them by Albert's new employer, Philips. Its windows look out on to a helipad and several times a day Lien watches as the helicopter lands like a dragonfly on the yellow 'H' that is painted on the concrete below her, its rotors crushing a neat circle in the surrounding grass.

Eindhoven is a hi-tech city. As well as being the home of Philips, it houses the Technical University, the Design School, and Brabantia, a firm that makes sleek pedal waste bins and other household products from stainless steel. Near the centre of town there is, from 1966, a huge concrete flying saucer called the Evoluon, which sits alongside a clock tower with rocket-like fins. People from all around the country come just to gaze at it, like crowds do in films when the aliens land.

Albert is a chemist, but he works in the Physics Laboratory, which for him is like a playroom with its wires, switches, tubes and screens. He has always loved this. Even in the war, while his family hid during the night in the ceiling of a house that was attached to a small factory, he built his own radio from scrap equipment and conducted experiments with chemicals that he found lying around. They are making such amazing things, he tells her: small stereos that you can carry and run off batteries, magnetic tape that stores images as well as sound. Each morning he cycles off like a schoolboy, eager for the day ahead.

Soon there are children to complete the picture. They appear one by one on the family photos in Lien's album. First a baby girl in white in the arms of her proud mother; then two children seated between the couple on the sofa, with Mum holding an arm to keep the little boy straight; then three, all laughing, squeezed together, with the youngest, another boy, holding hands with his brother in the middle. Batja in 1960, Daan in 1964 and, finally, Arjeh in 1970. They are happy. The boys do judo and football, and Batja is a great debater at school. Reports from the teachers say that they are doing well. The final photo in Lien's album of the family together is perfect: three beaming childish faces, Albert above them with a gawky grin, and Lien smiling blissfully with her eyes cast down at her lap.

Time passes. It is not right for her to work now that she is married with children. She sits as a volunteer on various committees, and in her spare time mixes with other housewives, who are mostly also Jewish and whose husbands also work long hours at impressive-sounding jobs. Life could hardly be better. They host dinner parties or invite families over so that the children can play. In the holidays they fly or take the sleeper train to pretty cottages in Austria or Italy or southern

France. And really she is not all that busy, at least not in the way that it was at home with Ma and Pa. There are all those modern conveniences – the fridge, the washing machine, the dryer, the vacuum cleaner – and there is also a lady who comes round to clean. Because of this, quite often she finds herself at the edge of some playground, or at home when the children are sleeping, with hours to spare. In the large modern kitchen of the house that they buy a few years later, Lien feels like a cut out picture of a perfect wife from a magazine.

Those hours of spare time are a luxury for her, but she tries her best to fill them with social engagements and charity work. This is partly to be useful, but it is also because the spare time brings questions and she has never asked questions before. They are inconvenient and sometimes frightening. Who is she really? Where does she belong? What is it that she believes?

Along with the questions there is, over the years, a new anxiety over the answers. Once, at Daan's nursery, they asked her to put a baby book together (a few little facts about the family that he could learn), but when they explained the idea it sent a sudden wave of panic through her and she had to leave. The past, which was once so easy to hide from, now looms ever darker, like a vast shadow that she knows lies behind her but that she dare not face. So she keeps on going to the coffee mornings and she keeps on smiling at the playground's edge.

All the same – as the decade passes, as Kennedy is replaced by Johnson and Johnson by Nixon; as history moves from the Cuban Missile Crisis towards defeat in Vietnam; as the Prague Spring is crushed; as Paris riots; and as people march to ban the bomb – at night the questions creep in upon her, even though the doctor has given pills to help her sleep. Aunt Roza told her how it happened: Lien's mother and grandmother, together, hand in hand.

She has never looked into it, but her mother must have been younger when she died than Lien is now.

'I ought not to be here.' It is the sentence that she cannot get out of her head. Like drumming it sits there in the background, growing ever more loud. And as it gets louder she feels that she does not belong to the world around her. She does not belong to the lovely house, to the lovely furniture and to the lovely kids. She brings a darkness with her. It becomes an effort to smile.

Albert goes to the synagogue, but the synagogue has stopped working for her. The potions and the conjuring – Shabbat, Rosh Hashanah, Hanukkah, Pesach, Yom Kippur – they feel like husks, with no content at all. And it frustrates her that Albert continues to follow these rules that have no purpose. He has no time for the questions she is asking, and he tells her simply to be happy and to carry on. But his mildness is now a kind of nothing, just like the words in the synagogue are nothing. Inside she feels that she is changing: a new being – fearsome, demanding, hungry – opens inside her like a seed.

Up to now, in life, she feels that she has made no choices, that she has had no real opinions, and that somehow this is all because she has not dared to look behind her at the past. But then, when she sees that past, in glimpses, she is frightened and she hears the sentence in her head that tells her that she should not be here, that she should have died in Auschwitz alongside all the others.

After a happy decade, once the 1970s start she is again free-falling, listless but fretful, cut out from the world. And with Albert she cannot even start to share this, because while she sits frozen, full of hidden turmoil, he is quite unchanging, tied to old conventions, keeping all his daily habits, kind but rigid, without understanding for her inner life.

*

Meanwhile, as Lien looks ever closer inwards, Ma van Es looks outward and places her worries there. In the diary that she kept up for around a decade, Ma writes of how she cannot understand the way that people all around her seem to exist in isolation, free from duty and appreciation of the good things they have. Though she often mentions her fondly, Ma thinks that Lien, like all of her adult children, is too introspective, asking unnecessary and pretentious questions while the world is under threat. Also, in her darkest hours, Ma is haunted by a fear of returning war:

> Last night I was hit by a terror. I hope that if something like this happens again I will be able to fight it because for the whole of last night and for the whole of this day I have seen in front of me what would happen if a third world war broke out. Pa would be the first to be taken by the Russians, or worse. And you all [meaning her children], I have never found you so lovely and all-consuming. And Marianne, if I should not be able to see her growing older, and Henk, such a fine young healthy boy, and Ali, who is expecting her second baby, and little Anneke. And all the others. Oh, what a terrible thing.

As she grows older, Ma feels that time moves ever faster, and yet, in the midst of her global worries, she still takes new people into her care. When her sister, Bep, gets divorced, for example, and arguments are raging that might be harmful for the children, Ma takes in her nephew and niece for half a year. It all takes its toll on her psyche. She knows that she is getting fatter, but she can never stick to her diets. As always, Ma worries that she is not an attractive woman, that she is not the right match for her strong and active husband.

In the end it is really with little children that Ma is in her element: she feels their illnesses intensely and she glories in their small moments of triumph. Seeing her foster-daughter and stepdaughter – Lien and Ali – pregnant gives her intense pleasure, and at the birth of Lien's 'gorgeous little girl' Batja she writes of overwhelming expectation and joy. Motherhood, for Ma, is a defining purpose in life.

This note on Lien's role as a mother, though, is amongst the last entries in Ma's diary. 'I am thinking of stopping with this book,' she writes a few pages later. 'I am writing so irregularly and it is not interesting I think.' Run-down and feeling less purposeful without young children, Ma is, she admits, increasingly prone to grumbling in spite of her best efforts to keep her spirits up.

By the start of the 1970s, Ma and Lien are quite distant from one another. They meet at birthday parties and perhaps at Christmas, but the contact between them rarely runs deep. When Lien calls on the telephone, Ma answers, 'I'll call you back,' but she rarely does.

Then on the evening of the Day of Atonement in September 1972, it is Albert's turn to give a talk at the synagogue. Lien will not join him. As so often, she instead sits at home, watching the rain as it runs in tracks down the windows, her head fogged by the sentence she cannot escape.

At 9.30 p.m. she hears Albert's key in the door.

'How was the talk you gave?'

'If you'd have been there,' he answers, 'you would have known.'

His irritation is not unexpected, but when he says this something strange happens inside her. It is as if a magic word has been spoken, as if a switch has been flicked. Lien gets up from the sofa and heads upstairs, her feet heavy, then crosses the carpeted landing, enters the bathroom and opens the cabinet that hangs above the sink on the wall.

To her at this moment it is the perfect solution. She almost smiles at its brilliance. What if, in an instant, she just wasn't there?

She normally does not like to swallow pills and cannot really do it. They just sit there on her tongue, the water washing over them, leaving a bitter taste in her mouth. That is why she has taken so few. That is why there are so many left. But this time it is easy. It is all so efficient. In no time at all the white plastic rectangles are empty and there is nothing left to push through the foil. With slow deliberate movements, she puts the packet of sleeping pills back in the cabinet and walks down the stairs.

Outside it is still raining. She sits down on the sofa. The sound of the rain is a comfort because it helps her to sleep.

25

There is a photo of Ben Spiero, Lien's cousin, that was taken at her wedding in 1959. It is the first image that I have of him since those baby snaps from the Pletterijstraat, where he sits, thumb in mouth, round-faced, on his mother's lap with Lien beside him in her checked dress with a white bow in her hair. On the photograph at the wedding he is in his mid twenties, seated at a table just after the dinner has finished. My grandfather is in shot directly behind him, looking animated in conversation with a group of other guests. Ben's face is a shock to me. A thick ugly scar runs from one corner of his cheek to the other, and the eye furthest from us stares out blankly at an odd angle, hooded and blind. The damage to his face was the result of a motorbike accident that happened years after the war had ended, but the way he drove was connected to a sense of abandonment, which Lien also felt. Like Lien he was handed over by his parents to the resistance. Like her, he

suffered horrors during the war. A short while after this photo was taken, Ben Spiero succeeded in hanging himself.

For some days it was touch and go whether Lien would survive the overdose. Albert rushed her to hospital, where she stayed for over a week. Then, in celebration of her homecoming, he organized a little party. 'The unhappiness is over,' he wrote on the cards that he sent to their circle of friends. As much as anything, the fact that these cards were written in all sincerity showed the distance between them, that he had failed to understand her, or perhaps that she had failed to explain.

'It was like being the guest of honour at my own funeral,' says Lien.

Ma's reaction is the opposite of Albert's. She is furious. Taking pills and abandoning your husband and children is an insult to everything she believes. After all the sacrifices that people have made for her, how could she be so selfish? What kind of person would do such a thing?

What kind of person? Yes, that is the question. What kind of person is she when you cut out what surrounds her, when you cut out the scientist husband, the synagogue and the comforts of a prosperous life? Does she really belong to the van Esses, or to the world of Jewish ritual, or to something entirely different that she has yet to find?

Her attempt at suicide was a terrible error, she can see that, and she promises her older children, aged eight and twelve, that she will never do anything like that again. But to go back now to the coffee mornings and the kosher cooking, to go back to leaving questions unanswered, that she also will not do.

In the years that follow, Lien works at her problems. There are various unsuccessful therapies, such as a time spent in analysis, with the psychiatrist sitting in a chair behind her as she lies there on his couch. It frightens her that she cannot see him.

'This man who started to kiss you,' he asks, 'am I right in thinking he is the man who saved your life?'

The sessions of psychoanalysis do not help her and they are abandoned, but there are other approaches that do. Lien finds solace in meditation, in the teachings of Buddhism, in Humanism and in discussions with new groups of friends. What is it, she asks herself, that she really wants from life? What is it that she believes? Is there a pattern to history from which we can learn?

Wanting to be stronger as a person, Lien decides to return to work. With Albert it is not easy. He does not see why anything has to change and, because of this, life at home starts to fill with tension and with petty rows. This is hard on the children, who, as so often happens in these situations, tend to blame themselves.

It is the spring of 1979 when the phone rings. Pa has lung cancer. Years of work with asbestos and many more of heavy smoking did not leave him with much of a chance and by the autumn he is dying in hospital and she is seated beside him on a visit as he lies there in bed. There is whiteness all around him, his face leaner than ever now that the cancer is eating him up.

She sits there and they speak of nothing. In all the years since she first came to stay with the van Esses, they have rarely been together alone.

Lien passes him a plastic cup of water that he holds and then spills with his blotched hands.

She does not say 'Thank you' or 'I love you' or 'Something did happen when you tried to kiss me like that in the Frederik-straat when I was twenty and it changed things for ever for me.' This family does not speak of such things. But then, what family does?

'I'll come and see you next week again,' Lien tells him.

'Yes, do that,' he says, almost without breath.

And then, three days later, Ma calls to tell her that Pa has died.

As expected, a white envelope edged with grey drops through the letterbox a week later. This will be the card with the funeral arrangements, but when she opens it the text cuts into her stomach like a knife:

Hendrik van Es
husband of
Jannigje van Es-de Jong

Dordrecht, 8 November 1906 – Dordrecht,
20 October 1979

Ali and Gerard
Kees and Truus
Marianne and Pierre
Henk and Dieuwke
Geert Jan and Renée

Grandchildren and great-grandchildren

They have listed all of Pa's children and their partners, but her own name is missing from the card. It is so unexpected that she can hardly believe it. Her fingers feel weak.

But it is not a mistake, far from it. The instructions are clear: there will be official mourning cars for Ma and the children, whereas Lien must travel with the aunts, uncles and other family members that follow behind. Pa was firm on the matter: Lien was not to be shown to the world as his child.

Albert cannot see the point of making a fuss about the arrangements. After all, she was his foster-daughter, which is different, and what does it matter what car you ride in or whether you are listed on some card? If need be it can be discussed at some later moment, but now is hardly the time. At the reception, he chats quite happily with the other mourners, staying longer than is necessary, while Lien shifts awkwardly between the tables of sandwiches, wondering when she might leave.

For Lien, it is obvious now that their marriage is over: she has changed but he has not. In the big house that they have bought to get more space from each other they avoid contact, have separate routines. She had wanted to explore the big questions, to meet different sorts of people, but he is set, unrelenting, in his ways. From his perspective, Albert cannot see why she makes things so difficult, why everything could not stay as it was at the start. In 1980 he leaves the household, taking a nearby flat, while she remains at home with their youngest son as they make plans to sell their beautiful villa, which sits at a sharp V-shaped junction where two roads meet.

So here she is, aged forty-seven, a divorced woman making a fresh start. Lien had qualified as a social worker on the day of her marriage, but it is only now, at the start of the 1980s, that she begins to work full-time. She takes a job with Eindhoven Social Services and, once the villa is sold, buys a modest house in a livelier part of the city. It is in a planned estate known as the White Village, designed in the 1930s by Willem Dudok, where busy playgrounds full of children blend in with terraces that have art deco curves. Neighbours here put yellow 'Nuclear Energy? No Thanks!' stickers on the quirky porthole windows that sit in the long identical lines of front doors. This makes it a kind of blend of the style that she shared with Albert and the messy communal warmth that she remembers from her childhood in Dordt. Her life here is not straightforward (the work that she does with families is difficult; her children have their problems as they grow up), but this existence is something that she has chosen and, for the first time in more than a decade, Lien feels that she belongs.

A few years later she embarks on a new relationship. He is someone she and her family have known since she first moved to Eindhoven, a widower named Bernard, who is known to everyone as 'Ber'. Although he is three decades older, it does not feel like it. Still youthful-looking, he has swept-back silver hair and wears shirts buttoned to the top without a tie. An amateur actor and director, Ber has a passion for art, books, opera, and also for the big questions in life. What she loves most is his childlike enthusiasm, the way that he can talk for hours, for example, about the characters in a play. As he prowls the stage in some piece of modernist German theatre, he seems eternally young.

By the summer of 1987 she and Ber have been a couple for four years. Then, all of a sudden, in the midst of rehearsals for his latest production (*The Wedding* by Elias Canetti), he becomes dizzy and gets headaches: it is a brain tumour. He has just a few months to live. Given the difference in their ages she was always likely to outlive him, but the change is far more rapid than she could have imagined. Once the doctors have decided that intervention is impossible, he is moved to a hospice, at first spending his weekends at home with Lien. By the start of the autumn he cannot remember her and needs feeding, mouthful by mouthful, as he lies blankly in bed, where he is visited by many friends.

It is with Ber on her mind that Lien drives to Dordrecht one morning that August to see Ma. The house that Ma rents is part of the big new estate in the south of the city, one of the many great building projects that Pa helped to establish. Number 15 Algolring is a four-bedroomed yellow-brick end-of-terrace, well maintained by the housing association and by a man who comes to do the garden once a week. In her early seventies, Ma is entirely healthy, kept vibrant by her interest in politics, her love of the grandchildren, and a firm determination to keep a clean, nice-looking house.

Lien has invited herself for coffee. She never feels terribly welcome when she phones up to arrange such visits, though Ma is very warm with Lien's children and also with Albert, with whom she has kept in touch. Lien's divorce, with which Ma was very disappointed, has not been forgiven, but the cautious distance between them runs much further back than that. Lien sometimes wonders what Pa said about that moment in the Frederikstraat, after which she left home for over a year. Was Lien's exclusion from the card and the ceremony of Pa's funeral related to that?

Ma stands at her big plate-glass window as Lien drives her Volvo into the cul-de-sac and then edges it backwards and forwards, trying to park in a smallish spot. Eventually, Lien opens the car door, clutching her bag and a bunch of white tulips, and smiles as she waves the flowers while walking up to the front porch. Ma waves back and then hugs her as she enters. She is at her best at such moments, being the hostess, welcoming people into her home. There is an easy joy in the way that she compliments Lien on the choice of tulips, in the way that she takes her coat and hangs it on one of the hooks in the hall. The house smells of coffee and lavender. Lien feels her toes on the spotless blue carpet after removing her shoes.

'I have just put the coffee on,' says Ma, heading into the kitchen, where the machine is making faint coughing sounds.

'And there is cream cake from the baker's – they do it nicely there,' she adds while unwrapping the tulips, whose stems she cuts with a pair of scissors on the worktop before arranging them in a vase.

Ma breathes a little heavily as she stands there working.

'Can I do anything to help?'

'You can put those on the dining table,' comes the answer as Ma moves towards the fridge.

So Lien carries the vase of flowers, first into the hallway, and then into a long room that is filled with light from the big windows at either end. Turning, she sees Ma through the serving hatch, which connects to the kitchen. Ma is whisking milk in a pan on the hob.

'I'll be there in a minute,' Ma calls, without looking round.

Lien wanders across to the seating area. There are two fairly new, dark brown sofas, a glass table, plus an armchair with an extendable leg-rest that matches the sofas. Against the wall is a unit of built-in shelves and cupboards in dark wood and glass. As always, Lien walks over to it and looks in at the lit-up glass menagerie of hedgehogs, swans, rabbits, owls and poodles, which cast little rainbows of broken light.

Ma enters with a tray on which two shop-cut triangles of cake sit on separate saucers. Glossy circles of egg-yolk-yellow apricot nestle amongst the folds of cream. The cups have happy domestic scenes printed on them, with apple-cheeked mothers serving trays of coffee and cake. They are like miniature portraits of Ma in her prime.

Using the glass jug from the percolator, Ma fills the cups and adds frothy milk, which she spoons across from the pan. In her own she puts two cubes of light brown sugar. Then, after a few mouthfuls of the rich cake, they begin to talk about Dordrecht and the family circle: changes to the bus timetable, restructuring at Geert Jan's workplace, the health of her friends, how Lien's children are doing. It is all perfectly friendly, but it is Ma who runs the conversation and there is no mention of Ber.

'Do you have plans for your birthday?' Ma asks after a moment of silence.

It is common for Lien to host a lunch or a small drinks party to mark the occasion, although Ma (who now rarely travels far beyond Dordrecht) often does not come.

'I won't do anything this year. Fifty-four is nothing special and with Ber in the hospice it doesn't feel right,' says Lien.

They talk a little more about other upcoming birthdays, where they will see each other, and then, after a second cup of coffee, it is clear that the visit is at an end.

There is a hug and three kisses and then Ma stands again at the big window as Lien edges the car backwards and forwards to exit the parking space. Once she is clear, Lien gives a final wave. Then there is a high whine from the engine as she reverses down the narrow street.

The weather is pleasant that September, with sunny days and temperatures in the mid twenties. Before and straight after work, Lien goes to Ber in the hospice, where he lies, suddenly immensely old-looking, in a raised surgical bed. No conversation is possible, so she sits there holding his hand, looking out at the gardens and welcoming visitors.

Every day, Ber's daughter, Miep, calls from Israel, asking for news on her father's health. Then, as the situation worsens, she fixes on a week to fly over and see him for what must be the final time. Lien and she get on well together, but there is little point in them both sitting there for so many hours, and, besides, it will be good for Miep to have some time with her father alone. So, for one weekend, Lien has a bit of free time.

As it happens, it all works out nicely. The weather is still gorgeous and so Lien suggests to a friend that they book a hotel at the seaside and go walking together for a couple of days. After all those months in the hospice it is just what she needs.

For this reason, on 7 September, Lien is walking across the dunes with the wind in her face, looking out at the van Speijk Lighthouse, which has stood on the sands of Egmond since 1833. Its copper turret blazes in the sunlight, and as they come closer they make out the golden mermaid on its weathervane. By the time they get back to the hotel's little foyer, the two of them are happy with tiredness. Then, just as they are about to head up to their bedrooms, they are greeted by the welcoming cheers of two old friends. This birthday gathering, planned in secret, comes as a complete surprise.

One of the friends is Esther van Praag, the sister of her stand-in foster-father, the man who would have been there with his wife to look after her if anything had ever happened to Ma and Pa. Esther has known Lien, as a kind of niece really, for a very long time.

The other woman, who rushes up to embrace her, is Took.

A widow for decades now, white-haired and nearly eighty, Took Heroma is still as vibrant as ever. She envelops Lien with a feeling of wonder, just as she did when Lien was a little child. There is that sense of her as a great personage – a former parliamentarian, a former delegate at the United Nations, a former member of the Labour Party's governing board – but also an intensity of contact as she asks her, with both hands resting on Lien's shoulders, about Ber.

The glasses for the wine are set out ready on a table in the bar, and they have made a restaurant booking, an easy five-minute walk away down the street. Lien is completely happy: the talk is on all her favourite topics, the food is perfect, they laugh till they are short of breath.

*

Ber passes away that November. His life is celebrated at a large and beautiful funeral, in which Lien plays a full part. There is sadness but also a sense of completion – a life well lived and a duty done.

Then, early in the new year, there is another van Es birthday: a party in a house in Dordrecht with wine and children and slices of cake. Lien arrives, gives her flowers to the hostess and mingles amongst family and friends.

Ma is there, seated in an armchair. Something is wrong though, because when Lien gets closer Ma stares darkly and turns her head. After a bit, Lien plucks up the courage to approach her, perching on a sofa to one side.

Ma's voice, normally so forceful, comes through very soft.

'I don't want to talk to you,' she says, turning to look into space. The two of them are so close together, almost touching, but they sit there locked in silence, cut off from each other and from the hubbub all around.

'But what is the matter?' asks Lien, frightened.

You can see that it pains Ma to speak.

'I only think it's very dishonest,' she says at last with her jaws locked together. Her words barely make sense. Then she adds, 'I heard all about it from Took,' and Lien understands, after a few seconds, that this is about her birthday party, which she had told Ma would not be happening but was organized anyway by Esther and Took.

Explanation is useless. Her failure to mention the party after it happened, it seems, is enough of a betrayal, and Ma, seeing the whole thing as a conspiracy, believes nothing that Lien says. When Lien will not move to sit elsewhere, Ma lifts herself with an effort and tells one of the other children that she wants to be driven home.

★

That night Lien writes a letter. It is the 'terrible letter' that Ma tears to pieces after reading it only once. For Lien, it is a letter of explanation: of the birthday party, of how important Ma is to her and of how much she loves her, but also of her mixed feelings towards Pa. Of that moment in the Frederikstraat when he tried to kiss her she says nothing, but she does say that she always loved Ma more than she loved him. Lien thinks that this will resolve the situation, but such letters are dangerous. Letters such as these are not read in the way they were intended. Their recipients will pull the most jagged phrases from them and the rest will flow, unnoticed, through their hands.

If I look for a moment from my grandmother's perspective, I think I can see the source of her anger, though this is not to say that her actions were right. She had no vocabulary for trauma. To her, Lien, as she returned from Bennekom, was just a difficult and rather sullen child. Later, Lien's attempted suicide and her divorce went against everything that Ma believed in. She found Lien self-indulgent. Moreover, Ma was saddened by the state of the modern world. And then for Lien to go out and be secretly happy with Took of all people and to write a letter of explanation in which Pa was treated with a lack of respect, this ignited an anger that had for a long time burned low.

Ma did not, I expect, think of Lien's exclusion from the funeral arrangements or of the many harsh words she had spoken to Lien over the years.

A day later a lilac envelope drops through Lien's letterbox at the Burghstraat in Eindhoven. The address is scratchily written 'To Mrs L. de Jong' and the stamps are pasted at awkward angles, one upside down.

Lien was reluctant at first to show me the letter. As she hands it to me, she averts her eyes.

Dordt 7.4.'88

To Lien

   As you know I do not like writing letters. They are always the cause of misunderstandings. But I still want to ask you not to call me etc., for a while. That seems to me, given the situation, the best way to proceed.

With best wishes
Mrs v Es

These are the last words Lien ever received from my grandmother, who died seven years later, the quarrel unresolved.

26

It is so trivial, an argument over a birthday party, when compared to a history that paired the two of them together against the backdrop of the Second World War. All the same, the row escalates quickly. Ma tells the rest of her children not to contact Lien, that Lien has written terrible things in a letter, that she will not ever again be in the same room as Lien. Attempts to persuade Ma to reconsider are met only by anger. Though some of Lien's siblings do at times reach out to her, the connection between Lien and the rest of the family is broken from this point on.

In June 1995 Lien hears from my mother of Ma's passing. Uninvited, she attends the funeral and listens to a colourless service in which Lien (and in fact the whole war and Ma's part in it) is left as a blank. She feels entirely cut out.

But perhaps there is such a thing as creative destruction? Starting with a counsellor at her work, Lien begins the task of rebuilding: long hours of therapy through which she slowly discovers a balanced sense of herself. She visits the Jewish Historical Museum and requests the dates of her parents' deaths and the details of how they died. Lien's 'Concrete Story of My Relations with the Van Es Family', the document that I first read in my hotel room in Dordrecht, is a product of this time.

There was also another breakthrough that came a little earlier. It was a kind of reunion, a Conference for the Hidden War Child, which in 1992 brought together more than 500 surviving child hideaways in Amsterdam. For three days in August, those who had gone into hiding as children exactly fifty years earlier got to know each other through workshops, speeches and poetry readings, through the sharing of photos on bulletin boards, through films, psychology lectures, and countless conversations one-to-one. Lien found it a moment of recognition because so many others there had, like her, been haunted for decades by the feeling that they did not belong in the world. The organization that ran the conference, the Society for Jewish Social Work, produced a daily newspaper to circulate amongst those attending, so that they could record their experiences and respond to those of others. As children who had grown up in isolation, almost all felt that the sharing of stories was something they had always lacked and craved.

Ed van Thijn, the mayor of Amsterdam, himself a wartime child hideaway, started the conference off with this theme of the 'untold story'. Though comfortable with public speaking, including public speaking about the Holocaust, he had, he told the audience in his opening address, been thrown into panic at the thought of having to tell them something personal. 'Even yesterday,' he said to the hall of 500 hideaways, 'I did not know what I should, or rather what I could, say.' Only at the last minute did it occur to him that to speak of oneself as a hidden child was, almost by definition, an impossible thing:

> To whom should we have spoken? Who was really able to listen to our story? The story of hiding has defined our whole existence, but we – at least most of us – have tried desperately all our lives to drive that story away.

Lien cried when she heard this, as did almost all the others around her in the room.

The Conference for the Hidden War Child was in retrospect the first stage in her move to Amsterdam, where she now feels that she has at last found her place. She has kept in touch with the Society for Jewish Social Work, which sends out a magazine and organizes non-religious trips and small-scale get-togethers for the roughly 30,000 Jews still living in the Netherlands, mostly in this city. Lien sits across from me in the chair that she bought with Albert all those years ago in the fashionable Amsterdam shop, looking content:

'After all that counselling and those nights of crying, it was finally over for me. I can talk about it now without emotion, though that might sound strange. In Buddhism there is this concept of waves in history and the way that people are caught up in them. You see that you cannot control everything and there is peace in sensing that bigger flow.'

She hugs her teacup, a little embarrassed by the grandness of her speech.

'Anyway,' she continues, 'once I could place what had happened to me in a pattern, things changed for me. I could make choices, like the choice to live here in Amsterdam.'

The magic of the city is still with me from this morning: its spires, bridges, and the lines of step-gabled houses shining across the water in the cold January light. Quite tranquil even at its centre, Amsterdam does seem like a place at peace with itself.

From her pretty white-walled house in Eindhoven, Lien moved first to a scruffy little worker's cottage in De Pijp, a youthful district known for its street market, cafés and rebellious, alternative vibe. Her friends were a bit worried for her, but Lien was happy. She bought a season ticket to the opera, visited art galleries, attended lectures on Buddhism, started meditation and yoga, and met many new people. Then, after fifteen years, she heard of a group of friends, many of them artists or social workers, who had a plan for living together in retirement. As a move it came a bit early, but the chance was perfect, so she asked if she could join them. It is in this block of apartments that we are speaking now.

Lien puts her cup on the table and pours some more peppermint tea.

'It was only then – I'm not good with dates, but it must have been 2003 or something like that – that I felt ready to face Auschwitz. I'd been so frightened of it till then. I thought: I can't do that. If I went with non-Jewish people I feared that something might be said that would hurt me. And then, if it was with other Jews, it would be this trail of collective trauma and I didn't want that either, so I just never dared. But I heard about a Buddhist teacher who took people to Auschwitz for a week's vigil, where it was possible to say something personal, and that felt like the right thing to do. They made a video of it. Shall we watch it together?'

And so, moments later, we are again seated at her desk, looking at her computer. It is just what we did for her testimony to the Shoah Foundation. Now, though, the Lien on the recording is much closer in age to the one beside me. What is also different from last time is that Lien is happy with the images that play out before us on the screen.

'I found it such a positive experience. I was given all the time I needed. People were crying. It was done with respect,' she says as the film begins.

There, through the hell-mouth gateway, amidst broken walls and lines of rusted barbed wire, stands Lien, her skin blue-white with cold. On the video there is sharp, chilling, discordant music that is somehow human and a voiceover that tells us the facts of what happened in this factory of death. The Buddhist group spent many long days together conducting their vigils. They stayed for a week, sleeping in a kind of hostel, sitting and standing for hours on railway lines, in the barracks and in the gas chambers themselves.

On the DVD, the scene changes and the camera pans to show windowless concrete rooms that are lit only by a few candles. Within them, people crouch and stare into the middle distance or whisper prayers with tight-shut eyes. Midway through, there comes the point where Lien is given her moment to address the vigil. She stands in the half-light of the former women's barracks, a wide circle of people around her, and speaks in English with a series of long pauses, her voice breaking now and again. Including the slight imperfections in grammar, these are the exact words that Lien speaks:

When I was eight years old, I went hiding and I said goodbye to my father and mother and I thought it was just for a few weeks.

And it went on and on and it did not end and I didn't see them any more.

My father was Charles de Jong and he died in Auschwitz and he was thirty-seven.

My mother was Catharine Spiero and she died together with her mother, Sara Verveer. My mother died when she was twenty-nine, and my – my grandmother was fifty-six.

The parents of my father were David de Jong, he became fifty-eight and died with his wife, Hesseline Lion, and she became fifty-seven.

My father had one sister. She became thirty-nine and she died at the same day as her children: Serina Mozes and David Mozes. Serina was my favourite cousin and she became fifteen and David was only three months older than I was. I always played with him and he became nine.

And they all died in Auschwitz.

Their father died in Sobibór. He became forty-four.

The brother of my mother became forty-four and died in Auschwitz.

Another brother was thirty-two and he died in the middle of Europe, and his wife was thirty-six and died in Auschwitz.

And their children – and their children, Nico and Robbie, died when they were four and three years, and the eldest became – lived – after the war, but he hanged himself after the war.

And then there was one sister of my mother and she became twenty-seven and died in Auschwitz.

And I want to tell you. And I missed them the rest of my life.

After this there is silence and soft crying as Lien's long list of names is enfolded by waves of many others:

Frieda Singer, Mordecia Singer, Golda Singer, Moshe Singer . . .

And on.

We sit for a while in silence. 'It is beautiful,' I say eventually, 'the way you name them.'

Lien nods.

'I was very happy with it,' she says.

That night, I stay with friends in Leiden. The first stage of research for my book about Lien is now over. In the morning I check a few last references in the university library and make plans for a return later in the year. When we planned this trip in December, Lien told me that she would not be free on the final day of my visit. Even as late as yesterday morning she did not actually say what she would be doing, feeling a little embarrassed, perhaps, at describing something as intimate and intense as the Buddhist discussion group that she will be hosting in her flat. Yesterday evening, though, she did tell me about it and about how important these sessions now are in her life. Lien suggested we could have lunch together beforehand. The Buddhist meeting does not start until 2.30. Before the members of the group start arriving, I could move to the front section of the apartment, which can be shut off from the sitting area with a set of glass doors. I could sit and work there before heading off, at about 4 p.m., to catch my flight.

So, over lunch, with sunshine cutting through the stained-glass artworks on the windows, we sit as friends together one last time for a while to come. Then, as the group will soon be arriving, Lien pulls the division across the room. This way, once the session has started, I can slip away through the side door without disturbing the people on the other side of the glass. We say goodbye to each other. I hug her. Till Easter, when I'll be back for another research trip, and sooner via a Skype call, we say.

Then Lien sets off to get the room ready and I take a seat at her desk. It seems a good idea to make copies of all the interviews, photographs and documents I have gathered. I will store these on her desktop, just to be safe. So I sit there, quietly porting the files across. After a bit, members of the group begin to drift past the window, ringing the doorbell and heading straight to the front room via the corridor as Lien welcomes them in.

When all this is finished I put a memory stick on Lien's desk, another in my pocket and a third in my suitcase. The memories that I have collected feel now like my most valued possessions. I recheck my ticket and confirm that I have my passport to hand. It is time to go. Before heading out, I move just quickly towards the glass doors that now divide the apartment, catching Lien's eye and giving her a little wave. Seated with the others, she smiles as she sees me. Then, taken up in the moment, she stands up and moves forward to open the doors. The glass folds away and she invites me in.

Lien addresses the people around her. 'This is my nephew, Bart,' she says. 'He is going to write my book.'

Epilogue: July 2017

'Without families you don't get stories.'

When I first heard these words just under three years ago I knew very little about my family's wartime history and I knew almost nothing about Lien. I also understood much less about my relationship with my own children, especially Josie, about whose troubles I had struggled to think or speak. Getting to know Lien has changed me. It has made me more reflective and less absolute. For the first time I feel I have seen someone else from the inside from the earliest stages of their life. I have also seen myself in another person, my grandmother. Not, of course, in her courage, but in some of her mistakes.

The way that Lien introduced me to her Buddhist group as a 'nephew' in January 2015 confirmed something special, the healing of a breach. I can claim no special credit for this. Lien has done the healing herself. Still, our meeting has proved to be the start of a series of fresh connections. I have since met up with her children and she has got to know mine. Last summer Lien came to visit us in Oxford, where she stayed at my parents' house, meeting my father for the first time in many years.

Lien and I meet often now as friends and keep up with each other's news. It was during her visit to Oxford that Lien first mentioned to my wife, with whom she developed an instant connection, that she was meeting up with someone, a man, who seemed nice. He was not exactly a new acquaintance. I had, in fact, seen his face on a photo on the very first day, back in December 2014, when I first met Lien.

At that point it was just a photograph amongst many others:

the school scene taken in The Hague in 1939 in which Lien, wearing a pinafore, sits with another little girl at a school bench, with two little boys to their right, wearing ties.

The picture, I later learnt, was given to her when she was twenty, and performing in a Christmas show at Middeloo College. After the performance, a lady who had been part of the audience came up to the stage.

'I think I recognize you. Are you, by any chance, Lientje de Jong?' she asked.

Lien, puzzled, said that she was.

The woman remembered her from The Hague. Lien and the woman's son, Jaap, had been at primary school together.

'I still have a photo of you,' she said. 'You and Jaap, both aged five.'

Jaap van der Ham, it turned out, was now also at Middeloo, on the same course as Lien. They knew each other, but neither remembered that they had once been classmates and even friends. A few days later Jaap's mother sent Lien a copy of the photograph, pointing out that her son was the boy with the neat side parting, shorts and long stripy socks on the far left.

Lien was not a great one for asking questions at this point in her life: the past was something on which she feared to dwell. Still, she and Jaap, although they moved in different circles, did talk on a few occasions about their shared childhood in The Hague. It turned out that they had been classmates for another two years after the photo was taken. Then, in 1941, Lien had to leave to attend the Jewish school. Jaap avoided the same move only by a fraction: his father was Jewish but his mother was not. For this reason, in March 1943, by which time Lien had already been in hiding for over half a year in Dordrecht, Jaap remained at home with his mother when his father was deported to Poland, never to return.

Lien kept the photo that Mrs van der Ham had given her,

adding it to the small collection that she had from her parents. Beyond this, though, the connection with Jaap was only a distant one. He had a steady girlfriend who soon became a fiancée, and though he was kind and charming, once the course at Middeloo was over, he and Lien lost touch.

When Lien and I met in December 2014, the photo of her as a little girl on the school bench with Jaap to one side was still a memento no different from the others. In October the following year, however, a letter was sent out by some of her former fellow students at Middeloo College in which a reunion of its old members was proposed. Jaap was one of those doing the organizing. Though Lien decided against attending, she did reply, asking how he was. There was, after all, the oddity that they had known each other as children in primary school. Her enquiry sparked an exchange of emails and then two meetings, the first in Amsterdam and the second in the village of Velp near Arnhem, where Jaap now lived.

On a bright May morning in 2016, Lien arrives on a train from Amsterdam to The Hague's Central Station. She is meeting Jaap again for the third time now. When they last met, in Velp, the two of them discussed their early years together and conversation moved to the Jewish school, which Lien said she would like to visit. Jaap, who remained living in this city until he was eighteen years old, still remembers where it stood. There is a new memorial now.

He stands there waiting in the high-ceilinged hall of the station. Although a little thickset and in need of a cane, there is still something of the schoolboy in him. He wears a flat cap and has clashing stripes on his shirt and jacket, which make Lien smile. There is a gentleness to him, an easy warmth as he moves forward to give her a hug.

Soon, on a terrace in the spring sunshine, they are drinking coffee and planning their route. First, Lien would like to pass by her old home on the Pletterijstraat, which was only a very short distance from their primary school. From there they can walk to the site of the memorial, and then have lunch. They have all day for this journey.

And so, an hour later, they stand in the red-brick archway with the door of number 31 Pletterijstraat before them. To the right, there are the concrete steps with metal railings that lead up to the landing, where there are doors for numbers 27 and 29. It was up on that landing that she used to sit with Lilly, their noses pressed against the ironwork, their feet hanging down. It was here in the hall that her mother parked her bicycle. It was down these steps that she ran to ask Mamma if she could tell the secret about going to stay somewhere else for a while. Lien and Jaap stand in silence, taking it in.

The place where their primary school once stood is now taken up by a block of apartments, dark brick and rather brutal, twelve storeys high. As 83-year-olds looking up at it they are more dwarfed by this building than they ever were, as little children, by the school itself. It feels right, being here with Jaap.

They talk together as they walk along the canal towards the centre of the city, traffic rushing beside them, its noise reflecting from the dirty windows of run-down shops. It does not need to be the big subject of the past that unites them. Conversation shifts easily between topics: a concert they might attend together; a song they remember singing in primary school; Jaap's plans for a holiday with his son in Israel; a sculpture exhibition here in The Hague this July. Now and then they stop and Jaap tells her about the things that once stood in the places where there are now hotels and offices with mirrored glass that shines in the sun: the old bakery, the greengrocer's, Lien's uncle's ironware shop.

And then they have reached it: the site of the old Jewish school. It is a pleasant square now, with modern apartment blocks looking down on to a cobbled pedestrian area that is planted with sycamore trees. There are rows of tables with sun parasols facing a sushi restaurant and, on one side, the imposing walls and gardens of a seventeenth-century church. The whole clutter of ramshackle buildings that stood here when they were children has gone. Jaap rests on his walking stick for a moment and surveys the scene.

The memorial is not conspicuous, but they find it under the sycamores: a nest of shiny stainless-steel tubing in the shape of a little cluster of chairs. As the two of them approach, they see that there are six of them, of different heights, with rungs like ladders. A bicycle is leaning against the one that is closest and, on the chair in the centre, a dark-haired girl is clambering, her face serious, determined not to fall. From a short distance, a woman looks on with an encouraging smile.

The memorial on the site of the old Jewish school is designed as a climbing frame, blending in with the hubbub of the square. Only if you look closely can you see that there are names and ages engraved on the steel tubing. They are the names of murdered children: 400 in all.

After their visit that day to the site of the former Jewish school in The Hague, Jaap and Lien have met up more and more often. This summer they went on holiday together to Spain, and they are now a couple, dividing their time between Amsterdam and the village of Velp. They enjoy country walks, museum visits, music, and spending time with their children and grandchildren, sometimes as a group. Now well into their eighties, they know this cannot last for ever, but they are happy. Lien feels connected to the world around her. She feels whole.

Acknowledgements

This has, from the beginning, been a work of partnership. The twenty-first of December 2014 was the first of many days that Lien and I spent together as this book evolved. After hours of recorded interviews there were hours of walks, meals, Skype conversations and email exchanges over which we discussed its numerous drafts. It is thanks to Lien's faith, honesty and wisdom that *The Cut Out Girl* has become a reality. Our deep friendship is something that I will always treasure.

As this is a book about families, it is a great pleasure to be able to thank family members on all sides. Lien's children – Daan, Batja and Arjeh – have been generous with their time and their memories. Getting to know them has been one of the many valuable consequences of writing this book. Their father, Albert Gomes de Mesquita, read and gave feedback on the chapters that describe his marriage and wartime experiences. He told me afterwards that he felt he did not come out very well from this story, but I hope and believe he is wrong about that.

It was thanks to my mother, Dieuwke, that I was able to make contact with Lien in the first place. From the beginning, she has worried that this project will upset people and damage the family's reputation but, in spite of this, she has continued to help with my research. The same is true for my father, Henk, who has told me a great deal about his childhood and has been an important source for my account. As with Albert, I am grateful for their open-heartedness and am confident that, seen in the round, this book will bring understanding rather than simplistic judgements on those who played a part in Lien's life.

My brother Joost, his wife, Sally, and their children have shown a great interest in the book; and my uncle Geert Jan gave me access to his mother's diary, which my aunt Greta kindly typed up for me to use. Some other relatives had no wish to be involved and I respect their reasons.

Jaap van der Ham helped with the epilogue.

On my mother's side there has been enormous generosity. Sabrina Meurs and Jan Willem Koekebakker appear briefly in these pages, but (through their friendship, insight and practical assistance) they have done far more than it is possible to record. I am also grateful to Corinne Meurs, Rob van Lummel, Steven van Lummel and Annemargreet Meurs, who put me up, cooked meals and were constantly positive about the importance of this work.

Beyond this, friends have been inspirational. Marianne Reijnhoudt, Frank Pot, Rajika Pot and Eric van Noort housed and fed me during numerous research trips. It was a privilege to share the book with them as it developed over time. Many other people opened their doors to me on my travels: Wout de Bond, Corrie Verhoef-de Bond, Marianne van der Top and Sascha and Ruud van Gageldonk to name but some.

Experts in the field have been exceptionally giving. Ad van Liempt, whose many books I have read and reread, took time to meet me and explain the workings of the National Archives in The Hague. Gert van Engelen did the same for Dordrecht, and Kees Heitink and Ad Nooij gave me access to their sources on Bennekom. This is not a book with footnotes or a bibliography, but it is, of course, dependent for a large part on research conducted by others. In this format it is not possible to acknowledge debts properly, but I would like to note my dependence on the work of Bert Jan Flim (who has written a great deal on the rescue of Jewish children during the Second World War in the Netherlands) and J. C. H. Blom, Dienke Hondius and Chris van der Heijden (especially on the Jewish experience after the end of the war).

The staff of numerous libraries and other institutions have provided assistance: notably the Dutch National Archives; Leiden University Library; the National Institute for War, Holocaust, and Genocide Studies (NIOD) in Amsterdam; The Hague Central Library; Dordrecht City Library; the Jewish Historical Museum in Amsterdam; the Resistance Museum in Amsterdam; Museum 1940–1945 in Dordrecht; and the Shoah Foundation at the University of Southern California, USA.

I began writing this book in January 2015. Right from that first moment, my dear friend Tore Rem has been very important. His comments on drafts and our many conversations gave me the confidence to carry on. Colleagues at Oxford have also been unfailingly positive. It was thanks to the suggestion of Peter McDonald (of St Hugh's College) that I began recording my interviews, and we have discussed this book over squash games ever since. Andrew Kahn, Louise Fawcett, Justine Pila, Marc Mulholland, Adam Smythe, Lorna Hutson, Sophie Ratcliffe, Peter McCullough, Paulina Kewes, and Catherine Clarke (at Felicity Bryan Associates), have given encouragement and advice. My colleagues in the English Department at St Catherine's – Kirsten Shepherd-Barr, Jeremy Dimmick, David Womersley and Ben Morgan – and, of course, the Master, Roger Ainsworth, have followed this project closely. The same is true of colleagues at other universities, amongst them Tiffany Stern, Andrew Hadfield, Douglas Bruster, Lukas Erne, Patrick Cheney, Michael Suarez and Indira Ghose.

In August 2015, thanks to the advice of James Atlee and the help of my former student Katherine Rundell, I sent a working draft of the first nine chapters of what would come to be called *The Cut Out Girl* to the literary agency Rogers, Coleridge & White, where, via Peter Straus, it reached David Miller. More than anyone else, it was David who reshaped what I had done up to that point. Over a series of intense late-night phone calls and conversations in pubs and restaurants he challenged me to be more innovative in the structure and contents of this book. Shockingly, David died (aged just fifty) a little more than a year after I met him, but his ambition and passion, his erudite reading suggestions, his probing questions and his sheer joy in literary writing will stay with me for life.

David introduced me to the world of trade publishing, where a great many people have helped me along the way. Among these I would like to thank Martijn David, Philip Gwyn Jones, Lisa Highton, Arabella Pike, Ravi Mirchandani, Alan Samson and Neil Belton, who all showed interest and gave advice on the book. Within Rogers, Coleridge & White, I'm grateful for the support I've had from Melanie Jackson, Laurence Laluyaux and Stephen Edwards, and also from Katharina Volckmer, Federica Leonardis, Matthew Marland, Miriam Tobin and Rosie Price. Most importantly, I want to thank Zoë Waldie, who took over after David's death as my agent. Her strength, kindness, insight and enthusiasm have been essential to me in the process of rewriting and book production. I owe her a lot.

Revising and editing has been an exciting process. My publishers (Juliet Annan of Penguin UK, Scott Moyers of Penguin USA and Haye Koningsveld of De Bezige Bij in the Netherlands) provided extensive suggestions as we moved from what Scott called 'Version 1.0' to 'Version 2.0' and beyond. Their collective input, along with the help of Catharina Schilder, Christopher Richards, Mia Council, Ellie Smith, Natalie Wall and Kiara Barrow, has made this a much stronger piece of work. The care and attention of that revision phase was also there during copy-editing, where Caroline Pretty (of Penguin UK) and Jane Cavolina (of Penguin USA) both did amazing work on the details of the text. Finally, I would also like to thank Cat Mitchell and Elizabeth Calamari for their efforts in promoting the book.

I began these acknowledgements with thanks for partnership and family. To finish, I will do the same. My wife, Anne Marie, has lived this book with me and has been the first reader of every chapter, often with tears in her eyes. Her deep insight and moral support have been an unfailing resource. The same is true of my children – Josie, Beatrice and Edgar – who have been there not only as readers but also as emotional anchors while I worked at reconstructing Lien's life. Readers of this book will know that there were moments where I felt a strong parallel between Josie's inner struggles and conflicts and the conflict between Lien and my grandmother. The two of us had some tough times together when she was a teenager, but they have made both of us wiser. I am immensely grateful for the generous and open-hearted perspective that Josie has had on this project from the beginning. Families are not straightforward – there will always be causes of sorrow – but families also give us the most powerful love.